The Body and Shame

The Body and Shame

Phenomenology, Feminism, and the Socially Shaped Body

Luna Dolezal

LEXINGTON BOOKS
Lanham • Boulder • New York • London

Published by Lexington Books
An imprint of The Rowman & Littlefield Publishing Group, Inc.
4501 Forbes Boulevard, Suite 200, Lanham, Maryland 20706
www.rowman.com

Unit A, Whitacre Mews, 26-34 Stannary Street, London SE11 4AB

British Library Cataloguing in Publication Information Available

Library of Congress Cataloging-in-Publication Data

Library of Congress Cataloging-in-Publication Data Available
ISBN 978-0-7391-8168-3 (cloth : alk. paper)— ISBN 978-0-7391-8169-0 (electronic)
ISBN 978-1-4985-1358-6 (pbk : alk. paper)

∞ ™ The paper used in this publication meets the minimum requirements of American
National Standard for Information Sciences Permanence of Paper for Printed Library
Materials, ANSI/NISO Z39.48-1992.

Printed in the United States of America

Contents

Acknowledgments

The completion of this book was made possible as a result of the support of several individuals and institutions. First, I would like to gratefully acknowledge the support of the Irish Research Council (and formerly the Irish Research Council for Humanities and Social Sciences) for funding my doctoral and postdoctoral research. Their generous support has made much of the research in this book possible. I would like to offer my sincere thanks to Tim Mooney for his encouragement and feedback and for overseeing the initial research that provided the basis for this book. I would also like to thank Chris Cowley, Brian O'Connor and Katherine Morris for their careful readings of my work and their thoughtful interventions. I am grateful to Maria Baghramian for her ongoing kindness and encouragement over the many years that I have known her. And also to Lilian Alweiss for her invaluable support as a research mentor. I also would like to acknowledge the support of the School of Philosophy, University College Dublin and the Department of Philosophy, Trinity College Dublin where I have had the good fortune to work while completing this manuscript.

Luna Dolezal
Dublin, 2014

Introduction

Shame as a topic of inquiry is compelling because it reaches to the heart of what it means to be human: each of us has experienced the pain of shame, it burns brightest in our memories ready to resurface, and to be relived, at any moment. We live our lives painstakingly avoiding shame; indeed, some thinkers argue that it shapes every action and encounter. As a result, shame helps make us who we are.

Although shame is an emotion that is always manifested and experienced through the body, some experiences of shame arise explicitly as a result of the body. Body shame, as I will designate it here, is a particularly interesting form of shame. An intensely personal and individual experience, body shame only finds its full articulation in the presence (actual or imagined) of others within a rule and norm governed socio-cultural and political milieu. As such, it bridges our personal, individual, and embodied experience with the social and political world which contains us. Hence, understanding body shame can shed light on how the social is embodied, that is, how the body—experienced in its phenomenological primacy—becomes a social, cultural, and political subject shaped by external forces and demands. In short, when investigating the nature of embodied subjectivity and the relation between the subject, body, others, and world, body shame is not only important, but is paramount.

As such, body shame will be the focus of this work. It will be argued that body shame is a process which can provide phenomenological insights into the manner through which the body is shaped by social forces, addressing a question not yet adequately answered by phenomenological accounts of embodiment: If my lived experience is one of agency, action, and intrinsically meaningful intentionality in the world, how is it that the diffuse, pervasive, and yet often invisible external socio-cultural forces have such a strong hold on the body? That is, what exactly is it that shapes the body according to external social, cultural, and institutional pressures? In short, through investigating body shame, I wish to perhaps offer an answer to the question recently posed by the phenomenologist Elizabeth A. Behnke: "Can there indeed be a phenomenology of the socially shaped body?"[1]

Despite its significance, shame often remains unacknowledged and hidden—itself *shameful*—and theoretical inquiries into the nature and significance of shame have been, until very recently, underdeveloped.[2] Perhaps in philosophy this is due, in part, to enduring attempts to connect with ideals and universals which are not corrupted by the changeability and irregularity of subjective human experience; and, furthermore, a traditional concern with the *meta*physical, that is, the immaterial and the incorporeal, that lies beyond the contingencies of the physical and social world. Shame is both embodied and social, and recent changes in philosophical inquiry, particularly the development of phenomenology, which investigates embodied and intersubjective relations, have provided a framework through which experiences such as shame can be investigated with philosophical rigor.

Phenomenology is unique in that it considers consciousness and the body together as aspects of an integrated and projective unity. Unlike the impersonal third-person, detached and scientific viewpoint which had been the dominant paradigm for theoretical investigation with respect to the body—and which is still relevant in some disciplines such as biomedicine—phenomenology takes first-person intuitive experience of phenomena as the starting point for its investigations. It attempts to determine the essential features of what we experience, recognizing the inseparability, and co-constitutive nature, of body and mind. Constantly questioning the world and attempting to uncover habituated structures of perception and action, phenomenology proposes an active and creative relation to the world.

Seeking to avoid arbitrary metaphysical hypotheses about the body or dogmatic ideas based on political or theological presuppositions, and turning instead to lived experience, phenomenology has reconfigured our philosophical understanding of embodiment and subjectivity. In doing so, phenomenology moves away from the questions that traditionally occupied philosophy, that which Foucault in his later writings referred to as the "formal ontology of truth."[3] Concerned with discovering 'truth,' which is allegedly ahistorical, atemporal, universal, and uncorrupted by the contingencies and irregularities of human experience, philosophy traditionally asks questions such as: "What is the world? What is man? What is truth? What is knowledge? How can we know something?"[4] Phenomenology moves away from these formal ontological concerns and offers a means to address the continuously pressing philosophical question: "What are we in our actuality?"[5] Phenomenology's short answer to this question is that we are *lived bodies*, or *body subjects*, and any understanding of the nature of human existence or features of that existence must consider the body and Being together. Phenomenology, hence, attempts to describe lived experience while recognizing its inherent complexity and ambiguity.

Essentially, the phenomenological approach is central to the ideas explored in this book. Through employing phenomenology, experiences such as shame will be reflectively and systematically considered from within, as lived phenomena with embodied, affective, and cognitive resonances, revealing important insights into the nature of subjectivity.

Alongside the development of phenomenology, a radical anthropological transformation in what it means 'to have' and 'to be' a body has occurred throughout the twentieth century. In modern Western society, dramatic changes in life span and standards of health, alongside previously unimaginable advances in biomedicine, technology, labor and work practices have radically altered the manner in which we experience and live through our bodies. As a result, in recent times, there has been much theoretical attention turned to the body and a proliferation of writing about embodiment from a variety of different disciplines.

The body, as such, has been regarded in a variety of ways. It is considered variously as a physical object, as a living organism, as a cultural artifact, as a scientific or biological entity and as an expressive subject, among many other descriptions.[6] How we understand, perceive or relate to the body is dependent on the antecedent perceptual style, or tacit frame of reference, which informs in advance a certain investigation. This perceptual style is necessarily socially and conceptually informed, whether it is philosophical, political, biological, medical, sociological, theological, and so on. Any attempt to make a thorough analysis of the lived body, and the nature or features of embodied subjectivity, must acknowledge that the body can be regarded from a multiple of different perspectives, and that these perspectives can offer distinct, or even contradictory views. The frameworks through which we view and investigate the human body yield multiple conceptualizations. As the philosopher Shaun Gallagher asserts, when discussing or analyzing the lived body, "[t]he philosophical task then seems to be to account for the unity of the various *Abschattungen* [adumbrations] of the body."[7]

My own theoretical curiosity about the body comes from my own experience and recognition that the body can be regarded and experienced in a variety of ways and a curiosity about how these various *Abschattungen* fit meaningfully together. My experiences as a body practitioner have led me to consider how introspective body practices, such as meditation and yoga, can have transformative potential for how one constitutes the world through action and perception. Practices such as yoga, which involve cultivating an *inner* awareness of the body can transform one's relationship to the *outer* body, which is enmeshed in frameworks of normative standards dictating appearance, behavior, and comportment. The individual experiences I have had through introspective body practices have not only demonstrated the inseparability of the body and mind, but also, interestingly, the inseparability of the self to others and to a broader rule and norm governed socio-cultural milieu. No amount of introspection can reveal a body or self untouched by an external milieu. However, the nature of the relationships between self-other and self-world can be examined and transformation and change are possible.

Furthermore, my embodied experience as a woman in Western late modernity has brought my body to my attention in a very different way. Often regarded as an aesthetic object seen in an objectified and alienated manner, my relationship to my body as an object has been difficult. At times obsessive, this relationship has centered around experiences of body shame. Within what would commonly be considered a 'normal' experience of the body—I suffer from no disability, disfigurement, pathology, or deformity—I have struggled constantly with body shame in various guises, as I surmise have many, if not most, women. I do not exaggerate when I say that it has been a defining part of my subjectivity and personhood, and continues to be so despite my extensive research and reflection on these topics.

As such, through my research and lived experience, I have come to appreciate the centrality of affect and inter-corporeality in defining and shaping subjectivity and identity. The human subject is not a self-contained subjectivity marching through life making a series of rational and conscious decisions, one after the other. Instead, our conscious life is infused with emotional significance and heavily shaped by normative forces within an intersubjective realm, and necessarily so. Emotion and affect are not barriers to reason and rationality, but in fact foundational to thought, identity formation, and decision making. In his book, *Descartes' Error*, Antonio Damasio demonstrates precisely this point: emotions are essential to rational thought.[8] Making wise decisions is dependent on emotion and feeling; they are necessary, as Damasio astutely argues, with assisting us to predict uncertain futures and to help us make sense of a complex and uncertain social world. Emotions are not just significant for individuals, but are also what binds the social world together. As Sara Ahmed discusses in her book, *The Cultural Politics of Emotions*, "emotions work to shape the 'surfaces' of individual and collective bodies."[9] Ahmed discusses the significance of emotions for world-making, particularly with respect to shaping bodies.

Hence, my recent philosophical research has centered around the body and emotion, and this interest has taken several paths reflecting the experiences that in many ways have shaped me. First, I have a strong interest in exploring the insights gained from the phenomenological study of embodiment, where the descriptions of lived experiences, which have a necessary affective dimension, are central and the interconnectedness of the body and self to others and to the world is acknowledged. Through a process of "awakening,"[10] similar to the insights gained through introspective body practices, phenomenology offers access to new conceptions of experience that reveal important *existential* truths which can elucidate the structures of existence and lived experience. Second, my experiences of my body as an object—an artifact of prevailing social norms regarding appearance and femininity— have drawn me to investigate how the body is shaped and constrained by socio-cultural and political forces and structures. I have been particularly fascinated by feminist discussions of embodiment, which explore the issues of normalization, internalization, objectification, alienation and body ideals. I have found great personal reassurance in feminist analyses that demonstrate that concerns around appearance are far from trivial for the women who experience them. On the contrary, these concerns are often a defining feature of subjective experience.

This work draws together these various strands of theoretical inquiry about the body and attempts in a broad sense to shed some light on the *why* and the *how* of embodiment, with a focus the affective dimension of bodily being. As such, this work attempts to address the questions: Why do we take on certain styles of embodiment? And, how does this occur? In doing so, the focus will be to discuss body shame as a process which can provide phenomenological insight into how the body is shaped by social forces.

NOTE ON METHODOLOGY

My methodology will be to consider the theoretical approach of phenomenology alongside social theory and social constructionism. While phenomenology is primarily concerned with hidden constitutive performances of consciousness that are not culture specific and are common to all human beings, social theory encompasses ideas which aim to explain social behavior, how societies change and develop, while exploring constructs such as power, social structure, gender, race and 'civilization.'[11] Social constructionism, in particular, is concerned with reflectively revealing historically and socially relative structures of knowledge and truth, demonstrating how they are the product of particular power relations. With respect to the body, social constructionism reveals how comportment and disposition are contingent on the power dynamics within social relations, some of which may be oppressive and devoid of rational warrant or justification. Looking at these approaches together is complementary because universal capacities (uncovered by phenomenological analysis) are always conditioned and restricted by contingent social forces (which can be described by social theory and social constructionism).

Broadly speaking, my methodology aligns with recent formulations of an emerging field of phenomenological inquiry, namely *feminist* phenomenology. Feminist phenomenology is an approach that combines insights regarding embodied experience, through phenomenological investigation, with reflections about the discursive structures which frame that experience, through feminist theory. As embodied experience is always shaped by a broad range of factors, which have political and social significance, such as age, gender, race, sexuality, ability, ethnicity, among others, feminist phenomenology attempts to reveal not only the taken for granted structures of lived experience, but also the sedimented or 'hidden' assumptions that inform our experience with respect to these categories.[12] As a result, exploring questions about the body, identity and social relations through phenomenology *and* social theory gives a richer and more complete account of the comprehensive conditions of situated embodied existence.

CONTEMPORARY RELEVANCE OF THE TOPIC

I did not initially intend to write a book about shame and I experienced some reluctance in doing so. As something which produces so much discomfort, we go to great lengths to avoid and circumvent shame. Indeed, as shame itself is shameful, just its mention can cause unease. Perhaps this explains how it is that, until the twentieth century, shame was for the most part not investigated with any seriousness within most disciplines and why, even today, I experience some reluctance in broaching shame as a topic of theoretical inquiry. However, I could not keep ignoring the significance of body shame. Not only is it a compelling topic for investigation in that it speaks to my personal experience, but my research has led me over and over again to consider body shame as key to understanding embodied subjectivity in terms of individual, intersubjective, social and political relations.

In fact, shame seems to be increasingly relevant to our contemporary social landscape and this is reflected in a surge in interest in shame research. In the psychoanalytic and psychotherapeutic setting, shame is now recognized to be ubiquitous.[13] The prevalence of psychiatric disorders which have shame as a central component, such as Body Dysmorphic Disorder (BDD) or Social Anxiety Disorder (SAD), are on the rise. In an image-saturated cultural landscape that is increasingly dominated with spectacle and obsessed with appearances, it is not surprising that body shame is of increased relevance to the contemporary subject of neoliberalism. In fact, some argue that shame is the central affect of neoliberalism, driving the machinery of the insecurity-consumption cycle. The "spectacle of the public putdown," as Philip Mirowski points out, has become a central cultural pedagogy as demonstrated by its predominance in reality television shows, tabloid newspapers, and popular magazines.[14] Cultivating experiences of insecurity and vulnerability, through shaming strategies, seems to be a powerful force of contemporary consumer culture.

The recent upsurge in affect theory, and its links to cultural politics, has demonstrated how shame is of inordinate relevance in social and political movements, where the oppression of marginalized groups is often not the result of legislation or overt political maneuverings, but happens more invisibly through the cultural deployment of affects like shame. In fact, movements such as 'Gay Pride' or 'Black is Beautiful' and events such as the Special Olympics demonstrate that shame, and overcoming shame (which is often centered on the body), has an important role to play in terms of the validation of subjectivity, both personally and politically. Becoming aware of shame—which is often unspoken, subliminal and invisible—and its consequences can be of great significance for the self and the broader milieu.

However, the relation between the embodied self, shame and the world is, as we shall see, not without complexity. On the one hand, shame is necessary, we cannot live or grow without it, nor should we endeavor to do so. Here, shame is an integral part of experience; it is everywhere, facilitating social interaction and making possible a coherent and stable social world. However, there are also times when shame can be limiting, where too much shame can be restricting and must be overcome for life to have the possibility of dignity and fulfillment. As a result, there are many competing ideas about shame: it is fundamental to the heart of being human: it gives us integrity, compelling us to act within socially sanctioned parameters and facilitating social order; however, at the same time, when shame centers on the body and self, it can be profoundly limiting and negative, inhibiting subjective experience; lastly, shame can be downright oppressive, it can be used to manipulate and disadvantage a social group, such as instilling the crippling insecurities and anxieties that plague many women with respect to standards of appearance and attractiveness. Overall, my reflections on body shame in this work will follow these diverging lines of inquiry: body shame as necessary in some instances and as compromising or oppressive in others.

I will introduce body shame as a philosophically significant force within the self, exploring the double movement at the core of the experience of all types of shame: it is painfully individualizing while uncontrollable relational. Shame, it will be seen, is a permanent, necessary and structuring factor of identity. However, it is a double-edged force; it contains the potential for individual and social transformation, while also containing the potential for world-shattering personal and social devastation. Shame is about visibility. When one experiences shame, one is seen (by oneself or others) to be doing something untoward or inappropriate. Through reflecting on shame about the body, this work will in fact give an account of the various modes of bodily visibility and invisibility that occur in lived experience. Through the following chapters, I will give an account of the phenomenology of bodily visibility, invisibility and (in)visibility as relevant to the features of embodied experience and also to the social and political realm.

Underscoring visibility, body shame is a particularly potent form of shame. Not only is the body the part of ourselves that is immediately observable to others, it is that which makes meaningful and oriented subjective experience possible. Describing not only the chronic shame of those who believe their bodies to be somehow defective or socially deficient, body shame also occurs in acute cases where during social interaction one's self-presentation falters or fails. What is more often described as embarrassment, shame, in this acute sense, is a mechanism of social control which ensures bodily order. Body shame is an important, though philosophically rarely explored, aspect of embodied subjectivity and social relations. Often an invisible and silent force, it is unacknowledged, but lurking, in much theoretical inquiry. In philosophical discussions regarding the nature of embodied subjectivity, shame, until very recent times has received little consideration. This lacuna is something I hope to address.

NOTE ON TERMINOLOGY

It is worth noting an issue regarding terminology when considering body shame. In its acute form, where shame arises as a result of minor and unexpected infractions as a result of the body or comportment, body shame is more commonly termed 'embarrassment.' There is a large body of literature discussing the differences between embarrassment, shame, and other negative self-conscious emotions. For the purposes of simplicity I will employ the term 'shame' throughout this work to indicate a whole range of negative self-conscious emotions including embarrassment, humiliation, mortification, chagrin, and so forth. Employing the term 'shame,' I do not wish to offer an exaggerated account of social reality and at times 'shame' may in fact indicate 'milder' or less intense affects such as embarrassment, chagrin, or social anxiety. Furthermore, throughout this work, I will often use the term 'body' as shorthand for body subject, that is, to indicate an incarnate and complex subjectivity. However, I do not intend the term 'body' to be a reductive one. Lastly, I will use the terms 'emotion' and 'affect' more or less interchangeably, while recognizing that affect designates an emotion that influences behavior or action.

WHO IS THIS BOOK FOR?

In writing this work, I have hoped that it may be accessible to scholars working in a wide range of disciplines. Although my approach to shame is largely philosophical, my hope is that I have introduced the theoretical frameworks that are being employed in such a manner that expertise in neither phenomenology nor social theory is a prerequisite for engaging with the ideas central to this text. As such, my hope is that those working in feminist theory, sociology, or cultural studies, among other humanities and social sciences, will find my discussion of phenomenology illuminating. Likewise, I hope that phenomenologists, who are not familiar with feminist scholarship regarding embodiment or the politics of race relations and cosmetic surgery, may find the latter chapters informative. As such, this text should be considered as introductory, in some sense, as it introduces a range of philosophical approaches and theorists. However, my aim in this work is to present an original thesis regarding the 'socially shaped body' through rigorously exploring the origins, manifestations, and consequences of body shame. In doing so, I hope to fill a lacuna in the current literature. Although there are many theorists who discuss the body and shame, to my knowledge there is no systematic theoretical account of body shame. Likewise, although the literature on cosmetic surgery is extensive, there is little writing connecting cosmetic surgery to body shame. Although the topics covered in this book are broad and somewhat eclectic, and this may be considered a drawback for scholars approaching this work from a particular discipline, I believe the theoretical scope of this work reflects the complexity and diversity of its subject matter. Shame, as a topic of inquiry, cannot be confined to one discipline or approach.

THE STRUCTURE OF THIS BOOK

Through a discussion of body shame, and the concomitant themes of bodily visibility, invisibility and (in)visibility, I will reflect on three related issues around shame and embodiment: first, how the body can be a source of shame; second, how the body experiences shame; and, third, how the body is, in turn, shaped by that experience. There are six chapters in this book. Chapters 1 to 3 will give an overview of the concept of body shame through exploring several philosophical accounts of embodiment. Through these chapters, it will be contended that body shame is a necessary and constitutive part of embodied subjectivity. Chapters 4 to 6 comprise of an analysis of how body shame plays a role in social relations, outlining a phenomenology of self-presentation and exploring the cultural politics of shame with respect to varying experiences of bodily (and social) visibility, invisibility and (in)visibility. In doing so, these chapters will explore shame and the body in the context of race relations and in a feminist analysis of shame and gender, with a critical focus on the practice of cosmetic surgery, a practice that demonstrates how the body can be literally shaped by shame. I offer a brief summary of each chapter here below in some detail.

   Chapter 1 will introduce shame as a philosophical and existential concept, in particular introducing the idea of body shame, which will be the main

focus of this work. In this chapter, I will give an overview of some philosophical conceptions of shame, defining the concept of shame in general and
of body shame more specifically. I will address issues related to terminology
and shame variants, outlining the basic features of the shame experience. I
will then turn to define and discuss body shame, examining acute and chronic
cases. Body shame is a complex experience which involves not only personal
and individual experience, but also intersubjective relations and the broader
social and cultural field. Therefore, while chapter 1 will offer a broad overview of shame within a general philosophical framework, the following two
chapters will examine four leading philosophical accounts of embodiment
through which the three layers or aspects of body shame—the personal, the
intersubjective and the socio-cultural—will be explored.

In chapter 2, I will begin with a phenomenological account of embodiment which gives primacy to individual experience. I will give an overview
of the phenomenological approach in general, reviewing the phenomenological attitude and the phenomenological reduction. I will also outline phenomenological descriptions of the characteristics of embodiment, through the
pioneering work of Edmund Husserl and Maurice Merleau-Ponty's description of the embodied subjectivity as developed in the *Phenomenology of
Perception*, particularly with respect to motor intentionality. From there, I
will enter into a discussion of bodily invisibility and visibility from a phenomenological perspective, discussing themes such as the body schema, body
image, skill acquisition and habitual action. These key phenomenological
features of embodiment will be seen to be integral to understanding and
elucidating the shame experience.

Although the phenomenological descriptions offered by Husserl and Merleau-Ponty give important insights into certain features of embodied subjectivity, this account, as I present it in chapter 2 is limited. In fact, I do not give
any sustained attention to Merleau-Ponty or Husserl's ideas on intersubjective embodied relations. Instead, for this, I will turn to the work of the
existential philosopher Jean-Paul Sartre, primarily his discussion of the body
and others in *Being and Nothingness*. Sartre's phenomenological ontology is
concerned with the role of the Other in the constitution of individual and
embodied subjectivity. Sartre argues, as we shall see, that reflective self-
awareness only arises as a result of intersubjective relations; the subject must
be 'seen' by others in order to be able to 'see' the self. In particular, I will
discuss Sartre's account of the Look in order to elucidate the role of visibility
(both literal and metaphoric) in intersubjectivity and shame. Interestingly,
unlike Husserl and Merleau-Ponty, shame is not insignificant to Sartre; he
discusses it at some length and posits shame as a structural, and necessary,
part of intersubjective embodied relations. Through Sartre's reflections, the
significance and role of body shame in intersubjective relations will be fur-

ther elucidated, especially with respect to the themes of social visibility, the seen body, objectification and alienation.

However, shame necessarily extends beyond personal and intersubjective experiences; it arises only within a context of shared social and cultural norms. Neither Sartre nor the phenomenologists spend much time considering how phenomenological characteristics of embodiment, such as the experience of bodily 'invisibility' or the formation of the body schema, are determined by broader social structures such as institutions and social customs. Hence, in chapter 3, I will turn to consider the ideas of Norbert Elias and Michel Foucault, two thinkers who give sustained attention to describing the social shaping of the body. Both Foucault and Elias use analyses of historical change and socio-cultural structures in order to better understand contemporary modes of body management. Criticizing phenomenological approaches to embodied subjectivity, Foucault offers a critical historical analysis of the manner in which bodies are embedded into social systems and institutions and how those structures can color and shape aspects of embodied life. As we shall see, in his account of the disciplined body, in his seminal work *Discipline and Punish: The Birth of the Prison*, punishment and fear of social retribution are key in understanding how the subject takes on certain styles of bodily being in order to comply with broader social norms and forces. Although Foucault does not explicitly discuss shame in his analysis of discipline and embodiment, key to his theory are several features of the shame experience, such as objectification, alienation, internalization, and normalization.

Norbert Elias, on the other hand, explicitly draws out how shame is an important mechanism at play when understanding how the body subject takes on modes of body comportment within particular social contexts. His theory of the civilizing process, described primarily in *The Civilizing Process* draws connections between the visible body, social control, body shame, normalization, and internalization, making salient the interdependence of bodies and the importance of belonging. As we shall see, the civilizing process is driven by a desire to avoid social exclusion or stigma and to secure and maintain social standing, facilitating acceptance and recognition within the social group.

There is an interesting tension between phenomenological and social constructionist accounts of embodiment, such as that offered by Foucault. These accounts seem to give two opposing, yet undeniably existent, views. On the one hand, phenomenology describes the body subject as a constituting agency, where the body acts as 'the organ of the will' opening a field of meaningful engagement with the world. On the other hand, social constructionism describes a body shaped and constrained by external social contingencies; the body that Foucault describes (in his early work at least) is, for the most part,

Yes, social science = no agency

docile and disciplined and there is scant attention paid to how the subject experiences the power structures which shape and tame the body.

Forging a connection between these opposing views through an understanding of the role of body shame and the phenomenology of self-presentation will be the focus of chapter 4. Through a discussion of the phenomenology of self-presentation it will be seen that shame is an integral part of social experience; it is everywhere, facilitating social interaction and making possible a coherent and stable social world. Although body shame is necessary and an inevitable part of human and social existence, there are also times when shame can be limiting, where too much shame can be restricting and must be overcome for life to have the possibility of autonomy, dignity, and fulfillment. Hence, I will finish chapter 4 with reflections on the cultural politics of shame, looking at how chronic shame about the body can be oppressive and used to manipulate and disadvantage marginalized social groups. My focus in this chapter will be race relations and exploring the consequences of embodied stigma.

In chapter 5, I will shift my focus to a discussion of recent feminist analyses of beauty and body norms, examining the crippling insecurities and anxieties that plague many women with respect to standards of appearance and attractiveness, particularly in the context of Western neoliberal consumer societies. In this chapter, I will discuss the relationship between shame, gender, and the female body, exploring the themes of objectification, alienation, and narcissism as they relate to the experience of female embodiment. I will then turn to examine beauty imperatives, normalization, and homogenization, discussing the manner in which women's bodies are subject to control through the internalization of social norms. From there, the relationship between shame and female embodiment will be considered. It will be argued that body shame plays a central role in female embodiment and that this can have negative consequences for women in terms of their agency, transcendence and subjectivity. In short, I will attempt to shed some light on why there are such profound gendered differences when considering the experience of body shame.

Chapter 6 will be concerned with a feminist analysis of cosmetic surgery and body shame. In this chapter, I will firstly discuss the notion of the body as a project, where the body is seen as an entity that can be self-reflexively worked on in ongoing projects of self-transformation and realization. I will then turn to discuss cosmetic surgery as part of this landscape of practices, exploring the manner in which cosmetic surgery is often regarded as a practice that can ameliorate psychological dissatisfaction with body image and alleviate chronic body shame. Examining the conflation of beauty and biomedicine as occurs in cosmetic surgery practices, particularly as it affects women, I will explore issues of normalization, internalization, and objectification. Considering body shame as a key component of women's decisions to undergo cosmetic surgery will be instrumental in highlighting concerns around pathology and normality in these practices, demonstrating that body shame is often exacerbated, rather than eradicated, by the cosmetic surgery industry. Finally, I will reconsider the arguments that cosmetic surgery offers some sort of psychological cure, demonstrating that if women are making decisions about cosmetic surgery from a place of body shame and emotional vulnerability, then the rhetoric of empowerment and personal responsibility frequently employed by the cosmetic surgery industry must be critically examined.

I will cover a lot of conceptual ground in this work, and naturally, due to space restraints, many of the topics I broach will not be able to be explored fully. In particular, I will not discuss child development or the formation of reflective self-consciousness in infants. I will not attempt to unify body shame with other varieties of shame,[15] nor will I spend any time differentiating shame from other self-conscious emotions such as embarrassment or guilt. Furthermore, I will not discuss at any length theories of emotions or of emotion types, nor will I entertain any psychoanalytic discussions of shame. Likewise, I will not discuss the origins, or exhaustively define, the features of the concepts of stigma, recognition, acceptance, and belonging. Although I will discuss intercorporeality and the interdependence of bodies, I will not explore the mechanisms of mimicking or intersubjective skill acquisition, nor will I discuss any theories of mind, though there has been much interesting work done on these topics within cognitive science and neuropsychology. In chapters 5 and 6, I will discuss the oppressive potential of chronic body shame. Although I have chosen to focus my discussion on beauty norms, female embodiment and cosmetic surgery, there are several other topics that are equally relevant and interesting that I have chosen not to discuss at length, such as race, eating disorders, sexual violence, disability, transgender, and old age, among other instances of embodied stigma. These omissions do not indicate in any way a lack of importance of these issues. Furthermore, in my analysis of chronic body shame, beauty ideals and cosmetic surgery, again due to space restraints, I will mention but not explore at length several issues in bioethics, such as autonomy, medical consent, medical necessity, and the treatment/enhancement distinction.

There are obviously many other theoretical approaches that could be taken when exploring body shame, especially as it is a topic of inquiry that straddles a multitude of disciplines. However, in this work, I hope to bring philosophical, and particularly phenomenological, reflection into dialogue with social theory, reconciling individual experience with patterned structures that are often outside of the realm of conscious awareness and intentional action. Although it is primarily as a result of my own interests and concerns that I have brought the concept of body shame to bear on contemporary feminist concerns regarding oppressive body norms, body shame has

wider implications for theoretical work on the body. In particular, understanding body shame introduces a new way of thinking about the social
constitution of the body.

NOTES

1. Elizabeth A. Behnke, "The Socially Shaped Body and the Critique of Corporeal Experience," in *Sartre on the Body*, ed. Katherine J. Morris (Baginstoke, Hampshire: Palgrave Macmillan, 2010), 231.
2. Phil Hutchinson's recent book *Shame and Philosophy* does something to address this
lacuna in the philosophical literature. However, Hutchinson does not explicitly address body
shame and its significance. See: Phil Hutchinson, *Shame and Philosophy: An Investigation in
the Philosophy of Emotions and Ethics*, (New York: Palgrave Macmillan, 2008).
3. Michel Foucault, "Technologies of the Self," in *Technologies of the Self: A Seminar
with Michel Foucault*, ed. Luther H. Martin, Huck Gutman, and Patrick H. Hutton (London:
Tavistock, 1988), 145.
4. Ibid.
5. Ibid.
6. For a discussion of the body as a "many-layered structure" see, for example: J. N.
Mohanty, "Intentionality and the Mind/Body Problem," in *Phenomenology: Critical Concepts
in Philosophy—Volume 2*, ed. Dermot Moran and Lester E. Embree (Oxon: Routledge, 2004),
324.
7. Shaun Gallagher, "Lived Body and Environment," in *Phenomenology: Critical Concepts in Philosophy—Volume 2*, ed. Dermot Moran and Lester E. Embree (Oxon: Routledge,
2004), 283. *Abschattungen* is a term employed by Husserl to denote the various aspects,
perspectives or profiles of a physical object. This object cannot be seen or understood all at
once, but presents itself through a range of possible views or *Abschattungen*. It is commonly
translated as 'adumbrations.'
8. Antonio R. Damasio, *Descartes' Error: Emotion, Reason and the Human Brain*, (New
York: Avon Books, 1994). For a detailed critical discussion of Damasio's account of emotions
as patterns of bodily changes and their role in guiding decision making and behavior see:
Matthew Ratcliffe, *Feelings of Being: Phenomenology, Psychiatry and the Sense of Reality*,
(Oxford: Oxford University Press, 2008), 108–112.
9. Sara Ahmed, *The Cultural Politics of Emotion* (Edinburgh: Edinburgh University Press,
2004), 1.
10. William R. Schroeder, *Continental Philosophy: A Critical Approach* (Oxford Blackwell
Publishing, 2004), 175.
11. Austin Harrington, "Introduction: What is Social Theory?" in *Modern Social Theory: An
Introduction*, ed. Austin Harrington (Oxford: Oxford University Press, 2005), 1.
12. See, for example: Linda Fisher and Lester Embree, eds. *Feminist Phenomenology*.
(Kluwer Academic Publishers, 2000).
13. See, for example: Helen B. Lewis, ed., *The Role of Shame in Symptom Formation*. (East
Sussex: Psychology Press, 1987).
14. Philip Mirowski, *Never Let a Good Crisis Go To Waste: How Neoliberalism Survived
the Financial Meltdown* (London: Verso, 2013), 133. See also: Martijn Konings, Martijn.
"Rethinking Neoliberalism and the Crisis: Beyond the Re-Regulation Agenda," in *The Great
Credit Crash*, ed. Martijn Konings (London: Verso, 2010), 23.
15. As shame experiences can be so diverse, the 'unity problem' for shame, where a common trait shared by all shame experiences is sought out, is a topic of much speculation. See, for
example: Julien A. Deonna and Fabrice Teroni, "The Self of Shame," in *Emotions, Ethics and
Authenticity*, ed. Mikko Salmela and Verena Mayer (Amsterdam: John Benjamins Publishing
Company, 2009), 35.

Chapter One

Shame and Philosophy

Introducing the Philosophical Significance of
Body Shame

Recognized to be of inordinate significance to human development and the organization of social structures, shame is studied widely across diverse disciplines such as anthropology, sociology, psychology, child development, classical studies and philosophy, among others. It has been variously described as the "master emotion,"[1] as "central to the development of identity,"[2] as an emotion of "social control,"[3] and as a "primary force in social or political evolution."[4] As an individual embodied experience, which arises as a result of intersubjective relations and, furthermore, is always contained within a nexus of socio-cultural and political norms and values, shame has implications not only for the self, but also for the other and for the broader milieu.

Shame is a fundamental fact of human life; a necessary part of embodied experience, it reaches the foundation of who we are, simultaneously revealing that which is most personal—our hopes and aspirations—while encompassing the generalities of our social world—culturally sanctioned norms and mores. Shame always has consequences, both individually and collectively; it always provokes change and transformation. As a topic of inquiry, it is compelling because it goes straight to the core of what it means to be human; everyone has experienced shame and been transformed in some way by that experience. It reveals our individual vulnerabilities while connecting us to a broader social nexus of value and meaning. In each personal experience of shame, we find the demands and concerns of the broader social collective.

Shame is perhaps one of the most compelling forces in human life. When dealing with shame, rationality and reason are often challenged; in creating

1

to protect ourselves from shame we will act against better judg-
d do so without hesitation. Consider Hanna, in Bernhard Schlink's
ɪ ɾ̥ɛ ɪ̥.. der.[5] In order to avoid the shame of being found out to be illiterate,
she quits several jobs, moves cities, estranges herself from friends and eventually accepts a life prison sentence for a crime she did not commit, rather
than admit that she cannot read or write.[6] Or consider young girls and wom-
en who regularly put themselves at risk of pregnancy or sexually transmitted
diseases because they are too embarrassed to ask their sexual partner to wear
a condom.[7] Or consider traditions which dictate that death is preferable to
living with shame. In the Samurai tradition, ritual suicide, known as *seppuku*,
is performed rather than living with shame or dishonour.[8] Rousseau in *The
Confessions* characterises the power of shame thusly: "I did not fear punishment, but I dreaded shame: I dreaded it more than death, more than the crime,
more than all the world. I would have buried, hid myself in the centre of the
earth: invincible shame bore down every other sentiment."[9] The power of
shame is beyond reproach. As these examples demonstrate, we go to inordinate lengths to avoid and circumvent shame, often without regard for rational
thought and reason. In short, shame is a powerful force in human life.

In this chapter, I will explore shame as a philosophical and existential
concept, particularly as it relates to the body. I will give an overview of some
philosophical conceptions of shame, delimiting the concept of shame in general and of body shame more specifically. I will address issues related to
terminology and shame variants, outlining the basic cognitive, social and
embodied features of the shame experience. In discussing body shame, I will
explore the cases of acute and chronic body shame, indicating the significance and importance of these experiences, especially when considering the
social shaping of the body.

DEFINING SHAME

Although shame has not received a great deal of sustained theoretical attention until relatively recent times, it has appeared in philosophical literature
since the Greeks. For Aristotle, shame is a "fear of disrepute"[10] which men
feel "before those whom they esteem."[11] In the *Rhetoric*, he asserts: "Let
shame then be defined as a kind of pain or uneasiness in respect of misdeeds,
past, present or future, which seem to tend to bring dishonour."[12] Since
Aristotle, philosophers have tended to characterize shame as an experience
that arises as a result of the subject being concerned with the opinions others
have of him or her as a result of some disgrace or transgression. Spinoza, for
example, avers that shame "is pain, with the accompaniment of the idea of
some action which we imagine others to blame."[13] Descartes similarly de-

fines shame as the feeling that arises when "the evil" that is in us "is referred to the opinion others may have of it."[14]

A standard philosophical analysis of shame follows these lines of thinking and characterises shame as an emotion of self-assessment which causes the subject to feel anxiety at the thought of how he or she is seen and judged by others.[15] However, the term 'shame' is often used inconsistently in philosophical, sociological and psychological literature. Many thinkers take for granted a folk (or everyday and unexamined) understanding of shame and use the term to denote a wide and varied range of experiences. Due to shame's inherent complexity and ambiguity, it is frequently conflated with other (some argue distinct) self-conscious emotions such as humiliation, embarrassment and guilt. Furthermore, there is some argument that the experience of shame has a cultural specificity which is reflected in the use of the term in various languages.

There are many issues concerning translation and cross-cultural applicability when considering emotion vocabulary in other lexical contexts. For instance, Aristotle's use of the Greek term *aidōs* (αἰδώς), most often read as 'shame,' has been variously translated as 'shame' and 'modesty.'[16] *Aidōs* carries a variety of meanings in Ancient Greek texts. It is commonly translated in various ways, for example as: shame; modesty; decency; respect; awe; reverence; veneration; ignominy; and disgrace.[17]

In contrast, Thomas Scheff remarks that when compared to other modern languages, the English definition of shame is quite narrow and extreme.[18] He points out that in other languages shame is defined more broadly and does not necessarily carry such negative connotations.[19] For example, some Asian languages have much broader emotional lexicons than English, with several terms that differentiate variant experiences of shame.[20] Chinese allegedly contains one hundred and thirteen terms to express shame and shame-related feelings such as: "losing face," "losing face terribly," "being ashamed to death" and "being so ashamed that even the ancestors of eight generations can feel it."[21] In contrast, Scheff also cites the Maori concept of *whakamaa*, a term that is used frequently in the Maori lexicon and refers to a wide range of experiences and feelings which are considered quite separate in Western languages, such as "shy, embarrassed, uncertain, inadequate, incapable, afraid, hurt (in its emotional sense), depressed or ashamed."[22]

These cultural and linguistic differences related to expressions of shame are not offered here to provide a comprehensive analysis of cultural variations in experiences of shame and its variants, but rather to indicate that perhaps there is some cultural specificity in how these experiences are socially constituted and interpreted.[23] For instance, analyses of cultural norms, such as that of the individual and the independent self in a Western context, reveal how Western models of shame are influenced by these ideals when compared with more collectivist ideals of some Eastern cultures.[24] In this sense, the applicability of the discussion of shame that is to follow should be largely limited to an Anglo-American Western context and lexical considerations should be carefully undertaken when moving to discussion in other languages and cultures.

A standard idea of shame, as described above, characterizes shame as an emotion of self-assessment which causes the subject to feel anxiety at the thought of how he or she is seen and judged by others. In this case, it is often linked to transgression and is also traditionally associated with visibility; shame is said to arise because one is seen by others to be doing something inappropriate, untoward or immoral. A Greek proverb from Euripides, *the eyes are the abode of shame*, is cited by Aristotle to illustrate this ocular nature of shame.[25]

Fittingly, shame is etymologically and historically connected with the body and nakedness, particularly the desire to conceal one's nakedness. In the biblical story *Genesis*, after the fall, Adam and Eve become aware of their naked state and cover themselves because they become ashamed of their nudity.[26] In Ancient Greek, *aidoia* (αἰδοῖον), a derivative of *aidōs*, is a standard Greek word for the genitals,[27] again connoting the reaction of wishing to hide or conceal oneself.[28] In English, the word shame comes from a pre-Teutonic word meaning 'to cover' where 'covering oneself' is considered the natural expression of shame.[29] Moreover, shame is often associated with the expressions of losing or saving face.[30] 'Face' in this sense connotes two simultaneous concepts: the visible aspect of the subject and an honourable position which commands respect and which the subject desires to protect, establish or maintain. A passage from Jane Austen's *Mansfield Park* captures this idea succinctly:

> Miss Price had not been brought up to the trade of coming out; and had she known in what light this ball was, in general, considered respecting her, it would very much have lessened her comfort by increasing the fears she already had, of doing wrong and being looked at.[31]

In short, shame is an emotion which is experienced by a subject when his or her perceived shortcomings or failings are observed by another. It is not incidental that shame is etymologically and historically connected with the body and visibility. In very broad terms, shame occurs when one is afraid, as is Miss Price, of 'doing wrong' and of 'being looked at.'

Despite shame being commonly associated with visibility, it is normally acknowledged that shame can also be a largely internal experience which can arise when no one else is present. In these cases, shame is a state of self-devaluation; it arises as a result of an internal mechanism of assessment.[32] The self is exposed to an internalized 'other' who holds the judgements and values against which the subject judges himself or herself.[33] This is the line

• The Sticker covering the blemish on the apple.
  shame?

of argument taken up by Julien A. Deonna, Raffaele Rodogno and Fabrice Teroni in their recent book *In Defense of Shame: The Faces of an Emotion*.[34] In this work, the authors argue that shame is not dependent on an audience, but instead arises purely because of the experience of being unable "to honor the demands consubstantial with being attached to certain values."[35] Ultimately, for these authors, the source of shame is one's own thoughts about oneself.

However, what the authors of *In Defense of Shame* put to one side in their account is the fact that values are embodied and necessarily socially constituted; human subjects are tightly woven into a web of social values and relations and, as shall be discussed in the phenomenological account of subjectivity in chapter 2, there is no meaningful way to keep distinct what one feels and thinks in relation to oneself without reference to the intersubjective realm and the broader milieu. Even though shame can arise in one's own eyes, the primary locus of shame is social, as Charles Taylor argues.[36] Values and norms do not appear out of nowhere, they are constituted and continuously modified by relations of embodied social interaction.

Hence, we cannot discount the importance of an audience (or the possibility of an audience) in the shame experience. It is not the case that a real (or even imagined) audience need be present for a shame experience to occur. However, the metaphors of an audience, of being seen and of visibility are instrumental in that they highlight the structural features of shame that involve the subject becoming aware of a discrepancy between a possible detached observer's description of their action, appearance or state and their own assumptions of these same features.[37]

Despite differing circumstances in which shame can arise, we can attempt to make some general statements about the various types of shame. Shame is necessarily a self-conscious emotion.[38] In shame, the subject must be able to regard himself or herself as the object of perception and understanding. Although shame is a self-focused experience and does not necessarily entail the concrete presence of others, it is inherently a social emotion and has an undeniably social dimension. In fact, not only is shame a social emotion, it has a necessary "inter-corporeality."[39] Shame arises in the interactions between bodies; it involves an intensification of the body's surface and its visibility. It is because we live through bodies, which are inherently ambiguous, relational and imperfect, that shame is a constant feature and possibility of social life.

BODY SHAME

As we have seen, shame has many faces; beyond a plethora of shame variants, such as guilt, mortification, embarrassment, humiliation and so forth, there are numerous antecedents for shame and there is no paradigmatic example of a shame experience. Shame has been aptly characterised as "the most mercurial of emotions."[40] It is as Kaufman observes, a "multidimensional, multi-layered experience."[41] Our lived experiences of shame are complex and multifaceted, often seeping beyond the realm of our conscious and rational experience.

However, what is clear is that the experience of shame has a wide remit and can be directed toward many aspects or characteristics of the self. One can feel ashamed of one's behaviour, personality traits, actions, states of mind, emotions, or even ashamed of one's situation or circumstances. However, I will reiterate that, for the purposes of this work, which aims to reflect phenomenologically on the socially shaped body, I will focus my discussion on a very particular manifestation of shame, that which I have designated 'body shame.'

Shame, like all other affective experiences, occurs through the body. Although it can have a clear cognitive dimension, shame, for the most part, is an embodied response. It overwhelms us physically, and common physical responses include a sense of physical exposure, coupled with a sense of wanting to hide or withdraw. However, while shame undoubtedly finds its expression *through* the body, shame, as noted above, is often also *about* the body. Indeed, the body, as Stephen Pattison notes in his recent work *Saving Face: Enfacement, Shame, Theology*, and "its appearance and functions are an important locus for shame."[42] Body shame is a particularly powerful and potent form of shame. Not only is the body the part of ourselves that is immediately observable to others, the body is also the seat of personhood, that which makes meaningful subjective experience possible. As the phenomenologists have argued—and I will turn to consider these arguments in chapter 2—the body is the ground of the self. As such, consciousness is necessarily embodied; no thoroughgoing demarcation can be made between the subject and the body. However, although *I am* my body, there is also a sense in which *I have* my body. In shame, a distance opens up between oneself and one's body; one becomes uncomfortable in one's own skin, so to speak.

Hence, body shame should be understood as shame that arises as a result of some aspect or feature of the body. My definition of the term 'body shame' is rather broad, encompassing shame that is straightforwardly about some aspect of the physical body, such as one's appearance, and also shame about less obviously physical aspects of body appearance, such as behaviour or comportment. This conception of body shame derives, in part, from the work of empirical psychologists, such as Paul Gilbert and Jeremy Miles whose book, *Body Shame: Conceptualisation, Research and Treatment*, explores the significance of shame about the body for psychological well being and in terms of social relationships.[43] I also draw inspiration for this conception of body shame from feminist thinkers—influenced by Simone de Beauvoir's seminal writings on shame and the female body in *The Second Sex*[44]—who have explored how shame about the body is deeply entrenched in female experience and has profound consequences in terms of identity formation and subjectivity. Furthermore, I am also indebted to the sociologists of 'everyday life,' particularly Erving Goffman and Norbert Elias, whose discussions about the role that self-conscious emotions—such as shame and embarrassment—play in embodied social interaction, made it clear to me that body shame is much more than one affective experience among. In fact, through reading the work of these thinkers, it became apparent to me that shame about the body, in terms of appearance, behaviour and comportment, plays a fundamental role when considering the phenomenology of the socially shaped body

Body shame, in short, can be understood to be shame that arises as a result of the body. It comes about as a result of some aspect of the body or bodily management, perhaps appearance, bodily functions or comportment. It is shame that is centred on the body, where the subject believes their body to be undesirable or unattractive, falling short of social depictions of the 'normal,' the ideal or the socially acceptable body. Although body shame can be straightforwardly about some aspect of the physical body, such as one's appearance, it also encompasses shame about less obviously physical aspects of body presentation, such as behaviour or comportment.

Body shame has a long history, and is connected to the origins of shame in Western thought. Historically, in Western culture, humanity has attempted to distance itself from the physical body and its animal nature has been shunned and repressed. Humans have traditionally celebrated their transcendence, not their flesh. As noted above, in *Genesis*, Adam and Eve recognize their nudity as shameful; shame of the body, of nakedness and sexuality, in this story, is the first true human act. As such, body shame is particularly powerful in that it disrupts our illusion of transcendence—the notion that we are more than *merely* animals—and reveals our undeniable and imperfect corporeality. Shame about the body has a significant social and cultural history and, as a result, it has significant existential consequences.

Body shame takes a variety of forms. For the purposes of my argument, I will discuss two distinct types of body shame: (1) acute body shame, and (2) chronic body shame. These two varieties of body shame are by no means completely distinct, and the conceptual demarcations which I will offer must always be considered merely as such. I separate acute body shame from chronic body shame thematically, largely for the sake of discussion. The complexities and realities of an experience of body shame may overflow the categories which I will offer here. Despite this, I believe these conceptual demarcations will be useful.

Acute Body Shame

First, acute body shame is linked to more behavioural aspects of the body, such as movement and comportment; it is related to self-presentation and bodily management. Commonly termed embarrassment, this type of body shame occurs in acute cases where, in social interaction, one's self-presentation falters, fails or falls short of socially desired modes of comportment; it often arises as a result of transgressions in behaviour, appearance or performance, or a temporary or unexpected loss of control of one's body and bodily functions. Sartre offers an example:

> I have just made an awkward or vulgar gesture. This gesture clings to me; I neither judge it nor blame it. I simply live it . . . But now suddenly I raise my head. Somebody was there and has seen me. Suddenly I realize the vulgarity of the gesture and I am ashamed. [45]

In this occasion, the social machinery falters or halts and a sense of unease pervades. Acute body shame usually occurs unexpectedly and without discursive preparation.

As noted above, acute body shame is often considered to be a type of embarrassment, and due to the large body of literature addressing the differences between shame and embarrassment, it is worth commenting on terminology here. There is an ongoing debate within empirical psychology and other disciplines regarding whether shame and embarrassment are distinct affects or merely variants of the same affect. Many empirical studies have been carried out in the attempt to meaningfully distinguish them. To summarize, key differences postulated between shame and embarrassment are related to: intensity; a moral component; the presence of an actual or imagined audience; a contagious element; an element of surprise; injury to one's self; and frequency of occurrence. [46] However, due to the ambiguities in emotions, and indeed in language to express emotions, experientially the boundaries between similar emotions, such as shame and embarrassment, may be imprecise and overlapping. As a result, finding absolute differences between these emotions is a difficult task, especially since both experiences are often mixed up with other affective states.

Typically, it is reported in empirical work, that the emotions that accompany shame are, for example, contempt, disgust, sadness, anger, fear and guilt, whereas embarrassment is accompanied by 'lighter' emotions such as awkwardness, foolishness, surprise and chagrin. However, relying on testimony in empirical work is particularly difficult when dealing with shame and embarrassment. In general, shame and embarrassment are more difficult to talk about than other experiences such as anger or sadness, and subjects participating in an empirical study may not explicitly be conscious of a shame experience because, as we shall see, shame is often bypassed or repressed. Furthermore, as Lauren Berlant indicates, a serious problem with working with emotion is that people's descriptions of emotions are often hyperbolic and melodramatic.[47] As a result, it is not clear that a subject's report of his or her own shame or embarrassment experiences will be accurate. Furthermore, it is noted that studies regarding antecedents to emotions may reveal people's stereotypes, or prototypes, of certain emotions rather than accurately reflect the emotions themselves.[48]

As a result of these ambiguities, there are often overlapping features between experiences of embarrassment and shame, and although we can generalize about differing antecedents and circumstances surrounding the two, a shameful experience may lead to embarrassment and likewise embarrassment may result in shame. Furthermore, an incident that I may find trivially embarrassing and easily forgotten, may be deeply shameful to another. For instance, if I stumble over my words while giving a public talk, I may feel nothing, or, at most, a twinge of embarrassment. However, that same experience may be deeply shameful for someone who has struggled with and overcome a speech impediment and has long associations of shame and failing around the issue of speaking clearly in front of others. However, for the purposes of this work, when discussing body shame, I will simply consider shame and embarrassment to be variations of the same affect, with perhaps varying antecedents, where embarrassment can be considered to be merely a milder, or less intense, form of shame.[49]

As such, the term shame, as I will use it, refers to a whole family of negative "self-other-conscious"[50] emotions including, but not limited to, shame, embarrassment, chagrin, mortification, humiliation, social anxiety and social discomfort. As noted in the introduction, through employing the term 'shame,' I do not wish to offer an exaggerated account of social reality and at times 'shame' may in fact indicate 'milder' or less intense affects such as embarrassment, chagrin or social anxiety. The experiences that I wish to indicate with my use of the term 'shame' are negative affective responses which arise as a result of the fact that we may be looked at (and judged or evaluated) by others.

Instances of acute body shame, as I have described it above, may be experienced by some as a deep mortification and by others merely a mild embarrassment. At times, these instances may be related to some physical aspect of the body or at other times to behaviour or comportment. Acute body shame acts as a regulating mechanism within social interaction. When it arises, it signals to the subject that she or he has transgressed some social boundary regarding socially acceptable appearance and comportment. As a result, acute body shame is a constant of social interaction, marking a threshold which keeps comportment and behaviour in check to ensure the 'flow' and 'harmony' of embodied interactions.

Body shame in the acute sense is not only normal, it is necessary. No one is spared these cases of body shame. These instances of acute body shame occur routinely and form an integral part of the social landscape. As Thomas Scheff remarks, shame "is an almost continuous part of human existence not only in crisis but also in the slightest of social contacts."[51] In this sense, body shame reaches everyone, it is not merely a concern of a self-conscious few, but rather, a structural part of subjectivity and social relations.[52] Although rarely discussed in philosophical literature on the body, acute body shame plays a key role, as we shall see, in skill acquisition, self-presentation, bodily management and the formation of the corporeal schema, not to mention in broader issues of social control and bodily order.

Chronic Body Shame

The second variety of body shame I will consider is chronic body shame. This arises because of more ongoing or permanent aspects of one's appearance or body, such as one's weight, height or skin colour. It can also arise because of some stigma or deformity, such as a scar or disability. Beyond appearance, chronic body shame is often linked to the body's functions and anxieties around commonplace occurrences such as acne, illness, bowel movements, aging, and so forth. In addition, it may arise around issues of comportment or bodily control, such as in cases of stammering or chronic clumsiness. Whatever induces it, this type of body shame comes chronically and repetitively into one's awareness, bringing recurrent or perhaps constant pain. Shame, in this case, is not experienced as an acute disruption to one's situation, but rather as a background of pain and self-consciousness, becoming more acute perhaps in moments of exposure or self-reference.

Consider the chronic shame of Pecola, in Toni Morrison's *The Bluest Eye*, the shame of being coloured, of her brown eyes and her perceived ugliness, obsesses her:

> Every night, without fail, she prayed for blue eyes. Fervently for a year she prayed. Although somewhat discouraged, she was not without hope . . . Thrown, in this way, into the binding conviction that only a miracle could relieve her, she would never know her beauty.[53]

In her social world, dominated by a white gaze, Pecola's shame is continuously fed and reinforced:

> She looks up at him and sees the vacuum where curiosity ought to lodge . . . The distaste must be for her, her blackness . . . Pecola unfolds her fist, showing three pennies . . . She holds the money toward him. He hesitates, not wanting to touch her hand . . . Finally he reaches over and takes the pennies from her hand. His nails graze her damp palm.

Outside Pecola feels the inexplicable shame ebb . . . Anger stirs and wakes in her; it opens its mouth like a hot-mouthed puppy, laps up the dredges of her shame.[54]

Chronic body shame is oppressive and compromising. It can lead to a diminished bodily experience where a constant preoccupation with the body affects one's self esteem and sense of self-worth. In contrast to instances of acute body shame, which are necessary and form an integral part of embodied social relations, chronic body shame can have a more oppressive landscape.

Chronic body shame is sometimes experienced to such an extreme that it is classified as a pathology. A psychiatric disorder known as Body Dysmorphic Disorder (BDD)[55] characterizes the most extreme form of chronic body shame.[56] Going by the diagnostic criteria for this disorder, BDD sufferers have a 'normal' appearance but believe themselves to be disfigured, defective or excessively ugly; there is an extreme preoccupation with an imagined or minimal defect in one's appearance. In BDD, this preoccupation causes significant stress and anxiety and leads to impairment in social and professional functioning.[57] BDD sufferers find that their shame over a particular body part hinders or affects their ability to engage with others and brings a constant pain and self-consciousness. In fact, body shame dominates the sufferer's existence. BDD is considered pathological because in reality the sufferer, by reasonable standards of evaluation, has nothing to be ashamed of: what a BDD sufferer perceives to be a disfiguring feature or characteristic of the body is in fact quite 'normal' or, in some cases, even attractive.[58]

However, the lines between pathology and normality are never easy to define. As we shall see, drawing the line between BDD and a 'normal' or 'reasonable' level of body shame and concern for appearance is not straightforward. In short, even for those not suffering from BDD, chronic body shame is an oppressive and compromising experience, with existential, social and political consequences.

CONCLUSION

It must be noted that all types of shame have a bodily component, even those which have nothing to do with the body or even the self. In fact, as Matthew Ratcliffe makes clear in his discussion of emotions in his book *Feelings of Being*, there are always "bodily feelings" associated with emotions, even when those emotions do not have the body itself, but "something external to it," as its intentional object.[59] For example, I may feel ashamed of the misdeeds of a family member, and even that shame will find its expression through my body. Shame is "a self-feeling that is felt by and on the body," as Sara Ahmed remarks.[60] Indeed, it has been suggested that shame is "the most body-centered of affects";[61] even Aristotle defines shame as a "bodily condition."[62] As with other emotions, in a shame reaction there are involuntary physiological responses. Blushing is perhaps the response most commonly attributed to experiences of shame and embarrassment; as Darwin famously avers, it is "the thinking what others think of us, which excites a blush."[63] However, blushing is not a necessary feature, nor by any means a unique attribute. With shame there are a myriad of physiological responses related to heart rate, perspiration, blood pressure, muscular tension, among others. As such, shame does not denote a merely cognitive experience, but instead, occurs as a somatic anxiety which manifests through particular physiological and phenomenological experiences. Although I will discuss certain embodied characteristics of a shame experience, it is important not to confuse the embodied experience of shame with the experience of body shame.

As we have seen, body shame is an experience which occurs within the individual subject. However, it can only arise as a result of intersubjective encounters, encompassed by a broader nexus of social meaning and value. Due to its intersubjective and social nature the consequences of body shame are by no means limited to the individual who experiences it. As Ahmed notes, "the very physicality of shame—how it works on and through bodies—means that shame also involves the de-forming and re-forming of bodily and social spaces."[64] In a fundamental sense, shame marks a threshold within social relations. It signals when the subject has transgressed some unspoken and internalized social code or norm. As a result, shame—as a force which moves not only individual bodies but also animates social norms—plays a key normative and constitutive role in embodied, intersubjective and socio-political relations.

Hence in the following two chapters, I will consider body shame across three distinct layers or levels. First, I will explore experiences of individual subjectivities, outlining a phenomenological account of the experience of body shame, primarily employing Merleau-Ponty's ideas about embodied subjectivity. Second, I will turn to Jean-Paul Sartre to discuss the significance of intersubjective relations in the constitution of embodied subjectivity, examining body shame as an event within intersubjectivity and intercorporeality. Finally, I will discuss the socially shaped body, through social theory, examining the ideas of Michel Foucault and Norbert Elias. In doing so, I will consider shame as an experience with transformative potential within a broader nexus of socio-cultural and political forces, norms and values. Through a philosophical discussion of the features and characteristics of body shame, it will be seen that body shame is an experience that can be viewed through a phenomenological lens in order to achieve a richer understanding of the socially shaped body.

NOTES

1. Thomas J. Scheff, "Elias, Freud and Goffman: Shame as the Master Emotion," in *The Sociology of Norbert Elias*, ed. Steven Loyal and Stephen Quilley (Cambridge: Cambridge University Press, 2004).

2. Gershen Kaufman, *The Psychology of Shame: Theory and Treatment of Shame Based Syndromes* (London: Routledge, 1993), 17.

3. Thomas J. Scheff, "Shame and the Social Bond: A Sociological Theory," *Sociological Theory*, vol. 18, no. 1 (2000): 97.

4. Donald L. Nathanson, *Shame and Pride: Affect, Sex and the Birth of the Self* (New York: W. W. Norton and Company, 1992), 15–16.

5. Bernhard Schlink, *The Reader*, trans. Carol Brown Janeway (London: Phoenix, 1997).

6. Hanna's shame is compounded by her involvement and ultimate complicity in a Nazi massacre. An alternative reading of this story is that she accepts the prison sentence—and ultimately commits suicide—not merely for the shame of her illiteracy, but due to shame about her Nazi past.

7. Rowland S. Miller, *Embarrassment: Poise and Peril in Everyday Life* (New York: The Guilford Press, 1996), 5.

8. Or see, for example, Bernard Williams's discussion of Ajax in: Bernard Williams, *Shame and Necessity* (Berkeley: University of California Press, 1993), 85.

9. Jean-Jacques Rousseau, *The Confessions* (London: Wordsworth Editions, 1996), 82.

10. Aristotle, *The Nicomachean Ethics*, trans. J. A. K. Thomson (London: Penguin Books, 2004), 110 (1128b).

11. Aristotle, *The 'Art' of Rhetoric*, trans. John Henry Freese (Cambridge: Harvard University Press, 1994), 215 (1384a).

12. Ibid., 211 (1383b).

13. Spinoza, *Ethics*, trans. G. H. R. Parkinson (Oxford: Oxford University Press, 2000), 219.

14. Rene Descartes, *The Passions of the Soul*, trans. Stephen H. Voss (Indianapolis: Hackett Publishing Company, 1989), 55. See also St. Thomas Aquinas, *Summa Theologae, Volume 21*, trans. John Patrick Reid (London: Blackfriars, 1965), 33.

15. This characterization of the 'standard philosophical analysis' of shame is offered by J. David Velleman and is intended to encompass the views of several philosophers including John Deigh, Gabrielle Taylor, Roger Scruton, Simon Blackburn and Richard Wollhein. See: J. David Velleman, "The Genesis of Shame," *Philosophy and Public Affairs* vol. 30, no. 1 (2001): 28–29n.

16. For example, in David Ross's translation of *The Nicomachean Ethics aidōs* (αἰδώς) is translated as 'shame,' whereas J. A. K. Thomson's translation is 'modesty.' See: Aristotle, *The Nicomachean Ethics*, 110, and Aristotle, *The Nicomachean Ethics*, ed. Lesley Brown, trans. David Ross (Oxford: Oxford University Press, 2009), 104–105.

17. James Morwood and John Taylor, eds., *Pocket Oxford Classical Greek Dictionary* (Oxford: Oxford University Press, 2002), 8. See also: Henry George Liddell and Robert Scott, eds., *An Intermediate Greek-English Lexicon* (Oxford: Oxford University Press, 1889), 19.

18. Thomas J. Scheff, "Unpacking the Civilizing Process: Interdependence and Shame," in *Norbert Elias and Human Interdependencies*, ed. Thomas Salumets (Montreal and Kingston: McGill-Queen's University Press, 2001), 104.

19. For example, the French have two terms, *pudeur*, which connotes modesty or shyness and is not considered a negative experience, and *la honte*, which is the emotion of crisis, similar to the English 'shame.' See Ibid.

20. See P. Shaver, S. Wu, and J. Schwartz, "Cross Cultural Similarities and Differences in Emotion and its Representation," *Review of Personality and Social Psychology* vol. 13 (1992).

21. R. S. Edelstein and P. R. Shaver, "A Cross-cultural Examination of Lexican Studies of Self-Conscious Emotions," in *The Self-conscious Emotions: Theory and Research*, ed. J. L. Tracy, R. W. Robins, and J. P. Tangney (New York: Guildford Press, 2007), 200. Cited in: Dan Zahavi, "Shame and the Exposed Self," in *Reading Sartre: On Phenomenology and Existentialism*, ed. Jonathan Webber (London: Routledge, 2010), 224–225.

22. Scheff, "Unpacking the Civilizing Process," 104. See also: Joan Metge, *In and Out of Touch: Whakamaa in Cross Cultural Perspective* (Wellington: Victoria University Press, 1986).

23. See also: Harald G. Wallbott and Klaus R. Scherer, "Cultural Determinants in Experiencing Shame and Guilt," in *Self-Conscious Emotions: The Psychology of Shame, Guilt, Embarrassment and Pride*, ed. June Price Tangney and Kurt W. Fischer (New York: The Guilford Press, 1995).

24. See: Ying Wong and Jeanne Tsai, "Cultural Models of Shame and Guilt," in *The Self-conscious Emotions: Theory and Research*, ed. Jessica L. Tracy, Richard W. Robins, and June Price Tangney (New York: Guilford Press, 2007).

25. Aristotle, *The 'Art' of Rhetoric*, 214–215 (1384a).

26. Velleman, "The Genesis of Shame," 27.

27. Liddell and Scott, eds., *An Intermediate Greek-English Lexicon*, 19.

28. Williams, *Shame and Necessity*, 78.

29. See the 'shame' entry in the Oxford English Dictionary. Also see: Ernest Klein, *A Comprehensive Etymological Dictionary of the English Language* (Amsterdam: Elsevier Publishing Co., 1967), 1430.

30. Williams, *Shame and Necessity*, 77–78. For a comprehensive discussion of the literal and metaphoric connections between shame and 'face' see: Stephen Pattison, *Saving Face: Enfacement, Shame, Theology* (Farnham, Surrey: Ashgate, 2013).

31. Quoted in: David Southward, "Jane Austen and the Riches of Embarrassment," *Studies in English Literature, 1500–1900* vol. 36, no. 4 (1996): 764.

32. Bernard Williams also discusses the issue of whether shame is autonomous, in the sense that it can arise from within without the need of external assessment, or whether shame is purely heteronomous, in the sense that it is only through the eyes (and values) of others that shame arises. See: Bernard Williams, *Shame and Necessity* (Berkeley: University of California Press, 1993), 82–84.

33. Paul Gilbert offers a distinction between 'internal' and 'external' shame to distinguish between shame that arises as a result of the evaluations of others (external shame) and shame that arises because of self-evaluation (internal shame). Although Gilbert's distinction seems to offer two varieties of shame, I will argue that in order for shame to arise in the external case as he defines it, the self must already agree with the evaluations of the external other. As such, internal and external shame as Gilbert formulates them are not distinct. For Gilbert's discussion of internal and external shame see: Paul Gilbert, "Body Shame: A Biopsychological Conceptualisation and Overview, with Treatment Implications," in *Body Shame: Conceptualisation, Research and Treatment*, ed. Paul Gilbert and Jeremy Miles (New York: Brunner-Routledge, 2002), 16–23.

34. Julien A Deonna, Raffaele Rodogno and Fabrice Teroni. *In Defense of Shame: The Faces of an Emotion* (Oxford: Oxford University Press, 2012).

35. Ibid., xii.

36. Charles Taylor, "The Person," in *The Category of the Person*, eds. Michael Carrithers, Steven Collins, and Steven Lukes (Cambridge: Cambridge University Press, 1985), 264.

37. This is a line of argument developed by Gabriele Taylor. See: Gabriele Taylor, *Pride, Shame and Guilt: Emotions of Self Assessment* (Oxford: Clarendon Press, 1985), 66.

38. Objections to the using self-consciousness as a measure to distinguish shame from other emotions are discussed by Dan Zahavi. See: Zahavi, "Shame and the Exposed Self."

39. Ahmed, *The Cultural Politics of Emotion*, 105.

40. Sedgwick, *Touching Feeling: Affect, Pedagogy, Performativity*, 97.

41. Gershen Kaufman, *Shame: The Power of Caring* (Rochester: Schenkman Boooks, 1992), 191.

42. Pattison, *Saving Face: Enfacement, Shame, Theology*, 62.

43. Paul Gilbert and Jeremy Miles, eds., *Body Shame: Conceptualisation, Research and Treatment* (London: Routledge, 2002). It should be noted that the accounts of body shame found in empirical psychology tend to focus on what I have termed 'chronic body shame' and do not address shame that arises as a result of failures in self-presentation, which I have termed 'acute body shame.'

44. Simone de Beauvoir, *The Second Sex*, trans. H. M. Parshley (London: Vintage, 1997).

45. Jean-Paul Sartre, *Being and Nothingness: An Essay on Phenomenological Ontology*, trans. Hazel E. Barnes (London: Routledge, 2003), 245.

46. For example, see: John Sabini, Brian Garvey, and Amanda L. Hall, "Shame and Embarrassment Revisited," *Personality and Social Psychology Bulletin* vol. 27 (2001); Mary K. Babock and John Sabini, "On differentiating Embarrassment from Shame," *European Journal of Social Psychology* vol. 20, no. 2 (1990); Dacher Keltner and Brenda N. Buswell, "Evidence for the Distinctness of Embarrassment, Shame and Guilt: A Study of Recalled Antecedents and Facial Expressions of Emotion," *Cognition and Emotion* vol. 10, no. 2 (1996); Tangney et al., "Are Shame, Guilt and Embarrassment Distinct Emotions?"; and Rowland S. Miller and June Price Tangney, "Differentiating Embarrassment and Shame," *Journal of Social and Clinical Psychology* vol. 13 (1994).

47. Lauren Berlant, Sina Najafi, and David Serlin, "The Broken Circuit: An Interview with Lauren Berlant," *Cabinet*, no. 31 (2008).

48. See, for example: Keltner and Buswell, "Evidence for the Distinctness of Embarrassment, Shame and Guilt," 168.

49. There are several thinkers who argue to this effect, citing embarrassment as merely a 'mild' form of shame. See: Gershen Kaufman, *The Psychology of Shame: Theory and Treatment of Shame Based Syndromes* (London: Routledge, 1993), 24. See also: W. Ray Crozier, "Social Psychological Perspectives on Shyness, Embarrassment, and Shame," in *Shyness and Embarrassment: Perspectives from Social Psychology*, ed. W. Ray Crozier (Cambridge: Cambridge University Press, 1990), 39–40; and Michael Lewis, "Embarrassment: The Emotion of Self-Exposure and Evaluation," in *Self-Conscious Emotions: The Psychology of Shame, Guilt, Embarrassment and Pride*, eds. June Price Tangney and Kurt W. Fischer (New York: The Guilford Press, 1995), 210.

50. Vasudevi Reddy, *How Infants Know Minds* (Cambridge: Harvard University Press, 2008), 145. Cited in Dan Zahavi, "Shame and the Exposed Self," in *Reading Sartre: On Phenomenology and Existentialism*, ed. Jonathan Webber (London: Routledge, 2011), 224.

51. Thomas J. Scheff, *Bloody Revenge: Emotions, Nationalism and War* (Boulder: Westview, 1994), 51.

52. It must be noted that there may be some pathological cases, perhaps in some cases of Asperger syndrome or Autism, where the subject may not experience body shame in instances that would customarily invoke it.

53. Toni Morrison, *The Bluest Eye* (London: Vintage, 1999), 35.

54. Ibid., 36–37.

55. Body dysmorphic disorder is listed in the DSM-IV and has been classified as a psychiatric disorder since 1987.

56. Thomas Fuchs discusses BDD as the "paradigm of a 'shame disorder.'" See: Thomas Fuchs, "The Phenomenology of Shame, Guilt and Body in Body Dysmorphic Disorder and Depression," *Journal of Phenomenological Psychology* vol. 33, no. 2 (2003): 234. In addition, see: David Veale, "Shame in Body Dysmorphic Disorder," in *Body Shame: Conceptualization, Research and Treatment*, ed. Paul Gilbert and Jeremy Miles (New York: Brunner-Routledge, 2002).

57. See: Katharine A. Phillips, *The Broken Mirror: Understanding and Treating Body Dysmorphic Disorder* (Oxford: Oxford University Press, 2005).

58. The most common preoccupations in BDD are perceived or slight flaws in the skin, hair, eyes, nose, mouth, eyelids, lips, jaw and chin; however, any part of the body may be involved (e.g. thighs, genitals, legs, stomach). Sometimes the complaint focuses on a perceived characteristic such as acne, wrinkles, scars, redness or asymmetry, for example; or, sometimes the complaint is non-specific, a general 'ugliness.' (See: Veale, "Shame in Body Dysmorphic Disorder," 268.) Furthermore, BDD sufferers tend to see their problem as physical, rather than psychological. As a result, they will often seek out the help of surgeons and dermatologists, and sometimes undergo expensive and unnecessary surgeries and treatments. The prevalence of BDD is hard to gauge; it is thought to be largely unrecognized or undiagnosed. Sufferers of BDD are often secretive about and ashamed of their physical obsessions; they may never reveal these obsessions to friends or loved ones for shame of being considered superficial or vain, or

for fear of drawing attention to the perceived flaw and compounding their already debilitating shame. Research has shown that about 1 percent of the general population have BDD, though this number is higher in certain groups, such as students, where it can be as high as 13 percent. See: Phillips, *The Broken Mirror*, 5.

59. Ratcliffe, *Feelings of Being*, 1.

60. Ahmed, *The Cultural Politics of Emotion*, 103.

61. Gail Kern Paster, *The Body Embarrassed: Drama and the Disciplines of Shame in Early Modern England* (Cornell: Cornell University Press, 1993), 2.

62. Aristotle, *The Nicomachean Ethics*, 110 (1128b).

63. Charles Darwin, *The Expression of the Emotions in Man and Animals* (Chicago: Chicago University Press, 1965), 309, 325. For a contemporary analysis of blushing see: W. Ray Crozier, "Blushing, Shame and Social Anxiety," in *Body Shame: Conceptualisation, Research and Treatment*, ed. Paul Gilbert and Jeremy Miles (New York: Brunner-Routledge, 2002).

64. Ahmed, *The Cultural Politics of Emotion*. 103.

Chapter Two

Phenomenology of the Body and Shame

Visibility, Invisibility and the 'Seen Body'

Phenomenology, as a philosophical approach, is concerned with revealing and describing the structures and conditions of conscious and embodied experience. Rejecting empiricist, detached or scientific viewpoints, phenomenology takes first-person intuitive experience of phenomena as the starting point for its investigations. Lived experience is central to a phenomenological investigation. As such, phenomenology is a particularly fruitful theoretical framework from which to examine the body and to uncover the structures of experience which underpin experiences of body shame, as described in chapter 1. The description of embodiment offered by phenomenology is important because it demonstrates that not only are the body and the mind inseparable and co-constitutive, overcoming a long tradition of dualism, but, in addition, that the subject (or *lived body*) and the world are also inseparable, in a constant exchange and tangle. This complexity of lived and embodied experience, as we shall see, is key to articulating the multi-faceted nature of body shame.

In this chapter, I will begin with an overview of the phenomenological approach in general. I will also outline phenomenological descriptions of the characteristics of embodiment, starting with the pioneering work of Edmund Husserl. I will then move on to discuss Maurice Merleau-Ponty's description of embodied subjectivity as developed in the *Phenomenology of Perception*, particularly with respect to his insights regarding motor intentionality and the body schema. From there, I will enter into a discussion of bodily 'invisibility' and 'visibility' from a phenomenological perspective. Visibility, as we

17

have seen, is a key part of the shame experience, especially with respect to body shame. I will explore the theme of bodily visibility phenomenological-ly, and in doing so will discuss features of embodiment such as the body schema, skill acquisition and habitual action. Following from these descrip-tions of the subjectively lived body, I will then turn to consider another aspect of embodied subjectivity, namely how the body is also able to be regarded as an object; it is available to be seen or regarded by the self and by others. To discuss the 'seen body,' I will turn to consider Merleau-Ponty's insights regarding intersubjective co-constitution in his later writings. I will also critically discuss Jean-Paul Sartre's insights regarding intersubjectivity and the Look in *Being and Nothingness*. Through exploring the see-er/seen relation in Merleau-Ponty's late ontology and the existential experiences of objectification, alienation and shame in Sartre's account, I will examine the social aspects of bodily visibility and invisibility. These phenomenological descriptions of the lived body and intercorporeal relations will culminate in a description of the phenomenological features of body shame.

EDMUND HUSSERL AND PHENOMENOLOGY OF THE BODY

In investigations into the nature of embodiment, how one understands, per-ceives or relates to the body is dependent on the perceptual style, or attitude, which is employed; certain qualities and attributes are revealed under the lens of a particular investigation or frame of reference. The body, as such, has been regarded in a variety of ways. It is considered variously as a physical object, as a living organism, as a cultural artefact, as a scientific or biological entity and as an expressive subject, among many other descriptions, depend-ing on which attitude is employed in its apprehension. The notion of 'atti-tude' is a key idea in the phenomenological approach as developed in the early twentieth century by Edmund Husserl. When a subject employs or adopts an 'attitude' or, to use Edmund Husserl's words, "mode of apprehen-sion,"[1] the reality which correlates with this perceptual style comes into view.

In order to give a phenomenological description of the body, examining the essential features of conscious embodied experience, a particular reflec-tive perceptual attitude must be employed, namely what Husserl terms the "phenomenological" attitude.[2] According to Husserl, in order to employ the phenomenological attitude, one must perform the "phenomenological reduc-tion."[3] In performing this reduction, one leaves aside social, cultural, scien-tific and other assumptions that could otherwise taint or colour our observa-tions. Through this "bracketing," the phenomenologist can attend to and describe the pure phenomenon as they are experienced.[4] Phenomenology, thus for Husserl, strives to be a presuppositionless form of enquiry. As such,

Husserl's phenomenological approach is usually characterized as 'transcendental' as it seeks super-empirical conditions of possibility that are operative without doubt. Employing this transcendental approach, Husserl endeavours to provide a description of the body as it is lived by the subject. He aims to elucidate how the body is not merely a "material thing" but rather, that which constitutes the "psychophysical subject."[5]

Rejecting the methodology of the empirical sciences which investigate the body as merely an extended material object, Husserl endeavours to provide a description of the body as lived flesh. The distinction between the body as a physical object and the body as a living organism is reflected in Husserl's use of the German terms *Körper* and *Leib*. *Körper*, which is etymologically related to the English word 'corpse,' is understood to mean "inanimate physical matter" and refers to the materiality of the body, that is, the body as a physical object extended in space. *Leib* refers to "the animated flesh of an animal or human being" and is usually translated as 'lived body,' carrying in this meaning the complexity of the experiential and subjective aspects of the body.[6] However, Husserl's distinction between *Körper* and *Leib*, does not imply that these aspects of the body are distinct. In fact, what Husserl is pointing to is that the lived body, or the body as it is experienced from within, is "constituted in a double way."[7] Husserl writes:

> [F]irst, it is a physical thing, matter, it has extension which are included its real properties, its colour, smoothness, hardness, warmth and whatever other material qualities of that kind that there are. Secondly, I find 'on' it and 'in' it, warmth on the back of the hand, coldness in the feet, sensations of touch in the fingertips.[8]

What this means is that our lived body, or *Leib*, is also experienced as 'matter' or as a 'physical thing.' In other words, the lived body is also experienced as a type of object. Although we can conceptually demarcate the lived body from the body as a physical object, in fact, we cannot separate them. Husserl famously uses the example of two hands touching each other to illustrate our double constitution. While the hand that touches is part of the lived body, or *Leib*, the hand that is touched is experienced, in part, as an object or *Körper*. However, the division between what is touched and what is touching can be reversed, one is infused with the other. What Husserl is indicating is that bodily experience is a necessarily double-sided affair, inner experience of the lived body always and necessarily is intertwined with outer experience of the object-body: we are *"Leibkörper"* to use Jenny Slatman's formulation.[9] In other words, the body is something that we *are*, but also in an important sense, something that we *have*. And this is a point, as we shall see, that is developed in Merleau-Ponty's thought and is significant when considering the phenomenological structure of the experience of body shame.

Husserl identifies several features of the *Leibkörper*, or lived body, which render it distinct from merely material objects. These characteristics can be schematised into four main features of embodied subjectivity. First, the living body is distinguished from other material worldly objects because it is sensitive: I sense "on" and "in" the body various tactile sensations of touch, for example, "warmth on the back of the hand, coldness in the feet, sensations of touch in the fingertips,"[10] and furthermore, I sense "kinaesthetic sensations" due to movement.[11] Husserl argues that the localization of these various types of sensation, which are absent in inanimate material objects, constitute the unity of the body and, furthermore, delimit its boundaries. Second, we find that, in contrast to other material things which are moved only in a mechanical and mediate way, the living body is immediately expressive and mobile: it is "an *organ of the will*, the *one and only Object* which, for the will of my pure Ego, is *movable immediately and spontaneously* and is a means for producing a mediate spontaneous movement in other things."[12] The body as freely movable is that which allows consciousness to be characterized by Husserl as an "I can" in contrast to the usual Cartesian formulation of a mere 'I think that.'[13] Third, the living-body is the "zero point" through which all spatial orientations are understood. The body is "a here which has no other here outside of itself, in relation to which it would be a 'there'"; additionally "all things of the surrounding world possess an orientation to the Body . . . The far is far from me, from my Body; the 'to the right' refers back to the right side of my Body."[14] All spatial orientations are conceived with respect to the size, shape and orientation of the body. In addition, the body is not merely the spatial centre around which the rest of the world is arranged, but it is also that which Husserl calls the "turning point" where physical causal relations are transformed into psychophysical relations, effectively constituting subjective experience.[15] Lastly, the body is the "*organ of perception*" and it "*is necessarily* involved in all perception."[16] It is through the body that all experience of the external world is made possible and manifest, and it is through movement that the sense of extended space is constituted.[17] The body has a "constitutive function as regards the constitution of sense-things, appearing spatial Objects."[18]

Through explicating these four main phenomenological characteristics of the body, Husserl helped to revolutionize philosophy's understanding of embodiment. Previously dominated by a dualistic paradigm, in rationalist philosophical writings the body was regarded as somehow separate to the 'true' self, which was considered to be immaterial: the soul, consciousness or the mind. Husserl's phenomenological description of the body demonstrates that the physical body cannot be understood reductively, nor as merely an appendage to the self, controlled in a conscious and mechanistic manner. Instead, the body constitutes spatial relations, perception, sensation and feeling, and most importantly agency and free will (through action). As such, the body is the ground for, and site of, meaningful existence.

Maurice Merleau-Ponty, in his seminal work *Phenomenology of Perception* (1945), develops Husserl's conception of the lived body into an existential phenomenology of the body, describing a non-cultural and non-linguistic body that is intertwined with and makes manifest our cultural and social existence.[19] Through taking a more existential approach to his phenomenological investigations of subjectivity, Merleau-Ponty argues that in order to understand and describe the nature of experience one must offer a descriptive yet situated characterization of the embodied experience of particular human subjects, in contrast to Husserl's transcendental and hence, putatively, culturally neutral, account. Hence Merleau-Ponty's description, although seemingly describing aspects of existence and experience which are pre-cultural and pre-social, attempts to remain bound up in the socio-cultural context in which it is explicated.

Perhaps the most significant contribution of Merleau-Ponty's phenomenological account of the body is his conceptualization of motor intentionality, a description of how we are oriented to a world which solicits our engagement through movement, action and perception. I will turn to give an overview of Merleau-Ponty's account of motor intentionality to set the conceptual foundations to be able to discuss the phenomenological experiences of bodily 'visibility' and 'invisibility' which are central in the experience and phenomenology of body shame.

MAURICE MERLEAU-PONTY AND MOTOR INTENTIONALITY

Employing Husserl's insight that consciousness is necessarily intentional, Merleau-Ponty extrapolates that, as the lived body is already infused with consciousness, intentionality cannot be restricted to a cognitive act, but instead envelops and involves the whole body. This motor intentionality implies that in waking life through motility the lived body is almost always engaged in some physical situation: "my body appears to me as a posture directed toward a certain existing or possible task."[20] And, following Husserl, in contrast to the usual Cartesian formulation of subjectivity, Merleau-Ponty argues that consciousness is not a matter of "'I think that' but of 'I can.'"[21] He argues that the "the perceiving subject is not [an] absolute thinker; rather, it functions according to a natal pact between our body and the world, between ourselves and our body."[22] The body, as subjectivity, is directed to the world in a posture of possible engagement.

In fact, there are no objects which escape this directional attitude; I can never experience anything as totally independent from my bodily engagement and orientation. Of course, I perceive objects and other bodies as separate and distinct from me, in this sense they are 'in-itself,' in that they are always separate from me and I can never know them in totality. However, they are always 'for-me': I situate my lived-body in space around them and in relation to them. I cannot see a glass bottle, for example, and observe, in an abstracted way, its material and form without immediately and pre-reflectively associating it with my body's history of experiencing such an object and hence projecting a possible future that includes the human act or acts which it can serve.

"Motor intentionality" is how Merleau-Ponty characterizes this posture of possible engagement.[23] For example, faced with a pair of scissors I do not need to consciously reflect on their form and shape and come to some abstract conclusion about what they are for before I grasp them and begin to use them. In illustrating the successful habitual motor action of the injured war veteran Schneider, Merleau-Ponty writes:

> [T]he subject, when put in front of his scissors and needle and familiar tasks, does not need to look for his hands or his fingers, because they are not objects to be discovered in objective space . . . but potentialities already mobilized by the perception of scissors or needle.[24]

The point being that in habitual action I do not consciously control my body or mediate its relation to the objects of its meaningful sphere: "[m]y body has its world, or understands its world, without having to make use of my 'symbolic' or 'objectifying function.'"[25]

We do not and (many argue) cannot move and act successfully if we thematically regard the body as an object, supposedly using rational and quantifiable judgements to control and manipulate it. As Merleau-Ponty makes clear when speaking of motor intentionality, there is no need for conscious reflection on the shape and location of my hands, or indeed that of the scissors, before I grasp the scissors and begin to use them. Merleau-Ponty argues that, once a skill is learned, successful action is intrinsically effected without thematization and that knowledge of the body is "pre-conscious knowledge" and that for "the normal subject" when engaged in motor intentionality there is no need for a "clear and articulate perception of his body."[26]

Motor intentionality is made possible, in part, by what is known as the body schema. The body schema is a system of motor and postural functions that are in constant operation below the level of self-conscious intentionality. In the most basic sense, the body schema is the subject's non-cognitive awareness of its position, orientation and movement. Merleau-Ponty fleshes out the idea of the body schema through his discussion of the "habit body."[27] Distinguishing between two levels on which the body operates, Merleau-Ponty makes the distinction between the "body at this moment" and the "habit-body" in order to elucidate how bodily intentionality can remain coherent and meaningful over time.[28] The body schema is renewed and rearranged through the sedimentation of tacit skills and techniques that make regular and repeatable (rather than purely spontaneous) action possible. Acquired habit, through skill acquisition, not only makes repeatable action possible, but also extends and enriches the capacities and capabilities of the body.

Furthermore, the body schema not only regulates and controls the body's posture and motility, but also how the body interacts with the objects and environment that constitute its immediate milieu. To illustrate this point, Merleau-Ponty gives the example of a blind man who uses a walking stick to aid in his manoeuvring around the physical world. After a while, the blind man uses the stick as though it were an extension of his own body. His body schema envelops the stick: "Once the [blind man's] stick has become a familiar instrument, the world of feel-able things recedes and now begins, not at the outer skin of the hand, but at the end of the stick."[29] The blind man has incorporated the stick into the body schema of his lived body. It has become "a bodily auxiliary, an extension of the bodily synthesis."[30]

The functionality of the body schema is fundamental to motor intentionality. Through acquiring habit and skill, the body schema is constantly rearranging itself in order to facilitate the experience of smooth motor intentionally prefigured actions. However, the body schema does not always function flawlessly. It is formed piecemeal over time through (sometimes painstaking) processes of skill acquisition. Successful engagement with the world involves certain learned techniques and skills: the blind man must have learned how to hold and yield his stick in order for him to use it successfully as an extension of his body schema. To the unpractised or unskilled user, the blind man's stick would not present an extension of bodily possibilities and capabilities, but rather may present a hindrance to, or confusion of, body action. Understanding the formation of the body schema, through the acquisition of habit and skill, is fundamental to Merleau-Ponty's account of motor intentionality.

Despite an acknowledgment of the importance of habit acquisition in the successful operation of the body schema and hence motor intentionality and perception, Merleau-Ponty does not fully develop an account of skill acquisition, nor does he reflect fully on the process of how the habit body is formed. Hubert Dreyfus's well-known account of skill acquisition is an attempt to fill this lacuna in Merleau-Ponty's own work. Dreyfus argues that in certain types of skill acquisition, the subject makes a self-conscious effort to acquire a skill that involves using or moving the body in a novel or unfamiliar way, perhaps learning to manipulate a tool or instrument. Although most skills are learned and acquired through complex processes of imitation in child development and not through "genuine intellectual operation,"[31] Dreyfus's phenomenological account of an adult acquiring a new skill through instruction is still instrumental in making explicit the mechanisms at play in skill acquisition, even if these mechanisms are often below the level of conscious reflection.[32]

Focusing on a motor skill, that of learning to drive a car, Dreyfus's model of skill acquisition tracks the learner through five stages of learning: novice; advanced beginner; competence; proficiency; and expertise.[33] Through these various stages, the learner starts by learning the rules of an activity on a cognitive level and then gains expertise through repetition and practice on the bodily level. In the beginning stages, the technique is performed with self-conscious effort and is characterised by faltering and stumbling, and explicit thematization of the body. Gradually, with repetition and practice the skill becomes embodied and, as such, integrated into the body schema, and no longer requiring conscious efforts or deliberation.

Eventually with proficiency, the subject can perform the skill without need for conscious reflection. Finally, with expertise, comes the flexibility and malleability to transfer skills to varied situations (once I learn to drive one type of car, I can drive many others), and the experience of flow in action. With flow, which is absorbed and skillful pre-reflective interaction with the environment, "[o]ne does not need a goal or intention to act. One's body is simply solicited by the situation to get into equilibrium with it."[34] Merleau-Ponty expresses it thusly:

> A movement is learned when the body has understood it, when it has incorporated it into its 'world,' and to move one's body is to aim at things through it; it is to allow oneself to respond to their call, which is made upon it independently of any representation.[35]

Furthermore: "my body is geared onto the world when . . . my motor intentions, as they unfold, receive the responses they expect from the world."[36]

On this account, Merleau-Ponty acknowledges that the body, self and world are necessarily intertwined, one cannot be said to precede the other. He argues that the "subject *is* his body, his world and his situation, by a sort of exchange."[37] Through motor intentionality, the lived body has a constant and ever-changing relation to the physical objects and people in its proximity. However, it is important to understand that this physical relation to objects is not a discrete interaction: I do not engage with objects as though they were objects of the natural sciences. My physical interaction with objects and with other bodies can be described by the physical laws of science, but it cannot be reduced to that description. Just as the blind man incorporates his stick, a scuba diver, for example, does not have an indifferent causal relation to his breathing apparatus, nor is a policeman's uniform an arbitrary accessory.

Each of these objects modifies the intentional attitude of the lived body, expanding and transforming the scope of possible activity.

However, it must be noted that body habits are not limited to those which entail the manipulation of some sort of instrument, object or tool (as all the examples thus far have involved). Indeed, *every* technique and attitude of the body, even ones that seem inevitable and 'natural' (for example, sitting, standing, walking, etc.) are learned and culturally specific habits shaped by certain socio-cultural idiosyncrasies.[38] One's general bodily 'style' is consti-tuted through habits, learned within a particular cultural milieu, that are sedimented in the body schema. Furthermore, it is important to note that the habit body is not an extra layer of abilities, rather it is a permanent and necessary condition of being embodied. Without habit and skill, movement, perception and indeed, *any* meaningful action would not be possible.

Hence, from the perspective of the performing subject, Merleau-Ponty and others argue that successful motor intentionality is not a result of con-scious action and choices with regard to moving the body. Instead, successful motor intentionality induces a certain sort of bodily transparency where the body does not explicitly appear in conscious deliberation, nor in the field of perception. It functions, to use Merleau-Ponty's expression, according to a 'natal pact' between the body and the world. This insight is important in that it demonstrates that the body is not controlled in either a mechanistic or purely conscious manner, overcoming dualistic notions regarding body and mind.

Hence, in phenomenological writings about embodiment, the 'healthy' or 'normal' body is often described as metaphorically 'invisible,' 'absent' or 'transparent' in that it is not explicitly noticed in action and perception. The basic idea is that when the body is in near or complete equilibrium with its surroundings, it seems to recede from conscious awareness. We have all undoubtedly had this experience, which Hubert Dreyfus terms "flow."[39] It happens regularly with skilled and habitual action, such as touch typing or driving, where a particular action can be performed automatically and with-out the need for conscious reflection on the physical body and its move-ments.

THE 'INVISIBLE' BODY

The notion that the physical body recedes from awareness when one is en-gaged successfully in motor intentionally prefigured action is one that Mer-leau-Ponty stresses. Merleau-Ponty discusses at length the case of Schneider, a World War I veteran who suffered from permanent brain damage as a result of an injury caused by a shell fragment to his head. Schneider's injury results in him being unable to perform certain abstract movements which previously came to him automatically and pre-reflexively.[40] Unlike the concrete, or habitual, movements described above of Schneider handling scissors—movements which are solicited by a familiar situation and a set of embodied skills or habits—Schneider can manage abstract movements (such as attempting a military salute in an unfamiliar context) only if he turns attention to his body and watches the limbs or body parts required to perform them.[41] Due to having to turn attention to the body, Schneider's movements are characterized by a self-conscious straining and lack of fluidity in motility. As a result of his injury, the 'invisibility' of Schneider's body has been disrupted; he cannot achieve 'flow.'

In more contemporary literature, Shaun Gallagher and Jonathan Cole refer to the pathological case of Ian Waterman (IW), who, as a result of large fibre peripheral neuropathy, has lost the sense of touch and proprioception from the neck down. Despite suffering from almost total deafferentation, resulting in almost all sensory nerve impulses to be interrupted, IW is not paralysed and retains the ability to move his body. However, what is interesting about the case of IW is that, despite not suffering from paralysis, IW initially lost the ability to move his body; at the onset of his illness he experienced a complete loss of motor and postural control. IW had to painstakingly re-learn how to move and perform everyday tasks by conceptualising his movements and using visual cues about body position. For IW, movement and posture require constant mental concentration and visual information.[42] Considering pathological cases like Schneider and IW puts into relief how in 'ordinary' (or at least non-pathological) motility the body remains, in some sense, absent from explicit conscious awareness.

Merleau-Ponty argues that bringing conscious or thematic reflection on bodily movement and motility, as Schneider and IW are required to do, is disruptive to the smooth flow of action. The body guides us but only "[o]n the condition that I do not reflect expressly upon it."[43] As soon as attention is turned to the body part which is involved in motility, it is commonly agreed that the act of awareness disrupts the fluidity of the motion, arresting the body in action. Hence, it is often argued that as my hands, for example, become "visual objects for me, they fall prey to the alienating regard, they cease to function, they stiffen involuntarily."[44] Therefore, in what is characterized as successful or normal motor intentionality, the body must remain 'invisible,' receding from awareness. This notion of body invisibility has been taken up and discussed by many other thinkers.

For example, in *Being and Nothingness*, Jean-Paul Sartre offers the example of a hand writing to illustrate this phenomenological experience of bodily transparency. In the act of writing, he argues, "I do not apprehend my hand . . . but only the pen which is writing; this means that I use my pen in order to form letters but not *my hand* in order to hold the pen . . . my hand has vanished."[45] Of course Sartre does not mean this literally; in writing my hand is still present, and I *know* this, but I know it with a pre-reflexive type of awareness that does not involve regarding the body in a separative way as an object of perception. Shaun Gallagher terms this experience of the body's absence in action and perception the "absently available body."[46] He writes:

> When the lived body is 'in tune' with the environment, when events are ordered smoothly, when the body is engaged in a task that holds the attention of consciousness, then the body remains in a mute and shadowy existence and is lived though in a non-conscious experience.[47]

In this sort of 'successful' bodily experience, the body seamlessly facilitates the subject's relation to the external environment, and as such it is largely unnoticed or, to use Sartre's oft quoted expression, *"passed by in silence."*[48] Implicit in this experience is a pre-conscious awareness of the position of the body and the ability to spontaneously move the body to act on the world, without it 'getting in the way.' Hence, in what many thinkers categorize as 'normal' or 'healthy' functioning, there is no need for the subject to attentively perceive his or her own physical structure, and it remains the silent, tacit background to projects and interactions in the world. This phenomenological corporeal absence is taken up and discussed at length by Drew Leder in his work *The Absent Body* where he explores the fact that while "in one sense the body is the most abiding and inescapable presence in our lives, it is also essentially characterized by absence." [49]

THE 'VISIBLE' BODY

Bodily invisibility, where the body recedes from awareness in action and perception, is dependent on the successful formation and functioning of the body schema along with the habit body. However, there are many experiences which can disrupt this sort of 'flow' experience. For example, in experiences of acute pain flow is often disrupted, and the body—or some part of the body—is brought sharply to one's awareness. Indeed, the rupturing of invisibility is often characterized in theoretical literature as occurring as a result of some sort of mundane and everyday performative failure such as pain, fatigue or illness; instead of flawlessly facilitating a relation to the external world, the body 'gets in the way,' so to speak. Many thinkers agree that the body is usually only noticed in instances, such as this, where it breaks down, fails or loses equilibrium with its surroundings. For instance, Gallagher stresses this point, reporting that:

> [A]ccording to most researchers, the body suddenly appears in the field of consciousness in certain "limit-situations," e.g., in fatigue, sickness, pain and

mental illness . . . In general the body appears when the organism loses or
changes rapport with the environment. [50]

Similarly, F. J. J. Buytendijk notes that "as long as we are healthy, nothing
strikes us *about* ourselves. However, when well-being is disturbed, one no-
tices one's own body." [51]

Hence, many thinkers argue that, in 'normal' circumstances, the body
remains absent to consciousness unless there is a forced reflection or attention brought on by some sort of pain or discomfort, such as fatigue, clumsiness, pain or injury. In these cases, the body becomes "conspicuous" as a
result of "localized changes in feeling." [52] Drew Leder terms this phenomenological experience of body awareness due to dysfunction "dys-appearance."
He writes:

> In contrast to the 'disappearances' that characterise ordinary functioning, I will
> term this the principle of *dys-appearance*. That is, the body *appears* as themat-
> ic focus, but precisely as in a *dys* state—*dys* is from the Greek prefix signify-
> ing 'bad,' 'hard' or 'ill.' [53]

In the case of dys-appearance, the body can be perceived in an alienated and
frustrated manner, as an obstacle to my relation to the world. We are all
familiar with experiences such as these where attention is brought sharply to
the body as a result of pain or discomfort. For instance, if I suffer a muscular
strain while playing tennis, my game is disrupted and my awareness is
brought sharply to my body, hindering the free and unreflective flow of my
movement. In these cases, instead of being lived through, the body becomes
part of the perceptual field; it is regarded, in some sense, as an object. As
Ratcliffe notes, in these instances the conspicuous body "is not just something that withdraws from within-world activity; it is also a change in the
sense of belonging." [54] In other words, a sense of alienation from the world
can pervade as a result of dys-appearance: one is no longer seamlessly engaged in one's activity nor in equilibrium with one's surroundings.

Although dys-appearance is usually discussed in philosophical literature
as occurring as a result of some sort of acute disturbance, such as sudden pain
or injury, it is important to keep in mind that dys-appearances may often arise
in a continuous manner as a result of enduring or even permanent conditions
such as in disability, pregnancy or chronic pain. In these cases, dys-appearances may become less disruptive as the body finds mechanisms to manage
or compensate. As such, there is a necessarily subjective element to any
discussion of invisibility owing to the variety of body experiences: what may
be experienced as an extreme instance of dys-appearance for one subject,
may be a good level of invisibility for another. Hence, bodily visibility and
invisibility, as I will discuss them for the remainder of this work, should be
understood in this incomplete, ambiguous and complex sense.

Despite these qualifications, bodily invisibility is a useful theoretical concept that has relevance when considering phenomenological descriptions of embodiment. It is certainly the case that the body, or at least parts of the body, are often experienced as 'absent,' or outside of conscious awareness. However, this invisibility should not be considered to necessarily indicate normal, healthy or successful motor intentionality. But rather, invisibility should be considered to be an experience that is often *favoured* by the subject, relative, of course, to the body's purposes.

In his discussion of motor action and perception, Merleau-Ponty describes how the subject favours certain conditions of perception, and furthermore, how the body works automatically to move and organize itself in such a way so as to 'optimize' the relation to the external world. Through the body schema, Merleau-Ponty argues, the body strives for 'equilibrium' with its milieu: the body is "a grouping of lived-through meanings which moves toward its equilibrium."[55] He writes:

> For each object, as for each picture in an art gallery, there is an optimum distance from which it requires to be seen, a direction viewed from which it vouchsafes most of itself: at a shorter or greater distance we have merely a perception blurred through excess or deficiency. We therefore tend towards the maximum of visibility, and seek a better focus as with a microscope.[56]

Through working automatically to achieve 'equilibrium' or optimize perception and action, the body facilitates the physical and perceptual relation to the external world.

In addition to working to optimize perception, the body also moves in such a way as to maximize invisibility, manoeuvring itself constantly to avoid the intrusion of the body into awareness through discomfort and pain. For instance, when walking, the body will move without conscious deliberation in such a way to avoid falling, tripping, stumbling or any other intrusion of bodily discomfort. Likewise, when handling a sharp object, such as a knife or a pair of scissors, one's hands will automatically handle the object in order to avoid injury or harm. In most physical activity, for the most part, the body arranges and manoeuvres itself in order to avoid or minimize dys-appearances such as physical strain or pain. Of course, at times, these adjustments or movements come into conscious awareness. However, more often, they form a silent and tacit background of activity. As a result, through striving toward 'equilibrium,' the body subject (often automatically and pre-consciously) attempts to achieve bodily invisibility in motor intentionality.[57]

Thus far, the phenomenological descriptions of certain features of embodied subjectivity offered here, such as motor intentionality, the body schema, invisibility, visibility and dys-appearance, have focused on individual experience, describing the body subject as though he or she exists independently, purely in relation to a world of objects and tasks. In fact, embodied human existence is bound up in relations with others and to fully account for a phenomenology of body shame, and other self-conscious emotions, we need more than just a description of individual embodiment, but also a description of the phenomenology of intersubjective and social relations.

In fact, both Merleau-Ponty and Husserl have developed accounts of the 'other' and the phenomenology of intersubjective relations and I will discuss certain aspects of these accounts in what follows. However, in order to elucidate the structure of embodied social relations, I am now going to turn primarily to the work of Jean-Paul Sartre, particularly his accounts of embodied being and the Look in *Being and Nothingness*. Although, there are problematic aspects to Sartre's account, and I will draw attention to these points, I have chosen to focus on Sartre's account of intersubjectivity because it directly uncovers the constitutive significance of bodily visibility and invisibility within social relations. Sartre's phenomenology of embodied social relations, through the Look, reveals how self-conscious emotions are at the core of our being, and furthermore, how the visibility of the physical body is central to our conception of ourselves. It is through experiences such as shame—where the body is *seen* and judged by others—Sartre argues, that we come to know ourselves.

JEAN-PAUL SARTRE AND THE LOOK: CONSIDERING THE 'SEEN BODY'

In *Being and Nothingness*, Sartre develops a comprehensive description of the lived body and intercorporeal relations, reflecting on the role of shame and objectification in the constitution of reflective self-consciousness. Sartre's phenomenological description posits intersubjective relations as a central and constitutive feature of embodied subjectivity. For Sartre, the encounter with the Other[58] is an ontological event which awakens reflective self-consciousness and the discursive realm. As a result, the phenomenological features of embodied subjectivity, as described above through the insights of Merleau-Ponty and Husserl, are discovered and given articulation only through relations to other subjectivities and, as such, being-for-others is given a constitutive status.

Sartre develops this account through his analysis of the 'Look.'[59] The Look arises when one embodied subjectivity encounters another. This encounter, for Sartre, is dominated by the visual field: one comes into contact with the Other's body, it can be seen. However, the Look for Sartre is not merely about being within the other's perceptual field; it is not a neutral *seeing*, but rather, it is a value-laden *looking* which has the power to objectify and causes the subject to turn attention to himself or herself in a self-reflective manner. When I am *looked at* by another, I am reduced to an object that is seen. Sartre's discussion of the Look in *Being and Nothingness* is illustrated by his oft-cited vignette of the voyeur overcome by jealousy kneeling by a keyhole to spy on his lover:

> Let us imagine that moved by jealousy, curiosity, or vice I have just glued my ear to the door and looked through a keyhole. I am alone and on the level of a non-thetic self-consciousness. This means first of all that there is no self to inhabit my consciousness, nothing therefore to which I can refer my acts in order to qualify them. They are in no way *known*; I *am my acts* and hence they carry in themselves their whole justification. [60]

In this example, Sartre describes the subject as pre-reflectively engaged in the act of spying, made possible through motor-intentionality and the successful arrangement of the body schema. Engrossed in the act of spying, his acts are simply *lived* and the body recedes from awareness; such as in the invisibility described above: "My consciousness sticks to my acts, it *is* my acts."[61] However, Sartre argues that with the appearance of the other, this invisibility is disrupted:

> But all of a sudden I hear footsteps in the hall. Someone is looking at me! What does this mean? It means that I am suddenly affected in my being and that essential modifications appear in my structure . . . First of all, I now exist as *myself* for my unreflective consciousness . . . I see *myself* because *somebody* sees me. [62]

The encounter with another, and the subsequent Look, confers the relation of "Being-seen-by-another."[63] Sartre argues that once we are captured in the Look of another we suddenly separate ourselves from the activity in which we are engaged and see the activity and ourselves as though through the eyes of the other; bodily invisibility is disrupted and I become 'visible' to myself, both in that I have awareness of my physical body and that I 'see' myself as though from a distanced perspective. In this way, the Look gives me a 'seen body' or, as Sartre puts it, an "outside."[64] I suddenly realize and *know* that I am vulgar; I am a voyeur; I am spying, and so on. Furthermore, I suddenly know that the other can see all these things about me too. This is what Sartre means when he says that the other "teaches me who I am."[65]

Although Sartre's account of the Look, and his voyeur example, is in fact multi-layered and complex, touching on epistemological, self-evaluative and ontological concerns when considering the constitution of embodied subjectivity, for the purposes of this discussion, Sartre's account is useful for illustrating the social dimension of bodily invisibility and visibility.[66] Of particular interest is the connection that Sartre makes between shame and the visibility of the body through the experience of being seen by another, or what we might term the 'lived seen body.' This of course has resonances to Husserl's conception of the lived body as necessarily intertwined with the material body: the *Leibkörper*. While the *Leib* is experientially lived through, there are always aspects of the lived body that can be regarded in an object- or thing-like manner. As inherently visible, the body is part of the fabric of the world and can be regarded as such.

Hence, an individual's physical exterior exists alongside his or her power to see. Lived bodies are simultaneously 'see-er' and 'seen.' This means that our 'own' body (experienced in its phenomenological primacy through the structures of motor intentionality and perception) will always be a thing among things, or a *Körper*, something that can be seen by oneself and by others in an object-like way. What this all points to is the apparent dual nature of the body, that despite being part of me, my body is, in fact, also part of the world. Merleau-Ponty expresses it thusly: "Visible and mobile, my body is a thing among things; it is caught in the fabric of the world, and its cohesion is that of a thing."[67] Merleau-Ponty, in his late work, is preoccupied with what he calls the "enigma" of the apparent duality of the body as both see-er and seen, or subject and object.[68] Our capacity for vision, *to see,* or to be the subject of perception in a more general sense, Merleau-Ponty argues, is intrinsically tied up with our capacity *to be seen*. He writes, "he who sees cannot possess the visible unless he is possessed by it. Unless he *is of it,* unless . . . he is one of the visibles."[69] Interestingly, this account of the visibility of the body, in Merleau-Ponty's later writings, is tied up with an ontological question about the constitution of conscious experience and our participation in Being. In his essay 'Eye and Mind,' Merleau-Ponty discusses the intrinsic connectedness of vision and mobility which, he argues, constitutes our very experience of Being and overturns any representationalist understanding of perception and thought. He writes:

> This extraordinary overlapping [of vision and mobility], which we never think about sufficiently, forbids us to conceive of vision as an operation of thought that would set up before the mind a picture or representation of the world, a world of immanence and of ideality. . . . Immersed in the visible by his body, itself visible, the see-er does not appropriate what he sees; he merely approaches it by looking, he opens himself to the world.[70]

Hence, the visibility of the body, for Merleau-Ponty, is not an incidental feature of our physicality nor the coincidence of how our perceptual organs are arranged. Instead, one's own body as seen by oneself enables our experience and understanding of the world in a fundamental sense.

However, above this deeper ontological story of the significance of the seen body as constituting a relation to Being in Merleau-Ponty's work, is a more mundane experience of how the body is regarded as one of the 'visibles': my body can be seen not only by myself—in this special case of simultaneously being seen and see-er—but is visible also *to others*. The centrality of the visibility of the body *for others* is acknowledged by Merleau-Ponty. He writes: "As soon as I see, it is necessary that the vision . . . be doubled with a complementary vision or with another vision: myself seen from without, such as another would see me, installed in the midst of the visible."[71] Fundamentally, Merleau-Ponty argues, we are "seers" or "beings who catch sight of one another, who see one another with eyes."[72] Furthermore, Merleau-Ponty suggests that being seen by others is necessary in order to have a complete view of oneself. He writes: "As soon as we see other seers . . . henceforth, through other eyes we are for ourselves fully visible; that lacuna where our eyes, our back, lie is filled, filled still by the visible, of which we are not the titulars."[73]

Merleau-Ponty's acknowledgment of the intersubjective nature of visibility as in some sense primary and constitutive resonates with Sartre's account: we are from the start visible to others and this constitutes a visibility of the self that we would not have alone, that is, I cannot see my own back or my own eyes. Merleau-Ponty writes: "to perceive part of my body is also to perceive it as *visible*, i.e. *for the other* . . . around each part of the body, [there is] a halo of *visibility*."[74] In fact, Sartre sees the visibility of one's own body (as seen by others) as a feature of experience that forms the foundation of his account of the constitution of embodied subjectivity through his discussion of the three ontological dimensions of bodily being. The first, 'the body as being-for-itself,' is the body as invisible in the sense described above in the voyeur example. That is, as engrossed in action or perception in the subject position, with the body receding from awareness. In the 'second' and 'third' 'ontological dimensions' of the body, I experience my body *as seen*. The second ontological dimension of the body's existence is the body-for-others (*pour l'autrui*). In this dimension, my body, according to Sartre, "is utilized and known by the Other"[75] and I realize that I exist as an object for the other. In short, Sartre is indicating the fact that through my own experience I have one kind of knowledge of myself and my body which is different from the knowledge given to me through the perspective of the other. Through the second dimension, I acquire a conceptual awareness of my body in an abstract way, as a knowing organism, with certain objective features (biological, physiological, cultural, etc.) in the world and in the midst of other bodies.

For Sartre, it is important to distinguish these first two ontological dimensions of the body as he asserts that they are incommunicable and cannot co-exist: "the nature of *our body for us* entirely escapes us to the extent that we can take upon it the Other's point of view."[76] Indeed, contra to Husserl and Merleau-Ponty who see the lived body as a complex intertwining of both subject and object—or see-er and seen or touched and touching—Sartre claims that either the body is an object or thing, among other things, or it is that which reveals things to me; however, it cannot be both at once. For Sartre, bodily invisibility and visibility, as discussed above, cannot occur simultaneously. As a result, in Sartre's account the subject is necessarily reduced to an object, that is objectified, in the relation with the other (who becomes the objectifying subject): to be seen is to be rendered an object. While this strong claim to objectification, as I discuss below, does not seem experientially accurate, what Sartre's account does make salient is the significance of the body as it is seen by another and how this is inherently related to self-conscious emotions.

Being-seen-by-another, for Sartre, is a constitutive part of experience. One gains knowledge of oneself, both ontologically and epistemologically, as a result of the Look of the other. This is what Sartre characterizes as the 'third ontological dimension of the body.' This dimension arises in some sense through the interaction of the other two: my awareness of my being an object for others means that I also "exist for myself as a body known by the other."[77] In this case, I cannot apprehend my own body as an object, but I can recognize the body of the other as an object and hence realize that my body can likewise be an object for others; that is, I recognise that the other is a *subject* for whom I am an *object*. In the third dimension, I experience my body not on my own and not as lived-through, but as it is reflected in the experience of it by others. This experience of the body is central in instances of body shame. I will call it the 'seen body.'[78]

It is worth noting that the 'seen body' is more than just a visible representation of oneself as seen from a distanced perspective; it is intrinsically bound to one's lived experience and the lived awareness that one is visible to others. It is more accurate to characterize it as the '*lived* seen body,' however for the purposes of simplicity I will denote this concept with the shorthand 'seen body.' The seen body can be likened to Charles Horton Cooley's conception of the 'looking glass self.' This term refers to a social and psychological process where people get a sense of self based on other people's perception of them and their bodies.[79] Paul Valery, writing contemporaneously with Sartre, describes this body as follows:

> Our [seen body] is the one which others see, and an approximation of which confronts us in the mirror or in portraits. It is the body which has a form and is apprehended by the arts, the body on which materials, ornaments, armor sit, which love sees or wants to see, and yearns to touch. It knows no pain, for it reduces pain to a mere grimace.[80]

The 'seen body' is distinct from the visible body in that it involves a view of the external body and is not concerned with salient internal bodily events. In contrast to the visible body, characterized by dys-appearances, the seen body "goes little farther than the view of a surface."[81]

The seen body is what one presents to the world and others in the visual field. This is important because the experience others have of my body is dominated by sight for Sartre: it is how others see (and judge) my comportment, aspect and appearance that is of interest in his analysis. As such, through awareness of my being-seen-by-another, I become reflexively self-aware of how I appear to others. Hence, for Sartre, our self-knowledge depends largely on objectifying responses from other people who make us objects of their judgements. Sartre famously argues that the origin of reflective self-consciousness is located in the perceptual encounter with the other: "I see *myself* because somebody sees me."[82]

OBJECTIFICATION AND ALIENATION

Objectification is a fundamental feature of Sartre's account of the constitution of reflective self-consciousness through the encounter with the Other. As we have seen, to become a self-aware subject, one must be rendered an object by the Look of another subject (whether that subject is empirically present or absent): "By the mere appearance of the Other, I am put in the position of passing judgment on myself as on an object, for it is as an object that I appear to the Other."[83] Through this process of being objectified, Sartre claims we can gain awareness of the self. In short, the other, through his or her "objectifying power . . . teaches me who I am."[84]

To be objectified in this sense involves a process whereby one person sees or treats another person as a type of object (rather than as a transcendence, that is, as a human being whose complexity eludes simple thematization). For Sartre this occurs on a physical level on some occasions: I can be reduced to a physical object, "flesh,"[85] as Sartre calls it: I am regarded as merely a body (or parts of my body), for example, when a doctor is examining me.[86] However, on other occasions, my object state is not focused on my body (as flesh), but instead, Sartre insists, on my "character,"[87] which Sartre takes to signify qualities of my temperament, personality or identity. The objectification of my character is likened more to thematization: instead of being regarded as a complex subjectivity, I am merely regarded as some aspect of my character: as a voyeur, a sneak or vulgar, for example. However, these aspects of character, Sartre is at pains to point out, are not in some way distinct from the body. Instead, "character is identical with the body"[88] and, as a result, one's own seen body is not populated merely with information about the physical attributes of the body, but additionally holds value judgements related to character. Indeed, it is not incidental that certain physical attributes are often considered analogous to certain character traits.

However, when I objectify the Other's body (or analogously, my body is objectified by the Other), this body does not become a material thing like any other inanimate object; instead, Sartre insists, "my perception of the Other's body is radically different from my perception of things."[89] To consider the body as an object, in this sense, would be to consider the body as a corpse.[90] In perceiving another body, I do not perceive a corpse which is subsequently animated, instead, Sartre argues, I can't help but perceive the Other's body as a meaningful, expressive object, which is a centre of reference around which the world is arranged:

> [W]e can not perceive the Other's body as flesh, as if it were an isolated object having purely external relations with other thises [sic]. That is true only for a corpse. The Other's body as flesh is immediately given as the center of reference.[91]

When I reduce this body to an 'object,' it becomes a special type of object, that which Sartre designates by the term 'transcendence transcended.' As Sartre argues: "The Other's body must not be confused with his objectivity. The Other's objectivity is his transcendence transcended. The body is the facticity of this transcendence."[92] Hence, objectification, for Sartre, seems to mean regarding the Other's body (and character) as an object, while at the same time holding in awareness that it is not an object (in the inanimate sense). Sartre's account of the perception of another lived body resonates with Husserl's account of the encountering of the Other. If I perceive another person, I do not just perceive the material facts of their *Körper*. Instead, I perceive an animate organism like myself, a *Leib*, or another subjectivity.[93] In short, the Other is always transcendence transcended and *never* merely object.

The negative experience of alienation can follow from objectification, but is not a necessary consequence. Alienation is an experience where the subject feels an estrangement from the self, or more precisely, the *possibilities* of the self. It occurs when I am conscious that my body is not for-me, but is instead apprehended by the other as an object without regard to my subjectivity. Consider the case of a female philosopher who is sexually objectified, perhaps through suggestive or explicit comments, by male audience members while attempting to present a conference paper. Her body becomes designated as alienated when it is apprehended by the Other in his world as merely a sexual object, and hence her possibilities in her world, as a philosopher or as an intellectual, are passed over. Alienation is not a necessary consequence of objectification, but instead arises when one is treated as an object in a way that alienates one's possibilities in a situation. In the case of alienation, objectification is oppressive and compromising. One is reduced to an object, something that can be bought or 'owned,' something that can be disregarded or hurt without consequences. Perhaps one is treated as a commodity, as inert, as having an impotent subjectivity, as fungible or as lacking autonomy and self-determination.[94] As the feminist philosopher Sandra Lee Bartky describes: "To be a victim of alienation is to have a part of one's being stolen by another."[95] Sartre argues that alienation occurs through certain affective states, such as shyness, embarrassment and shame, where the subject is, "vividly and constantly conscious of his body not as it is for him but as it is *for the Other*."[96] In short, alienation is when the 'seen body' comes to the fore and this conception of the subject (as determined by the Other) does not match his or her true intentions, desires or motivations.

Although the negative experience of alienation can follow from objectification, as noted above, it is by no means a necessary consequence. However, as Sartre tends to focus on the negative in his examples, alienation is for the most part conflated with objectification in his account. Indeed, it seems in Sartre's examples that every experience of objectification through the Look is negative, compromising and leads to alienation: "in the shock which seizes me when I apprehend the Other's look . . . suddenly I experience a subtle alienation of all my possibilities."[97] Sartre famously characterizes the encounter with the other as a conflictual relation, where a power struggle to maintain one's subjective status ensues.

For Sartre, the other appears in my world as a potential critic, a judgemental and antagonistic presence whose aim is to alienate and objectify me. In conceiving every intersubjective encounter to be infused with alienation arising from objectification, Sartre precludes an analysis of other non-antagonistic forms of interaction and reduces the complexity of human social experience to merely a "sinister dialectic of gazes,"[98] obviating an analysis of cases where objectification may be neutral, or even good or necessary.[99] In fact, there are many instances of objectification that do not necessarily lead to alienation. Consider this passage from Bartky:

> But surely there are times, in the sexual embrace perhaps, when a woman might want to be regarded as nothing but a sexually intoxicating body and when attention paid to some other aspect of her person—say, to her mathematical ability—would be absurdly out of place. If sexual relations involve some sexual objectification, then it becomes necessary to distinguish situations in which sexual objectification is oppressive from the sorts of situations in which it is not.[100]

In this case, being regarded as a sexually intoxicating body does not lead to being compromised or alienated, but within the context of a mutual sexual encounter, is rewarding and fulfilling. In a different setting, perhaps a classroom or workplace, being regarded as a sexual object would be oppressive and alienating. However, in a sexual encounter, this objectification is enriching and perhaps even necessary. As such, context seems to be the key factor when considering alienation through objectification.[101]

ie. objectification inescapable but not always bad

SARTRE AND SHAME

As a result of placing the experience of objectifying alienation—where one has explicit awareness of how the body appears to the judgemental and diminishing gaze of the Other—at the heart of his account of interpersonal relations, Sartre makes shame central to his analysis. Shame, for Sartre, is inextricably linked to the body. First, its presence is manifested in particular physiological symptoms: my shame "is my red face as I bend over the key-hole;"[102] or it "is an immediate shudder which runs through me from head to foot."[103] In this sense, shame makes me aware of my body because its symptoms (the shudder, the heat of the blush, etc.) are lodged there. However, beyond the symptoms of shame being felt on a physical level, shame, in Sartre's account, also brings *thematic* awareness to the body, as discussed above. I suddenly 'see' my body engaged in a particular action or appearing in a particular way; my seen body comes to the fore of my attention. It is this thematization of my body or exposed self that is key to shame arising: "I am ashamed of myself as *I appear* to the Other."[104] The same structure occurs, for Sartre, in embarrassment and other shame variants: "I can not be embarrassed by my own body as I exist it. It is my body as it is for the Other which may embarrass me."[105]

Shame, for Sartre, is an experience that arises as a result of an encounter with another person. Shame, in this case, arises when the other's Look reveals to me that I have transgressed some social expectation or norm. The voyeur is overcome by shame in the moment when he hears the footsteps behind him: "shame . . . is the *recognition* of the fact that I *am* indeed the object which the Other is looking at and judging."[106] This structure appears in several examples in *Being and Nothingness*: "I have just made an awkward or vulgar gesture . . . Somebody was there and has seen me. Suddenly I realize the vulgarity of the gesture and I am ashamed."[107] In these examples, shame is straightforwardly linked to judgment by another person who has witnessed a transgression on my part: "Shame is by nature *recognition*. I recognize that I *am* as the Other sees me."[108] I have done something wrong or inappropriate and I have suddenly become aware of this fact by the presence of another person—this is shame. In this case, shame arises unexpectedly and suddenly, without any necessary cognitive action on my part.

However, it seems that for Sartre shame must also be able to occur when one is alone, and is linked also to how *I* see *myself* (not necessarily to how a particular other sees me in a particular instance). The empirical presence of another is not necessary for shame to occur, as the voyeur example ultimately demonstrates: he hears the footsteps, lifts his head and it turns out that nobody is there. In fact, there are many examples in Sartre's account where the other is merely imagined or possible (there is a rustle in the bushes, or movement in the curtains).[109] Sartre's use of the capitalized 'Other' here is instructive. Some commentators claim the 'Other' merely indicates another person, albeit one who may not be specified. For example, Gary Cox asserts that the 'Other' is "Sartre's term for another person, particularly one who looks at me, sees me and judges me."[110] However, this formulation seems to be at odds with Sartre's own assertions. In Sartre's example of appearing "'in public' to act in a play or to give a lecture . . . the Other's presence remains undifferentiated."[111] Rather than signifying a person—an 'other' who can literally see me—the 'Other,' in this case, denotes a point of view from which the world is apprehended; it is not a "concrete and individualized being,"[112] but rather it is simply a point of view which is not my own. This point of view *can* belong to a particular person, and in this case the 'Other' can become the 'other.' However, it must be stressed that this point of view is not necessarily bound to any particular body or set of eyes.

As such, shame is also a self-evaluative experience for Sartre; it is clear that one can be alone in an empirical sense and still experience shame. However, Sartre recognizes that the metaphors of an audience and being seen are instrumental in that they highlight the structural features of shame that involve the subject becoming aware of a discrepancy between a possible detached observer's description of their action, appearance or state and their own assumptions of these same features.[113] Hence, in shame experiences, the self is simultaneously the agent and the object of judgement, observation and disapproval. The failings or transgressions of the self are exposed not only to the judgemental gaze of another, but also to an internalized other. In this sense, shame is more than just an affective reaction to public disapproval.

Sartre himself seems to give shame a deeper and more symbolic significance. Ignoring the moralistic and evaluative aspect suggested by his voyeur example, Sartre argues that shame extends beyond the everyday experience of transgression in intersubjective encounters or in social settings. Sartre calls this "pure shame"[114] and argues that it arises because I am disgusted or disappointed with the dependency or vulnerability I feel before the other:

> Pure shame is not a feeling of being this or that guilty object but in general of being *an* object; that is, of *recognizing myself* in this degraded, fixed and dependent being which I am for the Other. Shame is the feeling of an *original fall*, not because of the fact that I may have committed this or that particular fault but simply that I have 'fallen' into the world in the midst of things and that I need the mediation of the Other in order to be what I am.[115]

This ontological shame, as Sartre conceives it, seems to be a necessary feature of every Look and hence a permanent background to reflective consciousness. In this schema, shame that arises as a result of a social transgression in an intersubjective encounter or in a self-evaluative moment are meant to be conceived as examples of a more fundamental relation: the shame of having been rendered an object in the first place.

Sartre is at pains to relate this object state with the body, and he seems to tie pure shame intrinsically to concerns around bodily vulnerability. For Sartre, when the body is on display to the Other (particularly in its naked state), the vulnerability of objectification is manifested in the experience of shame. He refers tellingly to the 'original fall' in *Genesis*:

> Modesty and in particular the fear of being surprised in a state of nakedness are only a symbolic specification of original shame; the body symbolizes here our defenseless state as objects. To put on clothes is to hide one's object-state: it is to claim the right of seeing without being seen; that is, to be pure subject. That is why the Biblical symbol of the fall after the original sin is the fact that Adam and Eve 'know that they are naked.' The reaction to shame will consist exactly in apprehending as an object the one who apprehended my own object-state.[116]

Shame as Sartre describes it here, as related to bodily vulnerability, seems to be shame about the human condition in general: because we are thrown into the world and because we need the mediation of others to realize our being. Hence, 'pure shame' is not shame in an empirical sense; it is not an affective response to a situation where one has an awareness of the self or body as failing to meet some social expectations. Pure shame is not merely shame that is by-passed or repressed. Instead, when Sartre discusses 'shame' ontologically, he intends the term to signify something more fundamental: quite simply, the awareness of oneself "in general of being *an* object [for the Other]."[117]

SOCIAL DYS-APPEARANCE

Drawing inspiration from Sartre's account of shame and the objectifying and alienating Look developed in his voyeur example, Drew Leder reflects phenomenologically on social disruptions or dys-appearances that arise as a result of self-consciousness in social encounters. Developing his account of dys-appearance beyond the experiences of pain or other internal physical occurrences, Leder gives an account of what he calls "social dys-appearance."[118] He argues that, similar to the disruptions to motor intentionality and 'flow' that occur when the body is troubled by pain, illness or other salient bodily experiences, when the body is seen and judged by the others which constitute its social milieu, and when the gaze of the other is "highly distanced, antagonistic, or objectifying," one can become conscious of the body "as an alien thing."[119] When the body is objectified in such a way that self-consciousness arises, then body objectification can have the same disruptive effect as a dysfunction due to illness or pain, in that the body comes to the fore of attention and the external perceptual relation to the environment or world is disrupted or modified. Shame is one instance of social dys-appearance that Leder mentions in his account. The point being that bodily invisibility, through 'flow' and successful motor intentionality, as the phenomenologists describe it, is dependent on more than just physical well being and the absence of internal physical events such as pain, illness or fatigue, but is also dependent on social relations.

In short, social interactions have their own 'flow' and the invisibility of the body (in the phenomenological sense discussed above) has an undeniable social dimension: the body is only 'invisible' in social relations when one is 'in play,' to use the terminology of the social theorist Erving Goffman.[120] Flow in social relations occurs when one is "unoriented to and unconcerned about being under observation."[121] When one's body becomes a 'seen body' as a result of some breach in conduct, appearance or action—governed by the unspoken yet pervasive norms and rules regarding bodily comportment— then invisibility is ruptured and the body enters one's field of awareness in an explicit way; it becomes a 'seen body' through objectification, as Sartre's voyeur example illustrates. Hence, the conspicuousness of the body that arises in cases of body shame can perhaps be considered the paradigmatic case of social dys-appearance: not only is the body objectified and regarded from an antagonistic and distanced perspective, it is *seen*, but in addition this experience is extremely disruptive, interrupting the flow of motor intentionality and hence provoking 'visibility.'

PHENOMENOLOGY OF BODY SHAME

We are now in a position to consider a phenomenology of body shame. However, to avoid confusion, precisely what is meant by a 'phenomenological' description must be clarified as one must be careful when considering the term 'phenomenological' across various disciplines. In psychology, for instance, this term is used to refer to subjective experiences or the study of such experiences. Hence, in certain 'phenomenological' descriptions of shame in psychological literature, usually just the physical or psychological symptoms of the subjective experience of shame are described.[122] By contrast, in Husserlian phenomenology, 'lived experience' (*Erlebnis*) denotes a more complex concept, referring to relational intentionality. As such, a phenomenological description reveals the *essence* (or conditions) of experience. To provide a phenomenological description (in the Husserlian sense) of body shame, more than an understanding of the symptoms of shame is needed, and the essential characteristics of embodiment, as described above, such as motor intentionality, bodily visibility, invisibility, the body schema, the seen body and the structure of relations with others through the Look, must be considered.

As discussed in chapter 1, body shame is about visibility: in experiences of body shame, whether acute or chronic, some part of the body or some aspect of comportment is brought into awareness and is regarded (and judged) by the self or others. Body shame involves exposure and the 'seen body'; one is seen by oneself or by others (whose views and judgements one shares) to be 'doing wrong' or to be failing or flawed in some crucial way. However, it must be noted that shame is not anomalous, or only occurs when there is some mishap or fault in the flow of social relations. Shame is in fact constitutive and necessary. Shame is central to the formation of the body and to skill acquisition, both in childhood development and for adults. Dreyfus, in his account of skill acquisition, demonstrates that emotional involvement is key to the sedimentation of a body technique into the corporeal schema. In particular, self-conscious feelings such as shame and embarrassment, especially centred on the body, where one judges oneself according to standards constituted by some sort of external authority, are necessary to motivate skilled action. As Dreyfus argues, feelings of "remorse," of being "frightened," "disappointed" and "discouraged" arise as the subject experiences repeated failure.[123] Motivation to master the skill arises from wanting to avoid these negative feelings and to incur social approval. The idea that someone is evaluating one's performance, and that one may disappoint them or let them down, is fundamental to skill acquisition. Hence, to become competent, one must first struggle, falter and feel bad. Feelings of failure and shame, in the presence of an imagined or actual audience motivate the acquisition of skilled behaviour and hence the formation of the body schema. Self-consciousness is key in these experiences: in shame, the subject feels exposed to itself and to anyone present and this leads to a paralyzing inner scrutiny, a moment of extreme self-consciousness. As the clinical psychologist Gershen Kaufman describes it: "to feel shame is to feel *seen* in a painfully diminished sense."[124]

Hence, in situations where the self is exposed to the view of others, the body may be *seen* and regarded in a thematic way as the object of perception as in the social dys-appearances described by Sartre, Leder and others. In experiences of body shame, this occurs on two levels. Firstly, as body shame is about some aspect of the body or comportment, part of the body becomes conspicuous or *shameful* and attention is drawn to it. To foreshadow the discussion of cosmetic surgery to come in chapter 6, consider, for example, Michelle, a twenty-three-year-old woman who suffered from chronic shame about the shape of her nose before undergoing rhinoplasty. Michelle describes how her attention was continuously drawn to her nose, distracting her from other activities and disrupting the 'flow' of her social situations. She says:

It was like, my nose would just get really, sort of, *hot* and I'd be like, I've got to get to a mirror. . . . My boyfriend and I would be having a meal out and I wouldn't be thinking, y'know, about enjoying myself. I'd be worrying, does my nose look huge in this light.[125]

Second, compounding the feeling of being *seen* that arises as a result of shame about a physical feature, the shame experience itself also involves a whole slew of involuntary physiological reactions which, in addition, bring awareness to the physical body.

As discussed in chapter 1, shame is a 'bodily condition' and not merely a cognitive response. The physical symptoms that can arise in a shame experience are varied, as they arise from both sympathetic and parasympathetic responses in the body.[126] Goffman, in his extensive writing about shame, embarrassment and body management, offers a list of possible shame symptoms and responses:

[B]lushing, fumbling, stuttering, an unusually low- or high-pitched voice, sweating, blanching, blinking, tremor of the hands, hesitating or vacillating movement . . . there may be a lowering of the eyes, bowing of the head, putting the hands behind the back, nervous fingering of the clothing or twisting of the fingers together, and stammering . . . There are also symptoms of a subjective kind: constriction of the diaphragm, a feeling of wobbliness, consciousness of strained and unnatural gestures, a dazed sensation, dryness of mouth, and tenseness of muscles.[127]

I offer this list here, not as a definitive catalogue of shame symptoms, but rather to demonstrate that, although shame is *always* expressed through the body, it is difficult to describe a paradigmatic shame response; the symptoms and responses are numerous and varied, depending on a variety of factors. However, what is clear is that a shame experience is never merely cognitive, but instead manifests through corporeal expressions which draw attention to the body. Matthew Ratcliffe's discussion of the phenomenology of existential feelings is useful in understanding the physical component of the shame experience. Existential feelings, as Ratcliffe describes them, are both "feelings of the body" and "ways of finding oneself in the world." In other words, they are bodily states comprised of *feelings* that form a "background" through which experience is structured and made intelligible.[128] Existential feelings are a constant of our experience and shape our understanding of and relation to the world. When shame arises, our existential feelings—underpinning the physical 'symptoms' of shame, such as those described above—indicate that something has gone amiss or awry between our body and our relation to the world.

What is particularly interesting about shame is that these symptoms, as outward displays of shame, are themselves taboo. Revealing that one is expe-

riencing shame, through blushing, trembling, stuttering, and so forth, is *itself*
shameful.[129] As a result, shame symptoms provoke a shame spiral or
"loop,"[130] in which, when shame arises it incites more shame (about the
shame). Shame, as such, is an iterated emotion; its occurrence leads to an
intensification or multiplication of itself.[131] This "second-order"[132] shame
results from shame itself being a source of shameful anxiety. As a result,
shame is an emotion that is often fastidiously avoided and if that is not
possible, it is to be scrupulously ignored.

However, shame cannot always be avoided or ignored, and it often in-
trudes into daily life with disruptive consequences. As Goffman observes,
when an agent is overcome by shame or embarrassment he is in some sense
'paralyzed' by the symptoms of shame and "cannot . . . mobilize his muscular and intellectual resources for the task at hand . . . He is present with them
[others], but he is not 'in play.'"[133] Hence, just like the dys-appearances,
such as acute injury or pain, which can suddenly disrupt the smooth flow of
motor intentionality, instances of body shame have a similar disruptive effect: the body—or, again, some part of the body—comes to the centre of
awareness and is regarded in a separative way as an object of perception.
Body shame can disrupt 'flow'—whether it is an individual's flow in motor
intentionality, or the 'flow' of a social encounter—and cause attention to be
turned to the body, rendering it visible.[134]

Gershen Kaufman terms this experience of dys-appearance due to shame
"binding."[135] Binding arises as a result of visibility and involves a disturbance of smooth activity because some physical feature has brought attention
to the body, interrupting the intentional relation to the external world. In
addition, the physical symptoms of shame, themselves shameful, affect a
further disruption: "The binding effects of exposure, of feeling *seen*, acutely
disturb the smooth functioning of the self. . . . Exposure can interrupt movement, bind speech and make eye contact intolerable. Shame paralyzes the
self."[136] In the experience of binding, there is usually an arousal of an unpleasant feeling as a result of the predicament one finds oneself in, but also a
freezing into immobility in the humiliation one is experiencing.[137] Nietzsche
describes such an experience in the following manner:

> The feeling 'I am the mid-point of the world!' arises very strongly if one is
> suddenly overcome with shame; one then stands there as though confused in
> the midst of a surging sea and feels dazzled as though by a great eye which
> gazes upon us and through us from all sides.[138]

In this experience, there is the desire to conceal oneself, to shrink away from
others and the situation. Consider again Pecola from Morrison's *The Bluest
Eye*. Yearning for invisibility, her physical response to shame is palpable:

"Pecola stood a little apart from us, her eyes hinged in the direction in which Maureen had fled. She seemed to fold into herself, like a pleated wing."[139]

Arising as a result of this exposure and self-consciousness is the experience of an extremely negative affect within the subject; this affect is directed toward one's own estimation of oneself. The psychologist Silvan S. Tomkins writes that as a result of the "inner torment" of shame, one feels "naked, defeated, alienated, lacking in dignity or worth."[140] Gershan Kaufman echoes this sentiment, describing shame as a "wound made from the inside by an unseen hand" which leads to feeling "fundamentally deficient as individuals, diseased, defective."[141] To experience shame is "to experience the very essence or heart of the self as wanting. Shame is inevitably alienating, isolating and deeply disturbing."[142]

In addition, the negative affect of shame does not just impinge on the individual. Body shame has a peculiar 'contagious' character. In social relations, all the participants in a particular situation may experience feelings of embarrassment or shame when one person is overcome with the feeling themselves. As Goffman observes, in embarrassing incidents, when the flow of face-to-face interaction breaks down, all parties involved, "may come to feel ill at ease, nonplussed, out of countenance, [and] embarrassed."[143] Shame cannot, therefore, be considered an experience with consequences limited to an individual subject. Instead, it has a social dimension, in that it changes the character of a situation in which it has occurred and, in addition, can 'infect' others: what would otherwise have been a smooth social encounter becomes infused with awkwardness and uncertainty about social cues and roles. To avoid the discomfort that arises in instances of social dys-appearance, people go out of their way to avoid shame (or even mention past instances of shame),[144] even when this avoidance means harming or hurting the self.

Beyond remaining silent or being scrupulously avoided, shame can also be an "unidentified" or "hidden" emotion which does not enter conscious awareness but is nonetheless frequently present.[145] As shame is such a painful and disruptive experience, there is an intrinsic connection between shame and the mechanism of denial.[146] Although the experience remains available to consciousness, the person experiencing it is not able to, or perhaps simply will not, identify it as shame. In these cases, shame is 'by-passed' and other affects, such as anger, guilt or doubt, take over. Consider Pecola again, who replaces her shame with anger, albeit unsuccessfully in this case:

> Anger is better. There is a sense of being in anger. A reality and presence. An awareness of worth. It is a lovely surging . . . The anger will not hold; the puppy is too easily surfeited. Its thirst too quickly quenched, it sleeps. The shame wells up again, its muddy rivulets seeping into her eyes.[147]

When shame is replaced with another emotion, or when it is unacknowledged or hidden, it goes "underground."[148] As, Lashbrook explains: "Shame (and its various manifestations) despite its ubiquity, is subtle and hard to detect because its painful nature leads to the need to repress it."[149] Obviously, as an experience that can be by-passed or repressed, this presents a challenge to articulating a phenomenology of body shame and makes salient the fact that to understand a complex experience such as shame, much more than phenomenology is needed. For this reason, in the next chapter, I will turn to social theory in order to consider accounts of the social, cultural and political structures that frame shame experiences, rendering them intelligible even when they may remain experientially absent.

CONCLUSION

The power of shame is undeniable. Physical pain or discomfort is easily forgotten while the pain of shame, *especially* body shame, burns brightest in our memories ready to be relived at any moment, months, years or even decades after its occurrence. Indeed, even just the recollection of a shame experience can cause that shame to resurface. The desire to avoid body shame can by far surpass the desire to avoid pain. In fact, as Michelle cited above demonstrates, physical pain or discomfort is preferable to shame; undergoing rhinoplasty (a surgical procedure with serious risks such as disfigurement or even death and a long, painful recovery time) is preferable to living with the pain of body shame.

Avoiding and circumventing shame is a powerful (and often invisible) force in daily embodied life. The subject is constantly creating strategies to avoid incurring the antagonistic, reductive or judgmental gaze of the other. This occurs on a micro-level, in the minutiae of day-to-day encounters, in skill acquisition, in action and motor intentionality, and in more long-term strategies, such as Michelle's decision to undergo cosmetic surgery. Phenomenological invisibility is key. As the body is constantly engaged in strategies to achieve equilibrium, avoiding intrusions of 'dys-appearances' underpins action, perception and social interaction. Exploring how the body is able to be regarded as an object—available to be *seen* or regarded by the self and others which constitute one's milieu—further illustrates the phenomenological features of body shame. Through exploring the see-er/seen relation in Merleau-Ponty's late ontology and the existential experiences of objectification, alienation and shame in Sartre's account, the social aspects of bodily visibility and invisibility have been revealed.

Sartre, in casting the Look, visibility and shame as constitutive features of reflective self-consciousness, highlights the fact that a concern around self-presentation and bodily visibility is neither trivial nor insignificant. In contrast, Sartre demonstrates that embodied social relations are constitutive of reflective self-consciousness and form part of the very fabric of our being. It is not as though action and perception come first and then self-presentation follows as some sort of second order concern. Instead, they are entangled such that one cannot be said to precede the other. We can neither choose to turn away from others, nor to not present ourselves to others. The seen body, like the body schema, isn't optional or secondary to consciousness, but instead is an inherent part of the structure of reflective awareness. As such, self-presentation and body management play constitutive roles in subjectivity. Furthermore, body shame is a structural feature in the constant production of subjectivity and reflective self-consciousness.

Through his account of the Look, Sartre illustrates the necessarily social dimension of bodily invisibility. Beyond the 'invisibility' afforded by the physical body in instances of flow in habitual skillful action, invisibility depends in large part on the social field and one's relations to others within that field. Being seen by the other can disrupt one's experience of bodily invisibility, bringing thematic awareness to the body, affecting the social dys-appearance, as Sartre's voyeur example demonstrates. Sartre links shame to the body in a significant manner. It is through objectifying experiences of body shame that the subject gains awareness of the self. Shame (or the possibility of shame) as ubiquitous within intersubjectivity helps one construct a social identity. How the body is presented to others (present, imagined or absent) is fundamental for one's own conception of oneself, and furthermore through objectifying experiences of shame, one learns about oneself. These ideas resonate with Merleau-Ponty's own conception of the affective realm and his reflections of the visible body in his later work. For Merleau-Ponty the affective subtends all experience in the world, it forms a permanent substrate of our being.[150] Furthermore, being seen, for Merleau-Ponty, is not just about displaying my physical appearance, but is constitutive of a significant aspect of my being: it places my body into a realm of values and possibilities and elicits key affective responses from others.[151]

However, despite these insights into the constitutive nature of intersubjectivity, Sartre's and Merleau-Ponty's accounts remain incomplete. Although Sartre's account is embedded in and acknowledges a broader rule and norm governed socio-cultural and political field, he does not explicitly address how that broader milieu affects and determines the nature of intersubjective relations and how shame can only arise as a result of the normative forces constituted in a social, cultural and political realm. As we shall see, he has been criticized on this point. In addition, although Merleau-Ponty explicitly acknowledges the cultural embeddedness of the body subject, his account does not systematically describe the role that normative forces play in the phenomenology of lived experience. In order to elucidate the role of norms in the constitution of subjectivity and in experiences of body shame, in the next chapter I will turn to consider the work of Michel Foucault and Norbert Elias. Foucault and Elias are both social thinkers whose investigations, in part, centre around the body and the significance of how the body is seen and apprehended by others.

NOTES

1. Edmund Husserl, *Ideas Pertaining to a Pure Phenomenology and to a Phenomenological Philosophy—Second Book*, trans. R. Rojcewicz and A. Schuwer (Dordrecht, The Netherlands: Kluwer Academic Publishers, 1989), 150. Hereafter cited as *Ideas II*.
2. Husserl, *Ideas II*, 183.
3. Ibid. It should be noted that Husserl uses several terms to designate this operation, such as: 'the transcendental *epochē*,' 'the phenomenological *epochē*,' 'the transcendental reduction' and 'the phenomenological reduction.'
4. Husserl, *Ideas II*, 189, 380n. See also: Husserl, *Ideas I*, 60–62.
5. Husserl, *Ideas II*, 151.
6. See: "Translator's Introduction" in *Ideas II*, xiv. For a discussion about the difficulties in translating '*Leib*' and '*Körper*' see: Elizabeth A. Behnke, "Edmund Husserl's Contribution to Phenomenology of the Body in Ideas II," in *Phenomenology: Critical Concepts in Philosophy—Volume 2*, eds. Dermot Moran and Lester E. Embree (Oxon: Routledge, 2004), 238–239. In the English translation of *Ideas II*, these terms are distinguished orthographically, *Leib* appearing as 'Body' and *Körper* as 'body.' (I will preserve this distinction in citations, but I will not use it myself.)
7. Husserl, *Ideas II*, 153.
8. Ibid.
9. Jenny Slatman, *Our Strange Body: Philosophical Reflections on Identity and Medical Interventions* (Amsterdam: Amsterdam University Press, 2014), 133.
10. Husserl, *Ideas II*, 153.
11. Ibid., 154.
12. Ibid., 159. Emphasis in original.
13. Ibid.
14. Ibid., 166.
15. Ibid., 169.
16. Ibid., 61. Emphasis in original.
17. See: Husserl, *Thing and Space: Lectures of 1907*.
18. Husserl, *Ideas II*, 160.
19. Merleau-Ponty made a close study of the manuscript of *Ideas II* in 1939 when it was still unpublished and in archival form in the Husserl Archive in Leuven. See: Ted Toadvine, "Merleau-Ponty's Reading of Husserl: A Chronological Overview," in *Merleau-Ponty's Reading of Husserl*, eds. Ted Toadvine and Lester Embree (Dordrecht, The Netherlands: Kluwer Academic Publishers, 2002), 234–235.
20. Merleau-Ponty, *Phenomenology of Perception*, 114. Translation modified.
21. Ibid., 159.
22. Maurice Merleau-Ponty, "An Unpublished Text by Maurice Merleau-Ponty: A Prospectus of His Work," in *The Primacy of Perception*, ed. James M. Edie (Evanston: Northwestern University Press, 1964), 6.
23. Merleau-Ponty, *Phenomenology of Perception*, 127.
24. Ibid., 121.
25. Ibid., 162.
26. Ibid., 93.
27. Ibid., 95.
28. Ibid.
29. Ibid., 175–176.
30. Ibid., 176.

31. Maurice Merleau-Ponty, "The Child's Relations with Others," in *The Primacy of Perception*, ed. James M. Edie (Evanston: Northwestern University Press, 1964), 99.

32. Hubert L. Dreyfus, "The Challenge of Merleau-Ponty's Phenomenology of Embodiment for Cognitive Science," in *Perspectives on Embodiment: The Intersections of Nature and Culture*, eds. Honi Fern Haber and Gail Weiss (New York: Routledge, 1999), 105.

33. Ibid., 105–110.

34. Ibid.

35. Merleau-Ponty, *Phenomenology of Perception*, 160–161.

36. Ibid., 292.

37. Maurice Merleau-Ponty, *Sense and Non-Sense*, trans. Hubert L. Dreyfus and Patricia Allen Dreyfus (Evanston: Northwestern University Press, 1964), 72.

38. See, for example: Marcel Mauss, "Techniques of the Body," in *The Body: A Reader*, eds. Mariam Fraser and Monica Greco (London: Routledge, 2005).

39. Dreyfus, "The Challenge of Merleau-Ponty's Phenomenology of Embodiment for Cognitive Science," 111.

40. Merleau-Ponty, *Phenomenology of Perception*, 118ff.

41. Ibid., 119–120.

42. Shaun Gallagher and Jonathan Cole, "Body Image and Body Schema in a Deafferented Subject," in *Body and Flesh: A Philosophical Reader*, ed. Donn Welton (Oxford: Blackwell, 1998), 131. Jonathan Cole has well documented the case of Ian Waterman. See: Jonathan Cole, *Pride and a Daily Marathon* (Cambridge: MIT Press, 1995). Oliver Sacks discusses a similar patient in the case of the 'Disembodied Lady' who suffers from acute polyneuritis. See: Oliver Sacks, *The Man Who Mistook His Wife for a Hat* (London: Duckworth, 1985), 42–52.

43. Merleau-Ponty, *Signs*, 89.

44. Elizabeth A. Behnke, "World without Opposite/Flesh of the World (A Carnal Introduction)" (paper presented at the Merleau-Ponty Circle, Ninth Annual Meeting, Concordia University, Montreal, September 1984), 6. On this point see also: Matthew Ratcliffe, "Touch and Situatedness," *International Journal of Philosophical Studies* vol. 16, no. 3 (2008): 307.

45. Jean-Paul Sartre, *Being and Nothingness: An Essay on Phenomenological Ontology*, trans. Hazel E. Barnes (London: Routledge, 2003), 347.

46. Shaun Gallagher, "Lived Body and Environment," in *Phenomenology: Critical Concepts in Philosophy—Volume 2*, eds. Dermot Moran and Lester E. Embree (Oxon: Routledge, 2004), 278.

47. Ibid., 277.

48. Sartre, *Being and Nothingness*, 354. Emphasis in original.

49. Drew Leder, *The Absent Body* (Chicago: University of Chicago Press, 1990), 1.

50. Gallagher, "Lived Body and Environment," 273. It should be noted that Gallagher also mentions positive situations such as sport or dance. In the case of mental illness, Gallagher cites some examples in the literature of psychopathology where one may experience hallucinations with regard to how the body is perceived or sensed.

51. F. J. J. Buytendijk, *Prolegomena to an Anthropological Physiology*, trans. A. I. Orr (Pittsburgh: Duquesne University Press, 1964), 61.

52. Ratcliffe, *Feelings of Being*, 112.

53. Leder, *The Absent Body*, 84. In commenting on his choice of terminology, Leder writes: "Thus, the two words, *dys-appearance* and *disappearance* have an antonymic significance. Yet at the same time, the homonymity of these words is mean to suggest the deep relation between these two modes." Leder, *The Absent Body*, 86.

54. Ratcliffe, *Feelings of Being*, 112.

55. Merleau-Ponty, *Phenomenology of Perception*, 177. For further discussion on the body schema and equilibrium see: Katherine Morris, "Merleau-Ponty on Understanding *Other* Others," In *Body/Self/Other: The Phenomenology of Social Encounters*, eds. Luna Dolezal and Danielle Petherbridge (Albany: SUNY Press, Forthcoming).

56. Merleau-Ponty, *Phenomenology of Perception*, 352.

57. Naturally, this generalization is not intended to be a universal claim. There are certainly many cases where pain and discomfort are brought intentionally to the body, such as in self

harm, physiotherapy, body modification or other instances. For certain subjectivities, in certain circumstances, pain and/or discomfort may instead be the preferable state.

58. Sartre utilizes the capitalized 'Other' to denote not only another person, but, in general, a perspective which is not one's own. I will preserve this in citations and I will utilize 'other' to denote another possible subjectivity and the captialized 'Other' to denote a generalized sense of other than oneself.

59. I will employ the capitalized 'Look' throughout to designate Sartre's '*le regard.*'

60. Sartre. *Being and Nothingness*, 282–283. Emphasis in original.

61. Ibid., 283.

62. Ibid., 284. Emphasis in original.

63. Ibid., 281.

64. Ibid., 283.

65. Ibid., 298.

66. For a critical discussion of Sartre's account of the Look see: Luna Dolezal, "Reconsidering the Look in Sartre's Being and Nothingness," *Sartre Studies International* vol. 18, no. 1 (2012).

67. Maurice Merleau-Ponty, "Eye and Mind," in *The Primacy of Perception,* trans. Carelton Dallery (Evanston: Northwestern University Press, 1964), 163.

68. Ibid., 162.

69. Maurice Merleau-Ponty, *The Visible and the Invisible*, ed. Claude Lefort, trans. Alphonso Lingus (Evanston: Northwestern University Press, 1968), 134–135.

70. Merleau-Ponty, "Eye and Mind," 162.

71. Merleau-Ponty, *The Visible and the Invisible*, 134.

72. Ibid., 155.

73. Ibid., 143.

74. Ibid., 244–245. Emphasis in original.

75. Sartre, *Being and Nothingness*, 375.

76. Ibid., 382.

77. Ibid., 375.

78. The 'seen Body' is a term used by Husserl to describe the body as a visible object in the world. However, I will employ the term more specifically to signify the body seen *as though from the perspective of another*. See: Husserl, *Ideas II*, 155.

79. Charles H. Cooley, *Human Nature and the Social Order* (Glencoe, Illinois: The Free Press, 1956), 184.

80. Paul Valery, "Some Simple Reflections on the Body," in *Fragments for a History of the Human Body—Part 2*, ed. Michel Feher, Ramona Naddaff, and Nadia Tazi (Cambridge, MA: MIT Press, 1989), 399.

81. Ibid., 400.

82. Sartre, *Being and Nothingness*, 284.

83. Ibid., 246.

84. Ibid., 298.

85. Ibid., 367.

86. Ibid., 376.

87. Ibid., 372.

88. Ibid., 373.

89. Ibid., 369.

90. However, it should be noted that even a corpse is a special type of object not comparable to other inanimate objects such as tables or chairs. When encountering a corpse there is a recognition of its now defunct subjectivity: it is an object that used to be a subject.

91. Sartre, *Being and Nothingness*, 367.

92. Ibid., 374.

93. See: Edmund Husserl, *Cartesian Meditations: An Introduction to Phenomenology*, trans. Dorion Cairns (Dordrecht, The Netherlands: Kluwer Academic Publishers, 1977).

94. For a discussion of the various notions that are involved in the idea of objectification see: Martha C. Nussbaum, "Objectification," *Philosophy and Public Affairs* vol. 24, no. 4 (1995): 257. However, in this paper, Nussbaum does not meaningfully distinguish between

alienation and objectification, and seems to regard alienation as merely a type of objectification.

95. Sandra Lee Bartky, *Femininity and Domination: Studies in the Phenomenology of Oppression* (London: Routledge, 1990), 32.

96. Sartre, *Being and Nothingness*, 376. Emphasis in original.

97. Ibid., 288.

98. Martin Jay, *Downcast Eyes: The Denigration of Vision in Twentieth-Century French Thought* (Berkeley: University of California Press, 1994), 289.

99. Martha C. Nussbaum also discusses how objectification is a 'multiple' concept and in some cases can be positive or even necessary. See: Nussbaum, "Objectification."

100. Bartky, *Femininity and Domination*, 26.

101. See: Nussbaum, "Objectification," 271.

102. Sartre, *Being and Nothingness*, 301.

103. Ibid., 246.

104. Ibid.

105. Ibid., 377.

106. Ibid., 285

107. Ibid., 245.

108. Ibid., 246.

109. Ibid., 299.

110. Gary Cox, *The Sartre Dictionary* (London: Continuum, 2008), 157.

111. Sartre, *Being and Nothingness*, 305.

112. Ibid.

113. This is a line of argument developed by Gabriele Taylor. See: Gabriele Taylor, *Pride, Shame and Guilt: Emotions of Self Assessment* (Oxford: Clarendon Press, 1985), 66.

114. Sartre, *Being and Nothingness*, 312.

115. Ibid.

116. Ibid.

117. Ibid.

118. Leder, *The Absent Body*, 96.

119. Ibid.

120. Erving Goffman, *Interaction Ritual: Essays on Face-to-Face Behaviour* (New York: Pantheon Books, 1967), 101.

121. Erving Goffman, *Strategic Interaction* (Philadelphia: University of Pennsylvania Press, 1969), 11.

122. For example, see: Gershen Kaufman's chapter 'Phenomenology and Facial Signs of Shame' in Gershen Kaufman, *The Psychology of Shame: Theory and Treatment of Shame Based Syndromes* (London: Routledge, 1993), 3–29.

123. Hubert L. Dreyfus, "A Phenomenology of Skill Acquisition as the Basis for a Merleau-Pontian Non-representationalist Cognitive Science," University of California, Berkeley http://ist-socrates.berkeley.edu/~hdreyfus/pdf/MerleauPontySkillCogSci.pdf (Accessed 9 September 2014).

124. Kaufman, *The Psychology of Shame*, 17. Emphasis in original.

125. Quoted in: Debra Gimlin, "The Absent Body Project: Cosmetic Surgery as a Response to Bodily Dys-Appearance.," *Sociology* vol. 40, no. 4 (2006): 707.

126. Rowland S. Miller, *Embarrassment: Poise and Peril in Everyday Life* (New York: The Guilford Press, 1996), 17.

127. Erving Goffman, *Interaction Ritual*, 97.

128. Ratcliffe, *Feelings of Being*, 2.

129. The shamefulness of shame can vary for certain groups. For example, it is suggested by Aneta Stepien that shame is particularly shameful for men. As a result they are much more likely to repress, hide or deny shame, perhaps bypassing it for other emotions or experiences such as depression or anger. See: Aneta Stepian, "Understanding Male Shame," *Masculinities: A Journal of Identity and Culture* vol. 1 (2014): 7–27.

130. Thomas J. Scheff, "Shame and the Social Bond: A Sociological Theory," *Sociological Theory* vol. 18, no. 1 (2000): 90.

131. Helen B. Lewis, *Shame and Guilt in Neurosis* (New York: International Universities Press, 1971), 202. See also: Kaufman, *The Psychology of Shame*, 4, 20.

132. Robert G. Lee and Gordon Wheeler, eds., *The Voice of Shame: Silence and Connection in Psychotherapy* (San Francisco: Jossey-Bass, 1996), vii.

133. Goffman, *Interaction Ritual*, 100, 101.

134. Thomas Fuchs makes a similar point arguing that the lived body undergoes, what he terms, a 'corporealization,' where the spontaneous performance of the body is ruptured in experiences of guilt and shame. See: Fuchs, "The Phenomenology of Shame, Guilt and Body in Body Dysmorphic Disorder and Depression." On this point, also see: Katherine J. Morris, "The Phenomenology of Body Dysmorphic Disorder: A Sartrean Analysis," in *Nature and Narrative: An Introduction to the New Philosophy of Psychiatry*, eds. Bill Fulford, et al. (Oxford: Oxford University Press, 2003).

135. Kaufman, *The Psychology of Shame*, 18.

136. Ibid., 18, 19–20.

137. Miller, *Embarrassment: Poise and Peril in Everyday Life*, 16.

138. Friedrich Nietzsche, *Daybreak: Thoughts on the Prejudices of Morality*, eds. Maudemarie Clark and Brian Leiter, trans. R. J. Hollingdale (Cambridge: Cambridge University Press, 1997), 166.

139. Morrison, *The Bluest Eye*, 57.

140. Silvan S. Tomkins, *Affect, Imagery, Consciousness: The Negative Affects, Vol. 2* (New York: Springer, 1963), 118.

141. Kaufman, *The Psychology of Shame*, 5, 18.

142. Ibid., 18.

143. Erving Goffman, *The Presentation of Self in Everyday Life* (Middlesex: Penguin Books, 1959), 12.

144. See: Miller, *Embarrassment: Poise and Peril in Everyday Life*, 4–5.

145. Helen B. Lewis, *Shame and Guilt in Neurosis* (New York: International Universities Press, 1971), 203; Robert G. Lee and Gordon Wheeler, eds., *The Voice of Shame: Silence and Connection in Psychotherapy* (San Francisco: Jossey-Bass, 1996), ii.

146. Lewis, *Shame and Guilt in Neurosis*: 196.

147. Morrison, *The Bluest Eye*, 37–38.

148. Thomas J. Scheff, "Elias, Freud and Goffman: Shame as the Master Emotion," in *The Sociology of Norbert Elias*, ed. Steven Loyal and Stephen Quilley (Cambridge: Cambridge University Press, 2004), 231.

149. Jeffrey T. Lashbrook, "Fitting In: Exploring the Emotional Dimension of Adolescent Pressure," *Adolescence* vol. 35, no. 140 (2000): 754.

150. See: chapter 5 "The Body in Its Sexual Being" in Merleau-Ponty, *Phenomenology of Perception*.

151. See: chapter 4 "The Intertwining – The Chiasm" in Merleau-Ponty, *The Visible and the Invisible*.

Chapter Three

Shame and the Socially Shaped Body

Michel Foucault and Norbert Elias

In the previous chapter, the phenomenological approach was employed in order to describe the individual and intersubjective features of shame that is centred on the body. Examining the visibility and invisibility of the body, through phenomenological features of embodiment such as motor intentionality, skill acquisition and the body schema, it was demonstrated that shame that is centred on the body is key to understanding how the subject successfully negotiates both the physical and social world. Body shame is necessary for skill acquisition, the formation of the body schema and for setting up meaningful boundaries and limits for one's social and intersubjective interactions. Sartre's work further develops these insights, demonstrating that shame is ubiquitous in the constitution of the subject through social relations. It is through the Look that one discovers one's self and enters into moral and ethical life as a result of the objectifying and alienating responses of the Other.

However, as Sartre's project is primarily ontological, concerned with the conditions and structures of being, he does not fully consider the significance of the socio-cultural and political framework in which all intersubjective and social relations are embedded. When trying to uncover or illustrate ontological structures, Sartre fails to consider the normative frameworks through which subjects construct social identities. Indeed, it seems improbable that the voyeur had no awareness of the nature of his acts prior to undertaking them. He has not, as Marjorie Grene points out, "been dropped from heaven to watch and listen at the keyhole."[1] The voyeur has a whole social history which has shaped and given meaning to his situation. This point is particularly relevant when using Sartre's ideas to explicate shame, as shame can only arise within a framework of normative ideals, arising from one's social life, which instantiate binary codes around what is considered 'normal' and 'abnormal' or 'acceptable' or 'unacceptable,' and so on. Without considering this broader normative framework, Sartre fails to pick up on how the Look's effectiveness as an instrument of social control is tied to socio-cultural and political factors which envelop the structure of looking/being-looked-at or see-er/seen. Indeed, it is important just who is looking and just who is being looked at, and furthermore, as we saw with the discussion of alienation and objectification, the context within which this encounter occurs is central.

Simone de Beauvoir is critical of Sartre in this respect. In particular, she argues that Sartre overlooks the significance of gendered difference, neglecting to acknowledge possible imbalances in the dialectic of subjectification and objectification that arises in cases of the Look. The female body, de Beauvoir argues, and I will consider these arguments further in chapter 5, is more likely to be rendered object; her status as subject is more tenuous. As a result, she has less social power to deflect or defy the Look, and, concomitantly, she is more likely to feel ashamed or embarrassed about her body.[2] Franz Fanon makes similar arguments when discussing race. The raced body, within the colonial context, is again more likely to be rendered object, and his or her power to return the Look is considerably compromised as a result of certain normative conditions which render raced subjects disempowered within social relations.[3]

What these criticisms demonstrate is that the body cannot be considered to be a neutral entity, and the likelihood that one will experience body shame is connected to a broader network of value and meaning which envelops (and hence determines the nature of) actual intersubjective encounters. The vulgar gesture that Sartre mentions is only vulgar within a set of intersubjectively shared socio-cultural values. As such, shame can only find its full articulation within a normative framework, more than an encounter between two bodies is needed. Instead, a whole complex world of language, culture and normative values must be in place, where certain behaviours, actions or modes of being are prohibited and seen as deviant and others are socially sanctioned and considered 'normal' or 'acceptable.' Furthermore, each body subject does not have equal power when it comes to returning or receiving the Look. As a result, some bodies are more prone to shame than others. Hence, we find that each body is loaded with value and meaning while embedded within a complex nexus of signification within the socio-cultural and political spheres within which it finds itself.

In this chapter, I will turn to two social thinkers, Michel Foucault and Norbert Elias, to offer two accounts of how the body subject is embedded in socio-cultural and political world and hence how norms are transmitted through the body. Although Foucault and Elias locate their analyses within the developments of specific historical periods (namely, capitalism for Foucault and the court society for Elias), these accounts, as I am utilizing them here, are not intending to be merely historical or even sociological. Instead, they demonstrate how pan-cultural and pan-historical aspects of our subjectivity—our propensity for negative self-conscious emotions, our intercorporeality, our capacity for skill acquisition, and so forth—are shaped by the contingent normative values of particular socio-cultural and political spheres. All of the descriptions of individual embodiment and intersubjectivity thus far offered by Husserl, Merleau-Ponty and Sartre are inseparable from, and indeed intertwined with, this broader sphere. The phenomenal body is always loaded with social value—the configuration of the body schema in terms of which skills are acquired or cultivated within a certain individual, as we shall see, is by no means culturally or politically neutral. Furthermore, intersubjective embodied relations are always loaded with social meaning; the Look is never completely impartial. As a result, the socio-cultural political context cannot be effectively bracketed—as Husserl intended—when describing or discussing embodied experiences such as shame or intersubjectivity.

Both Michel Foucault and Norbert Elias consider the role of external forces on how the embodied subject is constituted. The body is important, if not central, to both their work. Although there are many differences in their approaches, they were both concerned with how standards for body management have developed over the course of Western history as a result of certain social and political developments, and the impact this has on conceptions of selfhood. They both wrote extensively about the seen body, concerned with the effect of objectification on the subject. Hence, in this chapter, I will turn to the work of Foucault and Elias respectively, drawing out the themes of internalization, surveillance, social control and the significance of body shame in the socio-cultural and political spheres.

FOUCAULT'S 'HISTORY OF BODIES'

Michel Foucault is often described as a critical historian of thought, and his theoretical work has been influential in a broad range of disciplines from philosophy to sociology to politics to literary theory, among others. In particular, his reflections on what it means to be an embodied subject in modern society have had far-reaching and profound implications. Foucault's theoretical writings span three decades and his work is varied in its approach and subject matter, from historical and empirical accounts of particular institutions, such as the asylum and the prison, to more theoretical works which seek to dismantle the theoretical underpinnings of classical philosophical endeavours, forging key concepts such as power, discourse and knowledge, to detailed historical and genealogical analyses of Ancient Greek and Roman mores surrounding sexuality. Despite the broad range of subject areas to which Foucault turned his critical attention throughout his career, he describes his overall objective to "create a history of the different modes by which, in our culture, human beings are made subjects."[4]

Foucault's work forms a critique of the various conceptions of the rational subject which, he argues, have dominated Western thought since the Enlightenment. His overall project has been to dismantle the notion of a fully unified, self-reflexive and rational subject characterized by capabilities of free agency which appears at the centre of much modern thought, for example in the theoretical subject of Husserlian phenomenology. Instead, Foucault explores the idea of the subject as a product of discursive and disciplinary formations. To be a subject, for Foucault, is to be subjected: the phenomenological description of the body as the 'organ of the will' is neither a complete, nor an accurate description of subjectivity. In fact, Foucault argues, against phenomenology, that the subject is determined by structures and configurations of power that are beyond the reach of transcendental consciousness.

When compared to Husserl, Merleau-Ponty or Sartre, Foucault takes an entirely different theoretical approach when considering the constitution and status of the embodied subject. Foucault entirely rejects the phenomenological approach which puts the subject, as a unifying ego, at the centre of theoretical enquiry. He contends that the phenomenological approach, centred on the perceiving subject, cannot give an adequate account of "who, what, or where we are," questions which are central to his philosophical project.[5] He writes:

> If there is one approach that I do reject, however, it is that (one might call it, broadly speaking, the phenomenological approach) which gives priority to the observing subject, which attributes a constituent role to an act, which places its own point of view at the origin of all historicity—which, in short, leads to a transcendental consciousness.[6]

Phenomenology, for Foucault, lacks the comprehensive breadth to consider the forces that influence and shape the body subject. As he puts it: "[p]henomenology has succeeded in making images speak; but it has given no one the possibility of understanding their language."[7] In other words, although we may see the effect of socio-cultural and political forces in phenomenological descriptions, we will not gain any critical understanding of the nature of these forces from these descriptions. Certain aspects of experience are so ingrained, and seem so natural or necessary, that it is only when they are considered from a distanced, or third-person perspective, that the contingency of these features may be appreciated and examined. Furthermore, Foucault argues that phenomenology lacks the ability to account for language and the influence of the unconscious mind, as described in psychoanalysis, in conferring meaning (if knowledge is to be strictly derived from the givens of lived experience).

Hence, in order to understand the subject—or to answer the question posed by Foucault: "What are we in our actuality?"[8] —Foucault takes an entirely different approach. Rejecting transcendental a priori theories of the subject, Foucault analyses the subject in terms of the socio-cultural, political and historical forces—particularly institutions, practices, modes of knowledge and conceptions of truth—that play specific roles in shaping and transforming bodies. He argues that the subject is not self-constituting and creative in action and perception, but instead is constituted by the various operations of power manifest in its milieu.

The body is central to Foucault's account of the subject. In fact, Foucault replaces the notion of subject with that of body. Conceived in radically anti-essentialist terms, the body is shaped by the contingent historical forces within which it is enmeshed. For Foucault, it is the intersection of the body with the world, experienced through the discursive and disciplinary modes that configure the social and cultural landscape, which make possible the experience (or what he might consider the illusion) of autonomous subjecthood in the first place. Foucault's philosophical and sociological project can be broadly defined as a social constructionist account of the body subject, in that he examines how certain bodily phenomena, such as comportment and appearance, are developed in and created by a particular socio-cultural and political context as result of particular power relations. Foucault has described his own work as consisting of a "history of bodies,"[9] radically arguing that the body is "totally imprinted by history."[10] I will turn now to consider Foucault's account of precisely how this bodily 'imprinting' occurs.

SURVEILLANCE, INTERNALIZATION AND NORMALIZATION

Foucault explores how bodies are shaped and transformed through his well-known descriptive and critical analyses of various social institutions, such as the correctional and medical systems. In essence, Foucault's philosophical project (at least in his early work) is to demonstrate how all individual and intersubjective experience occurs within and, furthermore, is determined by a broader nexus of forces and meaning. This nexus of meaning, Foucault argues, shapes embodied subjectivity; the body subject is, in a sense, created by the world, or what he considers to be the complex webs of power relations within which the body is enmeshed.

Following Sartre, Foucault is also interested in the seen body and the consequences of having the body, in particular appearance and comportment, under observation (and judgment) by Others. Employing Sartre's idea that the Look of the other objectifies and alienates the subject, fixing him or her according to the other's desires and definitions, Foucault explores the effect of an anonymous, institutional gaze. This gaze, he argues, pervades daily life and ultimately leads to the subjugation and domination of bodies. Ultimately, Foucault shares Sartre's inherently pessimistic attitude about social relations, and the Look he describes is negative, restraining and alienating, employed primarily as a means of control and domination.

Power is a key concept in Foucault's analysis of the subjugation of bodies. It is one of the most enduring and far-reaching concepts that has come from his work, and it is worth understanding what he intends by it. Conceiving of power as a force which circulates anonymously and which is created through institutional and discursive structures, Foucault argues that it should be understood as relationships of control which are produced through specific social practices in certain institutional settings. Power is never to be reduced to the motive force, intention or influence of any individual person. Rather, it is everywhere, invisibly and ubiquitously embedded in the social, cultural and economic structures which form the landscape of human interaction. Foucault writes:

> Power must be analysed as something which circulates, or rather as something which only functions in the form of a chain. It is never localised here or there, never in anybody's hands, never appropriated as a commodity or piece of wealth. Power is employed and exercised through a net-like organisation. And not only do individuals circulate between its threads; they are always in the position of simultaneously undergoing and exercising this power.[11]

Foucault argues that it is power which ultimately controls and shapes individuals through its hold on the body.

To illustrate the effects of power on the body, Foucault turns his attention to the manner in which the body is contained within certain social institutions. Famously, he explores the subjugation and domination of the body in correctional practices in the prison system in his seminal work *Discipline and Punish: The Birth of the Prison*. However, it should be noted that Foucault intends his reflections in *Discipline and Punish* to have a broader relevance beyond penal practices, and, as we shall see, to be in some sense metaphoric for the diffuse control found in other social institutions and broader socio-cultural and political contexts.

Constant surveillance and bodily visibility is key in Foucault's analysis of incarceration and punishment within the prison system. For Foucault, this is epitomized by the Panopticon, Jeremy Bentham's eighteenth century prison design. Inspired by a military school in Paris, Bentham, an English philosopher, reformer and social theorist, developed the design in 1785. The Panopticon has a circular design with rows of cells facing in toward a central watchtower. Backlighting within each cell renders the inmate visible to the tower at all times, whereas blinds within the tower prevent the inmates from observing their overseers. The design was intended to yield easy supervision and obtain power over the mind through surveillance made possible simply through architectural principles.[12]

Foucault's employment of Bentham's panopticon as a model of disciplinary power is the architectural realization of Sartre's most paranoid or vigilant characterization of the Look. It is the omnipresent gaze, simultaneously everywhere and nowhere, constantly objectifying and alienating the subject. Foucault describes the panopticon and its method of incarceration as follows:

> [A]t the periphery, an annular building; at the centre, a tower; this tower is pierced with wide windows that open onto the inner side of the ring; the peripheric building is divided into cells, each of which extends the whole width of the building; they have two windows, one on the inside, corresponding to the windows of the tower; the other, in the outside, allows the light to cross the cell from one end to the other . . . Each individual, in his place, is securely confined to a cell from which he is seen from the front by the supervisor; but the side walls prevent him from coming into contact with his companions. He is seen, but he does not see; he is the object of information, never a subject in communication.[13]

The panopticon's design ensures permanent observation of the prisoners with a minimum of manpower, relying on no external power structure other than the architectural and geometrical features of the building. The constant and permanent visibility of the prisoner, coupled with his inability to detect his observers (*he is seen, but he does not see*) results in the perfect realization of Sartre's most pessimistic fantasies regarding intersubjective relations: devoid of all power, the subject is completely vulnerable to the Look; scrutinized constantly, he is in a state of permanent alienation. As Foucault insists: "It is the fact of being constantly seen, of being able always to be seen, that maintains the disciplined individual in his subjection."[14]

Being under the constant gaze of a actual or possible overseer, the panoptic structure encourages prisoners to monitor themselves and exert self-control over their behaviour. Former implements of constraint and control, such as chains, manacles, whips, and so forth, become redundant. Foucault writes:

> [T]here is no need for arms, physical violence, material constraints. Just a gaze. An inspecting gaze, a gaze which each individual under its weight will end by interiorising to the point that he is his own overseer, each individual thus exercising his surveillance over and against himself.[15]

Hence, the panopticon, instead of trying to control the prisoner externally, through restraint, force or violence, manipulates the subject to use the internal discipline of self-control. The threat of punishment is key in this process. The prisoner must believe that there will be repercussions if he does not keep his appearance and comportment in line with the established rules or norms of his penal setting. Fearing punishment, incarcerated subjects become self-policing and self-monitoring. Individuals begin to regulate themselves. As Foucault explains, the major effect of the panopticon is "to induce in the inmate a state of conscious and permanent visibility that assures the automatic functioning of power . . . the inmates [are] caught up in a power situation of which they are themselves the bearers."[16] As a result of the actual or imagined gaze of an overseer who is exercising judgement, the inmates accept the rules of the institution and adjust their behaviour accordingly. Hence, in the panopticon, each prisoner develops a self-monitoring part of the psyche, an internalized 'other' which watches him- or herself as though from a distance, employing the stance of a judgmental and punishing overseer.

Internalization is a pivotal mechanism in this process. In his analysis of the panopticon, Foucault makes explicit the process of internalization which is never fully developed by Sartre in his discussion of the self-evaluative examples of the Look. Internalization can be considered to be the process by which one accepts and makes one's own, that is *internalizes*, a set of norms, rules and mores established by an external authority. Once internalized, these norms are integrated as part of one's 'normal' or 'natural' viewpoint and are taken to be the correct or right mode of being.

Foucault does not intend his discussion of internalization and self-regulation due to panopticism to be limited to the penal setting. Instead, he argues that the panopticon is symbolic of the organizational features of surveillance and control which are characteristic of all institutional structures:

> It is polyvalent in its applications; it serves to reform prisoners but also to treat patients, to instruct schoolchildren, to confine the insane, to supervise workers, to put beggars and idlers to work. It . . . can be implemented in hospitals, workshops, schools, prisons. Whenever one is dealing with a multiplicity of individuals on whom a task or a particular form of behaviour must be imposed, the panoptic schema may be used. [17]

In whichever institutional context, Foucault argues, panopticism ensures a particular form of behaviour from the subject, whether it is the skilled work of a labourer, the obedience of the school pupil or soldier, or the compliance of the medical patient. Outside of the carceral context, punishment and control are not the explicit aims of panopticism. Instead, institutions aim to inculcate and instill desirable patterns of body behaviour according to their needs: they produce good workers, obedient pupils, disciplined soldiers, docile patients and the like.

However, even outside the penal context, the threat of punishment is fundamental. Because the individual is constantly striving to avoid incurring punishment (of whatever form) through adhering to the rules and guidelines of an institution, norms become rooted in his or her psyche and body. In this way, the internalization of external rules renders norms invisible; the individual does not even realize that he or she is self-regulating. Social prohibitions are experienced as normal forms of behaviour which emanate from within, rather than coming from an external regulating force. As a result, over time, certain prohibitions become so commonplace that they come to appear natural and necessary; indeed, they come to be perceived as 'reality.' As a result of this process of surveillance and internalization, the subject eventually becomes 'normalized.' That is, their appearance and comportment adhere to standards imposed by institutional contexts according to prevailing norms.

Normalization is an important process in Foucault's account. He argues that the individual is constantly subjected to the binary standards of "normal" and "abnormal,"[18] and that this has arisen in part as a result of the rise in clinical medicine and psychiatry which provide clear categories through which individuals can be classified. These categories produce certain modes of acculturation and socialization which operate by setting standards against which individuals measure, judge, regulate, discipline and ultimately correct their behaviour and appearance. Essentially, normalization functions on the idea that there are 'normal,' and hence correct, modes of appearance and comportment; anything that deviates is characterized as abnormal and in need of remedy, bringing with it the threat of punishment.

The normal, for Foucault, derives primarily from the production of standards and models based on various methods of scientific classification. However, it is not a straightforward concept, containing two distinct and sometimes contradictory ideas which have been linked together somewhat arbitrarily. First, the normal contains the idea of the 'usual' or the highest statistical frequency. The normal in this sense is held in opposition to the 'irregular' or the 'unusual.' Second, the normal also carries the notion of the good or normative; it is what is right or proper.[19] In this normative sense, the normal is opposed to notions of 'inappropriate,' 'bad' or 'disgraceful.' Naturally, as what is typical (or occurs with the most statistical frequency) may not be desirable or good, normalization may have negative consequences, modelling itself on standards which are arbitrary or potentially harmful, through which populations and individuals can be assessed and can assess themselves. With respect to the body and its functions, there is a third sense with which the 'normal' can be articulated. Through the concept of "vital norms," as discussed by Georges Canguilhem, a sense of what is 'healthy' or 'normal' with respect to the physical body can be defined.[20] One has breached a vital norm when "the organism can no longer react creatively to new elements of its surroundings." In other words, "pathology" has become "a lived reality."[21] This third sense of the 'normal' as arising from 'vital norms,' while distinct, is closely tied to the first two senses of 'normal' described above, as what is defined as 'pathology' is based on scientific classification, statistical frequency and social norms regarding what is proper.

Regulation due to standards of normalization occurs on all levels and in all aspects of life. In schools, hospitals, workplaces and other social settings, professionals such as teachers, doctors, social workers, managers, and so forth, figure as the 'judges of normality' assessing and correcting individual behaviour against a normalizing set of standards and assumptions. For Foucault, this process of normalization is fundamentally linked to appearance and the body. Subjects do not merely begin to think in the same way, but eventually, all prisoners (or school children, factory workers, medical patients, etc.) begin to act the same and look the same. Normalization across a diverse group of individuals is achieved.

DISCIPLINE AND THE DOCILE BODY

Foucault uses the term 'discipline' to describe the process of normalization that occurs within institutional settings. Disciplines are methods of control and training which assure that the body complies to institutional demands. Foucault describes several organizational structures—such as temporal ordering through timetables, the bureaucratic documentation of individuals, the organization of architectural space and institutional rank—present in the prison and other institutional contexts which facilitate the practices of discipline.[22] These practices were developed to control and regulate the body by imposing on it certain prohibitions and obligations and, furthermore, by constraining its field of action.[23]

Disciplines, in short, facilitate certain types of skill acquisition and are in fact training regimes. The body is encouraged to acquire gestures, habits and behaviour patterns that maximize its success and minimize the threat of punishment in the institutions of which it is a part. The body "is manipulated, shaped, trained; . . . obeys, responds, becomes skillful and increases its forces" in order to service the institutions in which it is contained.[24] Foucault's account of discipline is conceptually linked to the rise and growth of capitalism: the productivity and economic efficiency of the body, trained as a submissive and productive source of labour, is key to the success of capitalist modes of production.

Foucault employs the notion of the body as "docile" to describe the productive and subjected body.[25] In stark contrast to Merleau-Ponty's conception of the habit body as that which expands one's capabilities and capacities to positively create and transform the world, Foucault's characterisation of the docile body sees habits or techniques inscribed on the body in a negative and compromising manner, constraining, limiting and inhibiting one's freedom and scope of possibility in the world. The docile body for Foucault is disciplined and subjected; it is trained and acquires body techniques in order to service the institutions within which it finds itself enmeshed, rather than to

enhance its own existence. Foucault's conception of the circumstances surrounding skill acquisition and the formation of the body schema, to use
phenomenological terms, implies an inherent passivity, receptivity and lack
of autonomy in the subject (at least in his early work). Skill acquisition
occurs within the context of institutions, to ensure their smooth functioning
and to meet their demands. Through the processes of surveillance, internalization and normalization, the docile and disciplined body is trained to a
large extent for others, not for itself.

EXAMINING FOUCAULT

Foucault's account of the disciplined and docile body is important in that it
demonstrates that external norms manifest on a corporeal level through the
processes of surveillance, internalization and normalization, features of embodied subjectivity and intersubjectivity largely omitted from the phenomenological
account. In contrast to Husserl, Merleau-Ponty and Sartre, Foucault describes a
broader framework, namely a socio-cultural and political milieu dominated by
discursive relations of power and knowledge, in which individual and intersubjective experiences are shaped and given significance. Foucault argues
that when we zoom out from the phenomenological description of the individual, we find a landscape of bodies not only interacting with each other,
but also plugged from the outset into institutions and social, cultural and
political systems which operate through a nexus of power relations and normative values.

However, in rejecting phenomenology when considering the constitution
of embodied subjectivity, Foucault's account, though insightful in many respects, gives a limited view of the human subject. Through his rejection of
phenomenology—in both the philosophical and psychological senses—Foucault almost entirely ignores the subjective experience of embodiment.[26]
Despite his great interest in sexuality and body disciplines, Foucault offers
little insight into how a subject feels and experiences power structures. As a
result, there is little regard given to experiences of action and perception, or
emotional and developmental experiences. Notably, despite his great interest
in social control through normalization, internalization and fear of social
stigmatization, Foucault does not explicitly consider the significance and
effect of self-conscious emotions, such as shame, acknowledged by other
social thinkers, as we shall see, to play a large role in social control.

Instead, in his early writings, particularly in *Discipline and Punish*, Foucault casts human subjects as socially constructed docile bodies, rather than
as individual persons with the capacity for emotional experience, thoughtful
autonomous action or as potential centres of resistance. As he describes it,
the body "is the inscribed surface of events . . . totally imprinted by histo-

ry."[27] Lacking the capacity for autonomous action, the disciplined body has no means to resist or transform the power structures within which it is enmeshed. Reading Foucault's early work, one is left initially with the impression that the body subject is a social automaton, haplessly determined by the mysterious power structures which are omnisciently and permanently present within the institutions of which it is a part.

Furthermore, in the panoptic schema, Foucault characterizes control as unidirectional and monolithic, emanating from a singular central authority figure. However, it is clear that our day-to-day experience does not reflect this model. Our own identities are not dominated by just one social role (prisoner, pupil, factory worker), instead, they are complex, multiple and ever-shifting. Moreover, much, if not most, of our experience occurs outside of rigid institutional structures dominated by a single authority figure. Unlike the prisoner in the panopticon, who is in isolation and does not come into contact with either his overseers or his peers, in daily life we experience a plethora of competing influences, from family, employers, friends, colleagues, peers, media, celebrity figures, and so forth. Indeed, it is not clear how training within an institutional context to serve the needs of a particular institution, such as the training of a factory worker, will prevent broader, more diffuse social influences in other aspects of life.

In his later writings, Foucault recognizes some of these shortcomings of his earlier work and attempts to remedy the characterization of power as a monolithic and unidirectional force which dominates the subject, ultimately arguing that discipline is not limited to institutional settings. He claims that in modern society an individual's behaviour is not regulated through explicit and overt oppression within an institution. Instead, control is achieved through standards of normality which are propagated through vast and diffuse networks of power relations which infiltrate every corner of life. Foucault employs the term "biopower"[28] to denote this non-institutional discipline which ensures regulation on all levels, personal and public, of human social life.

Biopower involves discipline, but it is not just about training the body within institutions. It is more insidious in that its target is the manner through which we live our bodies: "Unlike discipline, which is addressed to bodies, the new nondisciplinary power is applied not to man-as-body but to the living man, to man-as-living-being."[29] As such, biopower controls the means by which we construct our personal states and everyday lives, down to the smallest details. Foucault describes it as "numerous and diverse techniques for achieving the subjugation of bodies and the control of populations."[30] In short, biopower is about normalization. It ensures that the idiosyncrasies of individuals and everyday life follow universal categories, or norms, which are applicable across populations and demographic groups. However, even in his account of biopower, Foucault fails to explain how on a phenomenological and corporeal level, the disciplining of the body is achieved. Bodily control seems to occur through an unperceived, and perhaps imperceptible, process which is driven by power, a somewhat mysterious, ubiquitous and haunting force. Biopower is simultaneously everywhere and nowhere in particular. It infuses every personal state and intersubjective encounter, yet this concept remains a fairly ambiguous aspect of Foucault's work.

NORBERT ELIAS: THE BODY AND
SHAME IN THE CIVILIZING PROCESS

In order to elucidate the notions of power and biopower in Foucault's work, and to make clear the processes which drive body management and social control, I will now turn to consider the work of another twentieth century social thinker, Norbert Elias. Examining in detail the interdependence of bodies, especially with respect to the transmitting of norms and the achievement of social control, Elias develops his theory of the civilizing process. This theory draws connections between the seen body, social control, body shame, normalization and internalization, in part providing an illustration of Foucault's conception of biopower and making explicit the process of social control that Foucault identifies but does not fully articulate.

Primarily a sociologist, Norbert Elias was trained as a philosopher, and even studied under Husserl. His work, spanning over fifty years, from the 1930s to the 1980s, interlinks sociological investigation with psychology and history, analysing standards for bodily comportment and appearance as a result of changing historical and cultural norms. Like Foucault, Elias is also critical of what he sees as the traditional philosophical "subject of knowledge," conceived as an individual mind enclosed inside a container (the body) through which it has access to the "objects" which are "outside."[31] This conception of the subject of knowledge Elias terms '*homo clausus*'[32] and he argues that it is a basic philosophical motif running through Western philosophy since Plato, through classical philosophy of the Renaissance onward to Descartes through Kant and Husserl. The necessary sociality of the subject is something that Elias argues is lost in philosophical reflection, where the subject is not only a single and isolated mind, but furthermore, an adult mind. As a result, rationality and reason are lauded as a transcendental reality, rather than a historical contingency.

Elias proposes an alternative to *homo clausus*, that which he terms "*homo aperti*,"[33] which is the idea that individuals acquire their social identity through participating in complex social figurations that are developed through long-term social and historical processes.[34] The interdependence of bodies and subjects is a core concept in Elias's work and he argues that the isolated theoretical ego of transcendental philosophy cannot provide an accurate description of the human condition and the historical transformations which have shaped the physical and psychic conditions of the modern subject. Instead, Elias argues, along with Merleau-Potny and Sartre, that our sociality is necessary and that meaningful existence comes only as a result of our relations with others.

In some respects, Elias's work is an advance on Foucault's social constructionist conception of the body. Like Foucault, Elias is concerned with how modes of bodily comportment are contingent on certain types of social circumstances and configurations. However, in contrast to the social constructionist approach, where the body is taken to be determined by external social classifications and value systems, Elias sees the body as a biological and social entity which undergoes a lengthy developmental and educational process before it is fully accepted into its social milieu. How the body subject relates to and interacts with other subjects is fundamental to his analysis. Moreover, although he assesses the influence of socio-cultural and political norms on embodied subjectivity, individual experience is key in his analysis, with emotions, particularly body shame, playing a central role.

Elias is perhaps best known for his theory of the civilizing process which he sets forth in the two volume *The Civilizing Process*, published in 1939. In this work Elias's approach is primarily historical and sociological. He examines the development of modern Western society, from the Middle Ages onwards to the present day, in order to understand why certain modes of body management have taken hold. Exploring changes in what is sanctioned and prohibited in terms of body management and comportment over several centuries, Elias uncovers changes in the psychic structure and makeup of individuals with regard to self-control and self-restraint which come to dominate social interaction. These considerations are of obvious interest when considering Foucault's investigations, where institutional and social powers tame and shape the body, but it remains unclear precisely how this occurs.

The body is central to Elias's analysis of the civilizing process. Civilization,[35] for Elias, occurs as a result of bodily order and social control, through meticulous regulation of natural functions and bodily comportment. Thus, the civilized body has successfully internalized prevailing social and cultural norms with regard to appearance and behaviour and is able to scrupulously regulate and restrain bodily comportment within the confines of these norms. Civilization, in this sense, denotes the successful long-term transformation of external constraints into internal ones such that they come to appear natural and necessary.

In contrast to Foucault, Elias does not see the development of civilized or disciplined bodies as primarily a result of the rise of the systems and institutions of industrialised production and modern capitalism, which demand greater productivity and ever-increasing efficiency of the body. Instead, Elias believes that the beginning of the civilizing process is related to a moment in

European social history where the drive to acquire, and to subsequently maintain, social prestige through a focus on the body's appearance and comportment became paramount. In particular, he analyses the time from which the feudal lords of the warrior society of the early Middle Ages began to form what later became the court aristocracy, which Elias sees as a precursor to Western bourgeois capitalist society of the modern era.

Elias's fascination with and analysis of the court society serves best perhaps not as a historical or sociological account, but instead as an illustration of a particular type of social system—of which there are many other examples—which traces the development of models of conduct which dictate modes of self-presentation and body management. Like Sartre and Foucault, Elias's analysis centres around bodily visibility, the seen body, surveillance, internalization and objectification. Considering the seen body to be paramount within the court system, Elias charts how changes in manners and etiquette developed over time.

Constantly under "intense scrutiny," members of court, according to Elias, had to highly restrain and control their physical and emotional drives and regulate and monitor the body and its functions, internalizing ever-stricter and more refined codes of etiquette.[36] In the court society, highly detailed and refined codes which dictated body management were used to distinguish people and differentiate between one's relative social worth. Those who refused to follow court etiquette were shunned and subject to sanctions. As a result, there were huge social pressures among members of the court to observe and mimic others, adopting the correct form of behaviour:

> To keep one's place in the intense competition for importance at court, to avoid being exposed to scorn, contempt, loss of prestige, one must subordinate one's appearance and gestures, in short oneself, to the fluctuating norms of court society that increasingly emphasize the difference, the distinction of the people belonging to it. One *must* wear certain materials and certain shoes. One *must* move in certain ways characteristic of people belonging to court society. Even smiling is shaped by court custom.[37]

In this way, bodies, through the observable qualities of appearance and comportment, are the primary site of social value and estimation.

What is interesting about Elias's analysis is that he examines the most mundane and taken for granted aspects of embodied life, uncovering social protocols that are so thoroughly internalized and second nature as to be taken for granted as 'natural' or 'normal.' He examines how we manage our bodies and construct our personal states down to the smallest details. At first glance, Elias's choice of empirical material may seem surprising. He uses, above all, handbooks on manners and etiquette which explicitly outline proper protocols of etiquette. Through detailed study of various handbooks written over six hundred years and in five separate languages,[38] Elias notes how over time, the advice given by etiquette and manners books became more refined and complex, where eventually matters which had at one stage received explicit and detailed instruction, such as public excretion, eating with one's fingers, sharing a bed with a stranger, spitting and sexual behaviour, among others, were not even explicitly mentioned as they had been so completely eradicated or at least thoroughly relegated to behind the scenes of public life.

For example, considering table manners, Elias asks: "What is the rule use of the fork? . . . Why do we not use our fingers?" In the early Middle Ages, utensils were not in common use and the hands were employed at mealtimes; subjects would customarily eat from one common dish using their fingers to bring food to the mouth. However, over time this behaviour came to be seen as uncouth, uncivilized and barbaric. Indeed, the 1859 publication *The Habits of Good Society* indicates that it is "cannibal" to eat with one's fingers.[39] Today, the fork ritual is so ingrained in our everyday repertoire of body techniques, that it is entirely self-evident that, in a Western context, to use one's fingers to bring food to the mouth from a plate is uncivilized. (Excepting certain types of foods, such as bread or biscuits, which have their own rules of etiquette with regard to serving and consumption.)

Many other examples are given which demonstrate the embodiment of an increased level of revulsion with regard to one's own body and its functions and contact with the bodies of others. On public excretion, Erasmus's 1530 *De Civilitate Morum Puerilium* advises that: "It is impolite to greet someone who is urinating or defecating."[40] On sharing a bed with a stranger, La Salle's 1729 *Les Regles de la Bienseance et de la Civilite Chretienne* informs that it is indecent to "put your legs between those of the other."[41] On spitting, Erasmus advises: "Turn away when spitting, lest your saliva fall on someone."[42] As demonstrated by these examples, one main feature of the civilizing process, as Elias conceives it, is a distancing from the body's natural functions, so that embodiment is defined in opposition to the animal, and natural functions are scrupulously and meticulously socially managed and organized. Furthermore, a distance is forged between bodies, as it has become less acceptable to make physical contact, and bodily functions are socially managed, occurring in private spaces.

The examples Elias offers, often humorous in their frankness, serve to demonstrate how deeply ingrained today are the social norms and body techniques which in fact took centuries of explicit refinement to develop. Indeed, these norms are so ingrained, are so second nature, that as adults we do not need explicit instruction on how to conduct ourselves in matters of excretion, sexual behaviour, table manners and so on. On the contrary, these matters are executed silently and with expertise, without need of explicit mention. These highly detailed and refined codes which implicitly dictate body management are used to distinguish people and differentiate between one's relative social worth.

Is this rendering invisible the work of mothers, providing these lessons into kids?

Accruing social worth and prestige was driven by constant surveillance and the panoptic structure. In court, each individual felt as though he or she was under constant observation for any breach in conduct or appearance, however this 'gaze' did not emanate from any particular set of eyes. Norms became quickly internalized and individuals began to watch themselves. As Elias explains:

> [The] art of human observation is applied not only to others but to the observer himself. A specific art of *self-observation* develops . . . with observation of oneself with a view to self-discipline in social life. [43]

Over time, as the differences and divisions between classes became less rigid, Elias argues, these concerns around the seen body, body management and social value were not limited to the court aristocracy. Instead, the notion that appearance and comportment—dictated by highly refined and normalized standards of body management—were indicators of social worth was realized, in some form or another, on all levels of society.

Elias's analysis of the court society and changing codes of manners and etiquette makes salient the importance of social capital, and, in particular, body capital within social relations. Capital is a term usually associated with mercantile exchange and the economic and financial sphere, however, this term has been employed symbolically and in a wider context to signify a system of exchanges where various assets are exchanged or transformed within complex social networks of exchange and value. In particular, Pierre Bourdieu, the French sociological thinker who was directly influenced by Elias's analysis of the court aristocracy,[44] discusses the importance of social, cultural and body capital in the dynamics of power relations in social life, examining features such as social position, taste, class and other embodied dispositions and characteristics. Whereas economic capital is immediately convertible into a monetary form, non-economic forms of capital, such as social and cultural capital operate on a system of cultural exchanges which are not easily reduced to a strict system of valuation.[45] Cultural and social capital can bring 'value' to a social agent. As the body is the site of capital, Bourdieu terms the phrase "body capital"[46] to describe inherited and acquired bodily characteristics which can give an individual some social leverage or value.

Elias's analysis of the court society is in fact an account about securing and maintaining social capital, particularly in the form of body capital. As codes of conduct in the court became increasingly elaborate and refined, those in the upper echelons of court society endeavoured to increasingly distinguish themselves from their social inferiors. It was accepted that skill in etiquette, conversation and social relations were likely to help one accrue more social capital and advance a courtier's political and social career.

Therefore it was strategic to fastidiously follow prevailing norms in order to find advantage in matters related to friendship, marriage, politics and so on.

Motivated by the desire to establish and maintain social standing and body capital, behaviour arises, not as a result of causal restraint or compulsion, but rather through techniques of control that are available in and reinforced by the social field. Similar to Foucault's conception of biopower, Elias's analysis of changing standards of body management explores how constant surveillance occurs outside of any particular institutional context. Through the interaction between bodies and concerns around status and social standing, idiosyncrasies of individuals and everyday life follow universal categories, or norms, which are applicable across populations and demographic groups.

However, unlike Foucault, Elias does not rely on the ambiguous notion of 'power' to explain why the subject is compelled to conform to prevailing standards of body management.[47] Instead, for Elias, the structural concept of power, as Foucault employs it, is actually explained by emotional concerns related to threats to one's social standing within intercorporeal relations. Essentially, Elias argues that the subject has "deep-rooted fears" about losing his or her position and esteem in society.[48] These fears, which often may not even enter into conscious consideration, are that which motivate the internalization of external standards and the eventual normalization of appearance and comportment.

In fact, Elias's historical, sociological and philosophical investigation regarding changing modes of body management culminates in an analysis of the significance of body shame within embodied intersubjective encounters. When it does occur, social degradation or the compromising of one's social standing is manifested, Elias argues, as the "feeling of shame."[49] Shame is "a specific excitation, a kind of anxiety"[50] which occurs when someone acts or appears in conflict with prevalent social opinion. It is "fear of social degradation or, more generally, of other people's gestures of superiority" which causes shame to arise.[51] Shame, when it arises, indicates to the self that some rule or standard, almost always unspoken, implicit and internalised, has been transgressed. Elias asserts:

> [T]he person feeling it [shame] has done or is about to do something through which he comes into contradiction with people to whom he is bound in one form or another, and with himself, with the sector of his consciousness by which he controls himself.[52]

To avoid the unpleasant and disruptive experience of shame and the damage (to one's social capital) that it may bring, Elias argues that the body subject is constantly vigilant, ensuring that his or her appearance and comportment are in line with prevailing socio-cultural and political norms and standards.

Avoiding shame, embarrassment and other negative self-conscious emotions through successful self-presentation and impression management are unceasing concerns for the social subject. The threat of punishment, which is predominant in Foucault's account as the motivating mechanism for bodily conformity and docility, can be understood in Elias's account to be a fear of social degradation as a result of some failing in bodily appearance or comportment or, in short, the fear of body shame arising.

In Elias's account, the body subject acquires new skills and competencies in order to avoid shame. This echoes with the sentiments expressed in Dreyfus's phenomenological account of skill acquisition. Dreyfus alerted us to the fact that negative self-conscious emotions, such as body shame, play an important role in the formation of the body schema. Motivation to master an embodied skill arises from wanting to avoid negative feelings, dys-appearances and social disapproval. The idea that someone is evaluating one's performance, and that one may disappoint them or let them down, is fundamental to skill acquisition. Feelings of failure and shame, in the presence of an imagined or actual audience motivate the acquisition of skilled behaviour and hence the formation of the body schema. As a result, similar to Foucault's account of how the disciplining of the body occurs as a result of the drive to avoid punishment, the civilizing process is driven by a deeper desire to avoid social exclusion and shame in order to secure and maintain social standing.

CONCLUSION

The work of both Foucault and Elias provides a foundation from which we can reflect on the historical and cultural nature of the body which can further enrich the phenomenological accounts of embodiment and intersubjectivity offered by Husserl, Merleau-Ponty and Sartre. As we have seen, Foucault and Elias are both critical of the transcendental approach of some modern philosophy which ignores the interdependence and social embeddedness of the subject. As a result, they use analyses of historical change and sociocultural structures in order to better understand contemporary modes of body management. The role of history, society, culture and politics on the body is an aspect of theoretical investigation largely left aside by phenomenologists of embodiment who endeavour to describe first-person experiences of perception, motility and body intentionality, without fully considering the historical underpinnings which endow those aspects of embodiment with significance. Although Foucault and Elias locate their analyses within the developments of specific historical periods (namely, capitalism for Foucault and the court society for Elias), these accounts are not intending to be merely historical or even sociological. Instead, they demonstrate how pan-cultural and pan-historical aspects of our subjectivity—our propensity for negative self-conscious emotions, our intercorporeality, our capacity for skill acquisition, and so forth—are shaped by the contingent normative values of the socio-cultural and political sphere.

It becomes clear that the body is not only related to the world, and the objects of the world, through intentionality (as the phenomenologists so adeptly describe). The blind man envelops his stick, it becomes an extension of his bodily schema, and he can use it in a manner that does not require reflection nor explicit attention. However, behind this intentional relation there are a whole range of body techniques and habits which have been painstakingly acquired by the blind man, not only as a result of skill acquisition, but also through his relations to others, to institutions and as a result of the internalization of social norms which dictate appropriate bodily comportment. Indeed, meaningful motor intentionality is made possible only through a pre-existing social and cultural realm, composed of institutions, familial and social relations, social roles and a historical lineage through which body management norms have been developed and refined. Self-control and socialized bodily coherence is largely assumed and taken for granted in phenomenology, and reading social thinkers like Foucault and Elias demonstrate that self-control and bodily coherence are not only acquired through a lengthy process of child development and socialization but, furthermore, are also contingent on socio-cultural and political structures and forces.

Elias's analysis of changing trends in manners and etiquette yields insight into how a repertoire of skills and body techniques are acquired in order to respond to the variable needs of the social, cultural and political environments within which the body subject is necessarily enmeshed. Fear of body shame, and concomitantly of compromising one's social standing or threatening one's social bonds, drives the subject to train the body to habitually reproduce the distinctive conduct permitted by its milieu. Elias uncovers shame, and the concomitant desire to maintain one's social standing, as an important mechanism in ongoing social relations throughout history; it is that which motivates and facilitates changing modes of bodily conduct.

Although preceding Foucault's writings on biopower and panopticism by some decades, Elias's account of shame in the civilizing process can be read as an illustration of Foucault's conception of discipline and biopower through surveillance and perhaps gives a concrete way to explain the somewhat mysterious nature of power that circulates invisibly, anonymously and ubiquitously. The civilizing process is an account of how the smallest details regarding body management are shaped by prevailing norms and standards outside the rigid confines of an institution. Biopower, as Foucault characterizes it, surrounds and influences all body subjects and is, furthermore, infused with norms and standards for body management. Constant visibility, or panopticism, is key in this process. Following Elias's account of shame in the civilizing process, Foucault's conception of biopower can be read as a metaphor for body shame, or more specifically, the drive to avoid body shame. Nietzsche's characterization of shame as feeling 'dazzled as though by a great eye which gazes upon us and through us from all sides' evokes Foucault's carceral scene: in moments of transgression, the prisoner is paralyzed with the awareness that he is seen; in his cell he cannot hide from the central watchtower. To avoid punishment the inmate internalizes external rules and exercises self-restraint. In the same manner, the social subject avoids the loss of social standing (as manifested through the experience of shame) by internalizing external rules and exercising self-restraint.

However, unlike the isolated prisoner of the panopticon, who does not come into contact with other body subjects, physically separated from both his peers and his overseers, Elias demonstrates how the civilized subject is almost constantly in contact with other bodies and indeed, it is through this contact that norms and standards of conduct and appearance are transmitted. The interdependence of bodies is a key aspect of embodied subjectivity that is entirely absent from Foucault's account of panopticism, discipline and surveillance. The isolated body, described by Foucault, is inscribed by invisible power structures emanating from a monolithic authority figure. However, this does not reflect even the most rigid institutional structures where bodies are rarely, if ever, in complete isolation. By considering the individual in isolation, Foucault effectively ignores the significance of the interaction between bodies in intersubjective relations, failing to articulate the manner through which norms are shared and transmitted through intercorporeality. Indeed, even within institutional settings, skills and body techniques are often transmitted through explicit training or, at the very least, body habits and techniques are transmitted through complex processes of observation and mimicking. As Elias demonstrates, body norms are not mysteriously imposed by anonymous institutional structures, but instead, are shared and transmitted as a result of relations and interdependencies between individuals and groups. In short, bodies carry and transmit norms.

Furthermore, Elias demonstrates that it is not fear of institutional punishment that drives the subject to conformity. Instead, as bodies became the primary site of social worth and estimation, central to the social value system, fear of social degradation and the loss of social standing make it increasingly imperative for individuals to regulate and manage the body. Avoiding social exclusion and accruing body capital are central concerns for the subject, and these concerns are inextricably linked to the experience of body shame.

In the next chapter, I will review the main themes of the previous three chapters, offering an overview of the main features of body shame while exploring its phenomenological and existential significance. As a necessary feature of embodied subjectivity, involving personal, intersubjective and socio-cultural aspects of selfhood, body shame will be seen to be a conceptual tool that can link together the ostensibly opposing accounts of embodiment offered by phenomenology and social constructionism, which cast the body subject as constituting and constituted respectively. Ultimately, in chapter 4, I will argue that body shame can offer phenomenological insight into how the body subject is shaped by social forces without reducing the description of the body subject to one of social determinism, where the subject is figured as lacking autonomy and agency. In particular, I will outline a phenomenology of self-presentation in order to give an account of how the embodied subject is continuously—and constitutionally—engaged in conscious and unconscious strategies to manage how the body appears and is presented to others. From there, I will consider the cultural politics of shame, using the example of race relations and embodied stigma to more closely examine the impact shame can have as it circulates through the social and political spheres.

NOTES

1. Marjorie Grene, "Sartre and the Other," *Proceedings and Addresses of the American Philosophical Association* vol. 45, (1971–1972): 32.

2. See: 'Introduction' in: de Beauvoir, *The Second Sex*.

3. See: Frantz Fanon, *Black Skin, White Masks*, trans. Charles Lam Markman (London: Paladin, 1970).

4. Michel Foucault, "The Subject and Power," in *Michel Foucault: Beyond Structuralism and Hermeneutics*, eds. Hubert Dreyfus and Paul Rabinow (Hertfordshire: Harvester Wheatsheaf, 1982), 208.

5. Ibid., 285.

6. Michel Foucault, "Forward to the English Edition," in *The Order of Things* (London: Routledge, 2002), xv.

7. Michel Foucault, "Dream, Imagination and Existence: An Introduction to Ludwig Binswanger's 'Dream and Existence,'" *Review of Existential Psychology and Psychiatry* vol. 19, no. 1 (1984–1985): 42.

8. Michel Foucault, "Technologies of the Self," in *Technologies of the Self: A Seminar with Michel Foucault*, eds. Luther H. Martin, Huck Gutman, and Patrick H. Hutton (London: Tavistock, 1988), 145.

9. Michel Foucault, *The Will to Knowledge: The History of Sexuality, Volume 1*, trans. Robert Hurley (London: Penguin, 1998), 152.

10. Michel Foucault, "Nietzsche, Genealogy, History," in *The Foucault Reader* ed. Paul Rabinow (London: Penguin, 1984), 83.

11. Michel Foucault, *Power/Knowledge: Selected Interviews and Other Writings, 1972–77*, ed. Colin Gordon, trans. Colin Gordon et al. (Brighton: Harvester, 1980), 98.

12. See: Jeremy Bentham, *The Panopticon Writings*, ed. Miran Bozovic (London: Verso, 1995).

13. Michel Foucault, *Discipline and Punish: The Birth of the Prison*, trans. Alan Sheridan (New York: Vintage Books, 1995), 200.

14. Ibid., 187.

15. Foucault, *Power/Knowledge*, 155.

16. Foucault, *Discipline and Punish*, 201.

17. Ibid., 205.

18. Ibid., 199.

19. See: Martha C. Nussbaum, *Hiding From Humanity: Disgust, Shame and the Law* (Princeton: Princeton University Press, 2004), 218.

20. See: Katherine J. Morris, *Starting with Merleau-Ponty*, (London: Continuum, 2012), 71. Morris discusses how Canguilhem's concept of 'vital norms' aligns with Merleau-Ponty's discussion of the 'normal' body as discussed in the previous chapter.

21. Quoted in: Ibid.

22. Foucault, *Discipline and Punish*, 141–149.

23. Ibid., 136.

24. Ibid., 136.

25. Ibid.

26. This is a line of criticism developed by Bryan S. Turner. See: Bryan S. Turner, *The Body and Society* (Oxford: Blackwell, 1984), 245.

27. Foucault, "Nietzsche, Genealogy, History," 83.

28. Foucault, *The Will to Knowledge: The History of Sexuality, Volume 1*, 140.

29. Michel Foucault, *'Society Must Be Defended'*: *Lectures at the College de France, 1975–1976*, eds. Mauro Bertani and Alessandro Fortuna, trans. David Macey (New York: Picador, 2003), 242.

30. Foucault, *The Will to Knowledge: The History of Sexuality, Volume 1*, 140.

31. Norbert Elias, "Homo Clausus: The Thinking Statues," in *On Civilization, Power, and Knowledge*, eds. Stephen Mennell and Johan Goudsblom (Chicago: The University of Chicago Press, 1998), 284.

32. From the Latin for 'enclosed' or 'locked' human.

33. From the Latin for 'open' human.

34. 'Figuration' is a term that is used to convey the idea that human individuals are always bound to one another in a system of interdependencies and power balances which always endeavour to find a dynamic equilibrium. Norbert Elias, *What Is Sociology?*, trans. Grace Morrissey and Stephen Mennell (London: Hutchinson, 1978), 125–133.

35. It is important to note that the term 'civilization,' as Elias intends it, does not refer to a progressive and linear sequence of stages of human development, for example a progression from the less desirable states of barbarism or primitivism to the more enlightened mode of civilization. The normative or evaluative notions that often arise with the term 'civilization' must be put aside, as civilization does not denote a state of static achievement. Rather, it is a relational term which for Elias refers to an ongoing and never ending process of change based not on normative necessities but rather on historical contingencies. 'Civilization,' hence, is not intended to be value-laden; it refers to the formation of modern societies without corresponding judgements about whether the processes involved in formation are good or bad.

36. Norbert Elias, *The Court Society*, trans. Edmund Jeffcott (Oxford: Basil Blackwell Publisher, 1983), 55.

37. Ibid., 231–232. Emphasis in original.

38. See: Norbert Elias, *The Civilizing Process: Sociogenetic and Psychogentic Investigations, Revised Edition*, ed. Eric Dunning, Johan Goudsblom, and Stephen Mennell, trans. Edmund Jephcott (Oxford: Blackwell, 1994).

39. Elias, *The Civilizing Process*, 107.

40. Ibid., 110.

41. Ibid., 137.

42. Ibid., 130.

43. Elias, *The Court Society*, 105. Emphasis in original.

44. See for example Bourdieu's comments about Elias's analysis of the court aristocracy in the 'Preface to the English-Language Edition' in Pierre Bourdieu, *Distinction: A Social Critique of the Judgement of Taste*, trans. Richard Nice (London: Routledge, 1984).

45. According to Bourdieu, social and cultural capital can take two main forms: firstly, they can be objectified and exist in cultural objects such as museums, books, art works, social titles, and so forth; secondly, they can be embodied, that is they can exist through certain dispositions or skills, for example, the ability to play an instrument, proficiency in a sport or activity, manners, style, accent, stances, intonation and more subtle ways of moving and living through the body. Indeed, in the effort to acquire more embodied social or cultural capital, the subject

may be motivated to cultivate certain dispositions, a certain type of appearance or perhaps acquire a certain set of skills. See: Pierre Bourdieu, "The Forms of Capital," in *Handbook of Theory of Research for the Sociology of Education*, ed. J. E. Richardson (Santa Barbara: Greenwood Press, 1986).

46. Bourdieu, *Distinction*, 204.

47. It should be noted that, like Foucault, Elias is interested in the effect of power structures on embodied subjectivity. However, Elias's conception of power differs from that of Foucault. Elias's conception of power is based on the notion of the 'figuration.' This is a term that is used to convey the idea that human individuals are always bound to one another in a system of interdependencies and power balances which always endeavour to find a dynamic equilibrium. As a result, power relations are always a matter of balance between individuals and groups, and it is never the case that one group has absolute power over another. In essence, Elias's conception of power is that it results from relations between individuals and groups, it is ubiquitous, but has a dynamic two-sided character. See: Elias, *What Is Sociology?*, 74. For a discussion and comparison of Foucault and Elias's approach to power see: Ian Burkitt, "Overcoming Metaphysics: Elias and Foucault on Power and Freedom," *Philosophy of the Social Sciences* vol. 23, no. 1 (1993): 50–72.

48. Elias, *The Civilizing Process*, 368.

49. Ibid., 414.

50. Ibid.

51. Ibid., 415.

52. Ibid.

Chapter Four

The Politics of Shame

The Phenomenology of Self-Presentation and
Social (In)visibility

Self-presentation is a term that indicates conscious and unconscious strategies for controlling or managing how one is perceived by Others in terms of
both appearance and comportment.[1] Self-presentation, also commonly referred to as impression management, is, in part, a response to the embodied
subject's concern with the Look, gaze or judgemental, and perhaps punishing
or ostracizing, regard of Others within social relations, as we have explored
at length through the theories of Sartre, Foucault and Elias. Self-presentation
is an aspect of embodied subjectivity that manifests not only through conscious strategies of appearance management, such as Michelle's decision to
undergo rhinoplasty referred to in chapter 1, but also through implicit processes of the body schema, such as habituated modes of bodily comportment.
Self-presentation serves an important role in the social realm in that it ensures that one presents a coherent public image, where appearance and behaviour are predictable and intelligible over time and across various contexts.
As we shall see, the capacity to engage successfully in self-presentation is a
fundamental part of embodied subjective experience. Only with this capacity
can the self and others engage in social interaction meaningfully, establishing
the 'flow' of social relations and delimiting the boundaries and normative
codes of social interaction.

Self-presentation is intimately linked to body shame. The philosophical
theories of embodiment, explored in the previous chapters through the work
of Merleau-Ponty, Sartre, Foucault and Elias, have demonstrated the central
role of body shame across three levels or layers: the personal, the intersubjective and the socio-cultural and political. My contention through these chap-

ters is that negative self-conscious emotions that are centred on the body play a key role in helping understand how the body is shaped by social forces and can provide a means through which phenomenologists might provide a description of the socially shaped body. Self-presentation, as a way to understand how the embodied subject manages threats and instances of body shame, I argue, is central to this account.

Forging a connection between the two opposing views of phenomenology and social constructionism through an understanding of the role of body shame and the phenomenology of self-presentation will be part of the focus of this chapter. I will start by giving an overview of the insights of the previous chapters. From there I will develop an account of self-presentation and impression management, discussing aspects of social interaction such as habitus, body idiom, stigma, spoiled identity and the human drive for acceptance, belonging and recognition. I will then shift my focus in order to outline a cultural politics of shame, examining how body shame can be utilized as a means to oppress marginalized groups. Utilizing the embodied politics of race as exemplary, I will offer a phenomenology of the various aspects of bodily visibility, invisibility and (in)visibility as they are relevant on the personal, intersubjective and socio-political levels. My aim is to demonstrate that rather than being a secondary part of embodied subjectivity, after the more primary accounts of action and perception, self-presentation is in fact constitutive of embodied subjectivity. Furthermore, a phenomenology of self-presentation, acknowledging the central role of body shame in regulating how one appears to others, is key to giving a more complete picture of the phenomenology of embodiment, or how we live through, experience and 'possess' our bodies. My intention with these reflections is to demonstrate that how the body appears to others is by no means a trivial concern, but in fact central to one's social worth, political status and lived experience.

BODILY VISIBILITY, INVISIBILITY AND (IN)VISIBILITY

First, let us recall the philosophical accounts of embodiment offered in the previous chapters. In chapter 2, aspects of Husserl's, Merleau-Ponty's and Sartre's phenomenological accounts of the lived body were examined. As we have seen, phenomenological investigation into embodiment reveals the conditions of meaningful embodied experience, exploring features of embodiment such as motor intentionality, the habit body, the body schema, skill acquisition, dys-appearance and bodily 'invisibility.' Furthermore, Sartre's existential ontological account of the intersubjectively constituted body subject demonstrates the manner through which the subject's capacity for reflective self-consciousness is awakened through bodily visibility (through objectification) and the Look within intercorporeal encounters. In chapter 3, Foucault's social constructionist account of embodiment was explored, describing how the body subject is shaped and disciplined by discursive power relations within institutions and the socio-cultural and political realm, underscoring features of corporeal discipline such as surveillance, normalization and internalization. Also in chapter 3, we saw Elias's theory of the civilizing process, a historical and sociological account of how the body subject acquires changing modes of body management in order to secure recognition and body capital within social, cultural and political contexts. Although these four accounts of embodiment at times have competing ideas about the nature of subjectivity and its constitution, these accounts are by no means mutually exclusive, but in fact describe several attitudes, perspectives or *Abschattungen* through which one can regard or conceive of the body.

As noted in the introduction, my methodology in this work has been to consider the theoretical approach of phenomenology alongside social theory and social constructionism. While phenomenology is primarily concerned with hidden constitutive performances of consciousness that are not culture specific and are common to all human beings, social theory encompasses ideas which aim to explain social behaviour, how societies change and develop, while exploring constructs such as power, social structure, gender, race and 'civilization.' Social constructionism, in particular, is concerned with reflectively revealing historically and socially relative structures of knowledge and truth, demonstrating how they are the product of particular power relations. With respect to the body, social constructionism reveals how comportment and disposition are contingent on the power dynamics of social relations, some of which may be oppressive and devoid of rational warrant or justification. Looking at these approaches together is complementary because universal capacities (uncovered by phenomenological analysis) are always conditioned and restricted by contingent social forces (which can be described by social theory and social constructionism).

Furthermore, while providing a critical overview of these philosophical theories of embodiment, the previous chapters have also provided an analysis of the concept of body shame. In chapter 1, body shame was introduced as a philosophical concept, with a description of the cases of acute body shame and chronic body shame. Throughout chapters 2 and 3, body shame was described variously as: a personal and phenomenological experience; an event within intersubjective encounters; and as a feature of socio-cultural and political normativity and control. While body shame appears explicitly in some philosophical and theoretical accounts of embodiment—in particular, as we have seen, it is a structural feature of intersubjective relations for both Sartre and Elias—it often remains an unarticulated or underdeveloped concept, despite its great relevance when considering the recurring themes of bodily visibility, invisibility and the 'seen body' which arise in the philosophical accounts of embodiment considered above.

Bodily visibility is a key concept when considering embodied subjectivity. A multi-dimensional concept, bodily visibility, and concomitantly invisibility and the seen body, have featured in all the accounts of embodiment considered in the previous chapters. As we have seen, the body can become 'visible' in a phenomenological sense. In experiences of dys-appearance, for instance, the physical body becomes salient and comes to explicit thematic awareness as a result of pain, dysfunction or sensation. Instead of being experientially 'absent,' the body is regarded in some sense as an object of consciousness. The related experience of bodily *in*visibility, in this phenomenological sense, indicates the experience of successful pre-reflective motor intentionality, where the body achieves 'flow' when it is in equilibrium with the surrounding environs and is experienced as transparently lived-through.

Another facet of bodily visibility occurs within the social field. Social visibility involves the 'seen body.' This body, as Sartre indicates, arises as a result of one's experience of Others and understanding that in the same manner that the Other can be an object for me, I can also be an object for the Other. The seen body is the surface of the body as regarded by Others (or oneself), or from some distanced perspective. Visibility of the body, in this sense, can arise in intersubjective encounters where one experiences the distanced, judgemental or antagonistic gaze of another. In these experiences, appearance or comportment is brought to thematic awareness in a negative and self-conscious manner. Objectification and alienation become possibilities which can disrupt the flow of social relations or the flow of one's motor intentionality. Hence, the seen body can lead to bodily visibility in the phenomenological sense, as in the social dys-appearances discussed by Leder. As a result, bodily 'visibility' is a complex experience that involves both salient internal events (such as pain or discomfort) mixed together with an awareness of the appearance or outer aspect of the body and its movements.

As noted in chapter 2, the body subject's lived experienced is characterized by efforts to sustain invisibility, and hence 'flow,' in motor action and social interaction. Sander Gilman's concept of 'passing' is useful to understand this idea. "Passing," as Gilman indicates, is a type of "silent validation" where one is "accepted *without comment*."[2] Passing blends the notions of social and bodily visibility *and* invisibility together. Gilman explains, "Such a notion of 'passing' is not becoming 'invisible' but becoming differently visible—being seen as a member of a group with which one wants or needs to identify."[3] The idea is to remain visible, to remain in play in social interaction, but at the same time to look and act just like everyone else, and hence not draw undue attention to oneself; that is, to be "seen but not seen" or to achieve a state of being "(in)visible."[4] Bodily (in)visibility and, concomitantly, the 'flow' of intentionality within social relations are disrupted when attention is drawn to the body in a self-conscious manner, such as is experienced in body shame.

Bodily (in)visibility indicates that one's appearance and comportment are in equilibrium with normative social expectations and the subject remains 'in the game,' so to speak. In this sense, social visibility and invisibility become intertwined into one concept: (in)visibility. (In)visibility indicates that the subject is 'visible' in social relations, he or she is 'in play,' but at the same time, remains unremarkable: acknowledged as a social agent but not judged or objectified.

Although both dimensions of bodily visibility are not necessarily negative experiences—there are many instances where objectification does not lead to alienation, or where attention is brought to the body in pleasure rather than pain—the negative articulation of body visibility has important consequences. A disruptive experience both phenomenologically and socially, bodily visibility is usually avoided or circumvented by the subject. In fact, as we have seen, invisibility—where motor action occurs seamlessly and social relations flow without disruption—is often the favoured state. In addition, the subject is always engaged in strategies to avoid shame or social dys-appearances, hoping to stay in the flow of social relations as a full co-subjectivity. As a result, we can conclude that subjectivity involves constant strategies to achieve and ensure bodily (in)visibility.

Through exploring a possible phenomenology of body shame, we saw that both instances of bodily visibility are instantiated in the shame experience; the body is visible in that the physical symptoms of shame make it salient and dys-appearance occurs, while, at the same time, it becomes visible in that some external aspect of the body, whether appearance or comportment, is regarded by an Other (whether present or internalised) in an antagonistic manner and the body is objectified; hence, social dys-appearance also arises. With these dys-appearances and the experience of visibility, comes an extremely negative affect. In shame, one feels deficient, defective and anxious about one's social standing and social bonds. Body shame, as a result, is an extremely disruptive experience, one that is usually avoided at all costs.

However, despite its negative and undesirable character, body shame cannot always be successfully circumvented. In fact, it is an inevitable and structural part of embodied subjectivity. This is something that Sartre draws out in his account of the Look and the intersubjective constitution of reflective self-consciousness. Being objectified by the other, through the Look, gives the embodied subject self-awareness. Experiences of shame (or the possibility of shame), which are inevitable and ubiquitous, give rise to a self-evaluative structure in consciousness. As Sartre demonstrates, through encounters with others who can see us and judge us, we awaken the capacity to see and judge ourselves.

Both Foucault and Elias develop this line of thought in their accounts of the disciplined body and the civilized body respectively. Foucault and Elias demonstrate how the personal and intersubjective experience of self-evaluation through body shame occurs within a broader normative framework through the mechanisms of surveillance and internalization. In efforts to avoid punishment, shame and incurring social disapproval, the body subject internalizes prevailing social norms regarding appearance and comportment. Hence, the ideas explored in the work of Sartre, Foucault and Elias demonstrate that impression management and self-presentation are central to embodied life. Indeed, it is not as though (bodily experiences of) action and perception come first and then self-presentation follows as some sort of second order concern. Instead, these features of experience are entangled such that one cannot be said to precede the other. We can neither choose to turn away from others, nor to not present ourselves to others, nor can we choose to disregard the socio-cultural and political normative context within which we are enmeshed. The seen body, like the body schema, isn't optional or secondary to consciousness, but instead is an inherent part of the structure of reflective self-awareness. As such, self-presentation and impression management play constitutive roles in subjectivity. Furthermore, body shame is a structural feature in the constant production of subjectivity and reflective self-consciousness. I will now turn to discuss the drive for (in)visibility through self-presentation and impression management within social relations.

THE BODY IN SOCIAL RELATIONS: BOURDIEU, SARTRE AND MERLEAU-PONTY

The coherent and competent body described by both phenomenology and social constructionism is, in fact, a body that has undergone a lengthy developmental process of socialization and acculturalization, as Elias indicates in his account of the civilizing process. This is an ongoing and lifelong process of body management, skill acquisition and self-presentation within intersubjective relations, involving the formation of the body schema, the habit body and the seen body in line prevailing normative expectations. As we have seen, body shame, resulting from an explicit awareness of how one appears to others, is key to this process.

As noted in chapter 2, even the techniques, postures and attitudes of the body that seem somehow inevitable and 'natural' (for example, sitting, standing, walking, etc.) are learned and culturally specific habits shaped by certain socio-cultural idiosyncrasies. One's general bodily 'style' is constituted through habits, learned within a particular cultural milieu, that are sedimented in the body schema. Bourdieu's account of "habitus"[5] is useful to understand the manner through which one lives one's body through style, disposition and practices. The habitus is a set of embodied dispositions that are acquired as a result of one's past and present circumstances, such as one's culture, upbringing or education. The habitus can be considered to be an embodied history, sedimented in the habit body, and comprises of a set of embodied dispositions that shape one's perceptions, practices, judgements and actions. Bourdieu asserts that the habitus "designates a *way of being, a habitual state* (especially of the body) and, in particular, a *predisposition, tendency, propensity or inclination.*"[6]

The habitus determines our manners of acting, feeling and thinking. In short, it is our social and cultural history carried within our dispositions and which shapes our present mode of being. It shapes how one makes choices to act in particular manners and not in others. Obviously, the habitus is an evolving set of structures, which are never fixed or static. Forming a link between the past, present and future, the habitus also links the individual person, and individualized tendencies, with broader social influences and structures; it is "the social embodied."[7] The concept of habitus is a useful manner through which to understand the cultural specificity of the habit body, as described by Merleau-Ponty. The habit body is not an extra layer of abilities and practices, but rather forms the condition of the possibility of being in the world. Furthermore, the habit body is not a neutral set of bodily capacities, but is necessarily laden with social value and meaning; it is a habitus. Merleau-Ponty himself recognized the cultural embeddedness of the body subject, discussing how the life of consciousness is underpinned by an "intentional arc" that subtends "our past, our future, our human milieu, our physical situation, our ideological situation, and our moral situation."[8] It is through this idea of the habit body being shaped by the social field that Merleau-Ponty repeatedly insists on the intertwining of self, others and world.

As a result of the habitus, we have a general bodily style, simultaneously idiosyncratic and collective, determined in part by the human milieu within which we find ourselves. This bodily style is expressed both in terms of appearance and comportment. In order to ensure that our body is in line with prevailing standards regarding body management, and to avoid breaching the normative standards that explicitly and implicitly permeate one's social field, hence possibly incurring the threat of social exclusion as described by Elias, the subject must maintain a sense of how the body appears to others. Maintaining and managing one's seen body, or what is commonly referred to by the term 'body image' in psychological and philosophical literature, is a central, and constitutive, part of embodied subjectivity.[9] Body image, in this sense, is one's subjective experience of how the body appears (to Others). It is a complex phenomenon which is constructed by individual perception, intersubjective responses, affect and shared social experiences. As Martin

Dillon explains, "My body-image is my image of myself: as image, it is object, as myself, it is the subject that I am."[10] The body image, understood as the seen body—my preferred terminology as 'body image' carries many conflicting conceptualizations—can be both the body as objectified by the judgemental and limiting gaze of the other and the functional image of the body we have when it is in flow in physical action and social relations. As we saw in chapter 2, for Sartre, it is only through the encounter with the other that the body can be regarded as an intentional object for certain attitudes and beliefs, and through which an explicit, public 'seen body' can be formed. This visual aspect of oneself plays a key role in one's embodied identity, perceived social worth and continuous social interactions.

However, for Sartre, the seen body is formed through objectifying and alienating encounters with others. It is worth commenting here on the pessimistic nature of Sartre's account of intersubjective relations. While Sartre has a very worked out account of the significance of the seen body, or the idea of how (one believes) the body appears to others from some distanced perspective, his account has been heavily criticized for offering a very lopsided view of social relations. Almost all of the examples that Sartre offers of social encounters are tinged with a pessimistic and misanthropic attitude with regard to interpersonal relations. It is widely acknowledged that Sartre tends to focus on negative encounters where subjectivities find themselves in conflict or in some compromised state, and furthermore, that he insists on dichotomizing the subject-object positions within these encounters. Many of Sartre's critics resist the idea that the essence of all intersubjective relations is conflict and he is often criticized for his misanthropic attitude. Merleau-Ponty was particularly critical of this aspect of Sartre's ontology believing that it provides an inaccurate and inhuman description of embodied social relations which are more complex and ambiguous. Commenting on Sartre's account of the Look, Merleau-Ponty writes:

> The other transforms me into an object and denies me, I transform him into an object and deny him, it is asserted. In fact the other's gaze transforms me into an object, and mine him, only if both of us withdraw into the core of our thinking nature, if we both make ourselves into an inhuman gaze, if each of us feels his actions to be not taken up and understood, but observed as if they were an insect's.[11]

Merleau-Ponty suggests that it would be more accurate to characterize alienation as arising from objectification as one example, among perhaps many, that can characterize intersubjective encounters: "This is true: this objectivation [sic] by the look is a profound truth . . . But it is a particular case of a more general relation."[12]

Other commentators also suggest that there are many other modes of relating which don't necessarily lead to objectification and alienation or a dichotomizing struggle between subject and object. For example, Marjorie Grene suggests that there are many situations where the Look is not threatening; she asks us to consider the "rare but still indubitable experience of mutual understanding, of the reciprocal look of peers; or the look of mother and infant, where the one protects and the other is protected."[13] There are countless instances where an encounter with the other leads to what Leder terms "mutual incorporation."[14] He writes: "As long as the Other treats me as subject—that is, experiences *with* me the world in which I dwell, mutual incorporation effects no sharp rift."[15] In this vein, van den Berg offers an account of the "accepting look" of the Other which "gives me the almost exceptional right to be myself as a moving body."[16] Moreover, the sociologist Erving Goffman likewise offers a description of social interaction that is not self-conscious, denoting this experience as "euphoric interplay,"[17] arguing that there are many occasions that people are "unoriented to and unconcerned about being under observation."[18]

In addition to these qualifications to the negative articulation of the Look, there are other theorists that argue that ontologically our relations with others are characterized by an ethical opening, rather than an antagonistic struggle between subjectification and objectification. Notably, Emmanuel Levinas develops this line of thought in his phenomenological ethics, arguing that the pure alterity of the Other can never be assimilated or reduced to an object for the self. Ultimately, Levinas's project is to articulate an ethics which puts ethical responsibility, as arising from the encounter with the Other, as integral to subjectivity.[19] Rosalyn Diprose likewise argues that at the level of prereflective intercorporeality, our relations with others are characterized by generosity, rather than antagonism. Generosity, Diprose argues, "is a being given that constitutes the self as affective and being affected [and] that constitutes social relations."[20] Diprose invokes Merleau-Ponty's claim that through perception, agency and subjectivity the body is 'open' to the bodies of others and this openness constitutes a corporeal generosity, a to-and-froing of embodied exchanges.

ERVING GOFFMAN, STIGMA AND THE BELONGINGNESS HYPOTHESIS

In fact, Goffman and other theorists argue, against Sartre, that for the most part social relations are characterized by non-objectifying relations which ensure 'flow' and harmony within intercorporeal interactions. This is made possible because the lived body is constantly engaged in strategies of self-presentation and impression management. Self-presentation, hence, can be understood to be the conscious and unconscious bodily strategies, made possible by the body schema and the habit body, that the embodied subject continuously employs to ensure social (in)visibility, or to ensure that the body remains present and visible in social encounters, avoiding instances of body shame which might disrupt the flow of interactions.

The relationship between the visible aspect of oneself and the society and social relations within which the self is visually represented and received, is theorized at length by Erving Goffman. In his work, Goffman forges a strong link between creating a desired impression in others, achieving success in social encounters and the experience of self-conscious emotions such as shame and embarrassment. The focus of much of Goffman's writing is the management of social life through face-to-face encounters, particularly examining how orderly behaviour is so fastidiously maintained within social interaction. Through his dramaturgical presentation of social life—making great use of the metaphors of the theatre such as acts, roles, audiences, props, on stage and backstage areas—Goffman argues that social life is a series of stages that each induce a different performance from the subject, depending on context. The order of social life is maintained through each 'actor' attentively playing his or her part through careful management of the body, expression and communication.

In concordance with Elias, Goffman argues that individuals manage and control their bodies, in a sense constructing and managing their habitus, in order to conform to leading social standards with the aim of facilitating successful social interaction. Public order and the harmonious co-existence of embodied subjects results from shared modes of conduct and behaviour. Successful intervention, as Elias likewise argues, requires a high level of embodied competence in controlling movements, expressions and body language.

Goffman posits the idea of a shared "body idiom"[21] which is a shared style of bodily comportment that members of a society adhere to in order to maintain the smooth functioning of intersubjective situations and spaces. These "shared vocabularies" of body idiom are conventionalised forms of non-verbal bodily behaviour which are largely undetermined by the individual, and furthermore are prescribed to without any conscious choice or reflection on the part of the subject.[22] Furthermore, once a body idiom is adopted, the subject can employ it without need for conscious reflection, the idea of 'control,' as offered by Goffman, not implying sustained, conscious effort. Within interpersonal and social encounters, the individual sustains complete, unending and thorough command of the body, behaving within the parameters of socially acceptable behaviour: "During interaction the individual is expected to posses certain attributes, capacities, and information which, taken together, fit together into a self that is at once coherently unified and appropriate for the occasion."[23] Furthermore, it is not just a matter of sustaining control but, just as importantly, being seen by others to do so. Any transgression of the shared body idiom leads to shame and embarrassment, and instances of social dys-appearance:

> At such moments the individual whose presentation has been discredited may feel ashamed while the others present may feel hostile, and all the participants may come to feel ill at ease, nonplussed, out of countenance, embarrassed, experiencing the kind of anomy that is generated when the minute social system of face-to-face interaction breaks down.[24]

Self-presentation and impression management, as described here by Goffman, are basic concerns for the embodied social subject. Maintaining the flow of social situations through the micromanagement of self-presentation is achieved often without the need for conscious efforts or deliberations. Acute shame, or perhaps more accurately, the possibility of acute shame arising, acts as the regulating mechanism in those encounters.

Although, Sartre's account of human interaction as dominated by objectifying responses between subjectivities, as described above, proves inaccurate when considering Goffman's account of 'euphoric interplay,' or the flow of interpersonal interactions, what Sartre's account does alert us to is the presence of the *possibility* of shame, objectification and alienation in every encounter. Shame is by no means an anomalous experience which only occasionally disrupts social relations or is merely the concern of a self-conscious few. On the contrary, all human contact is pervaded and infused with embarrassment and shame, either realized or anticipated, and there is no social encounter which is excluded from the possibility of shame. Negative self-conscious emotions are not deviances from normal or natural interaction, nor are they anomalous or trivial in human experience, but rather, as Goffman insists, shame "is a normal part of social life . . . embarrassment is not an irrational impulse breaking through socially prescribed behaviour, but part of this orderly behaviour itself."[25] The phenomenologist, Erwin Straus, offers a similar characterization of shame as ubiquitous, arguing that shame is "continuously active."[26] He writes: "Shame is not merely active at certain times and under certain circumstances. When someone is ashamed, it is a sign that the permanent safeguard of shame has been breached."[27] As a result, the possibility of acute shame, embarrassment and other negative self-conscious emotions is vital for the continuance of an uninterrupted flow of social interaction.

However, it must be remembered, as Elias's account of the civilizing process demonstrates, that impression management and self-presentation involves much more than the micro-management of bodily behaviour and comportment, but centrally concerns the 'seen body' and the unconscious and self-conscious management of how the surface of the body appears to Others. Goffman was highly alert to this aspect of impression management. His well-

[margin handwritten note: Shame is the normal function.]

known work on stigma offers an analysis of how physical appearance is central to the embodied and existential drive for social harmony. Stigma, Goffman argues, is "the situation of the individual who is disqualified from full social acceptance" as a result of some aspect of appearance that deviates from that which is considered to be "ordinary" and "natural."[28] Stigma is about visibility and "bodily signs" which expose "something unusual and bad about the moral status" of the individual.[29] Stigma arises when an individual's bodily identity within a social group does not correspond to normative expectations of the attributes that the individual should posses. The stigmatized person "is reduced in our minds from a whole and usual person to a tainted and discredited one."[30] The stigmatized person likewise holds this belief: "the standards he has incorporated from the wider social group equip him . . . to agree that he does indeed fall short of what he really ought to be."[31] Social worth is intimately linked to stigma and the avoidance of what Goffman refers to as 'spoiled identity.' Being stigmatized is an undesirable and deeply troubling situation, as the "normals," that is, the non-stigmatized individuals, "believe the person with a stigma is not quite human [and] exercise varieties of discrimination [that] reduce his life chances."[32]

Body shame, of course, is central to this process. All deviations from the 'normal,' with respect to appearance, become potential occasions for shame. As Goffman remarks, with stigma, "shame becomes a central possibility."[33] Stigma is not an unusual or infrequent occurrence, affecting a few unfortunates in society.[34] Instead, it is a necessary feature of the 'normal,' as the normal only comes into relief against that which is considered abnormal or unnatural. As a result, to avoid the discrimination and social punishment that stigma incurs, most of us, most of the time, attempt to appear 'normal.' What is 'normal' for any individual is determined by a complex interaction between social norms and individual attitudes and values.[35] However, what is clear is that ideas of normality circulate within social relations, having a concrete impact in terms of self-presentation. In line with Foucault's account of normalization arising as a result of power relations, Goffman demonstrates how fear of punishment, instantiated as a threat to social bonds, is a powerful regulating force in embodied social relations and interactions. Stigma is a fear of social death, a fear of being put 'out of play.' Through the hypervisibility of the body, stigma paradoxically incurs another species of bodily *in*visibility. As a spoiled identity, the stigmatized person is often not accepted into social relations, they are seen, but then *seen through* or rendered invisible.[36] This sort of invisibility, as we shall see below, has serious consequences, personally and politically, for the embodied subject.

Goffman postulates that the central concern in the stigmatized person's life, which can be extrapolated to be the central concern in any subject's life, is to overcome this social invisibility; it is a question, as Goffman remarks, "of what is often, if vaguely, called 'acceptance.'"[37] Acceptance and concerns about belonging to a social group are revealed as basic and often invisible drives in intersubjective interaction. We are all constantly engaged in strategies to manage the impression others have of us in order to secure our position within our social group. Self-presentation is not just about accruing and augmenting prestige, social standing and body capital, as Elias's account of court society emphasizes, but rather a basic or more fundamental need for a sense of social inclusion and belongingness.

There is extensive literature in evolutionary psychology discussing the human need for belonging and its central place in shaping the concerns and motivations for the embodied subject. Roy Baumeister and Mark Leary argue for the "belongingness hypothesis" which demonstrates a fundamental human drive to seek out rewarding interactions and establish social bonds with others in the context of long term and intimate relationships.[38] The belongingness hypothesis proposes that the need for "frequent, affectively pleasant interactions" with others is a fundamental interpersonal concern.[39] Having a sense of belonging within a community is in fact a foundational aspect of our beings. As Rosalyn Diprose argues, belonging is not merely a social or political concern, but is *ontological*: "the ontology of belonging points to the existential necessity and ethical force of community."[40] The body is ontologically inclined, Diprose argues, "toward or open to others."[41]

Axel Honneth discusses this need for belonging—the ontological 'inclination' toward others—through the concept of recognition; a concept which moves out of the ontological into the social and political spheres. He argues that as humans we are constantly involved in the "struggle for recognition."[42] We are all strategic agents who actively (albeit not necessarily consciously) strive to manage the impression others have of us in order to secure recognition within our social group. For Honneth, the struggle for recognition has three phases or strata: first, the demand for love, confirming one's basic needs and creating the basis for self-confidence; second, the demand for rights, where one recognizes others as independent human beings with reciprocal rights, creating the basis for self-respect; and third, the demand for recognition as a unique individual, which is the basis for self-esteem. Within intercorpereal relations, the struggle for one's own recognition—and concomitantly conferring recognition to others—is a central component of self-presentation. Recognition, Honneth argues, is the "making visible" of a person "with the aid of suitable actions, gestures or facial expressions, to the fact that the person is noticed affirmatively in the manner appropriate to the relationship in question."[43] Through expressive responses it is made "clear publically to the person in question that she has been accorded social approval or possesses social validity."[44]

Potential threats to social bonds, and hence the potential to not be recognized within one's social group, through shame experiences, are cause for significant distress: "behind the feeling of shame stands not the fear of hatred

...ar of *contempt* which, on an even deeper level of the unconscious, ...pells fear of *abandonment*, the death by emotional starvation."[45] The fear of being ostracized is likened to *death* by some thinkers. This association is by no means arbitrary, nor extreme; there are very high stakes involved when breaching social norms and when one's sense of belonging and recognition are compromised. Goffman's *Stigma* opens with a letter to the agony aunt Miss Lonelyhearts. Written by a sixteen-year-old girl born without a nose, the letter recounts how she is completely ostracized from social life as a result of her bodily defect. Even her parents find it difficult to accept her. She ends the letter desperately asking if suicide is her only option.[46] As Jane Megan Northrop notes, in cases of stigma and the breaching of societal norms, "social death and actual death are imminently convergent."[47] As a result, it is no wonder that shame is avoided fastidiously and that all of the features of embodied subjectivity described by phenomenological thinkers, such as the body schema, the habit body, motor intentionality, skill acquisition and the drives for (in)visibility, are shaped by our fear of shame.

THE CULTURAL POLITICS OF SHAME

Body shame, underpinned by a basic human need for belongingness and recognition, infuses all social relations, acting as a threshold to maintain social order, social groups and the coherence of intersubjective and political life. While acute body shame is a necessary part of human experience, too much shame can have negative consequences. In fact, there are times when body shame can be oppressive, especially when it becomes chronic, as noted in chapter 1. Instead of being instrumental for realizing the full expression of embodied social life, chronic body shame can be disempowering and compromising, threatening one's basic sense of recognition and belonging within a social group, ultimately leading to experiences of social invisibility, as described by Honneth. When this occurs systematically, or as part of the oppression of a particular social group, then body shame can become highly political.

What must be kept in mind, especially when considering the role of shame in the political sphere, is that shame is not experienced in the same manner by all subjects. In fact, the propensity to shame, and its consequences, is very much dependent on one's position within a social group. While Sartre describes a process of objectification and subjectification between two equal subjects in part of his discussion of the Look and shame, this account does not acknowledge that power relations are easily lopsided between subjects. In fact, Sartre's account seems to be entirely devoid of any nuances regarding social stratification or the consequences of imbalanced power relations. What Sartre's account does not acknowledge is that some subjects, such as Pecola in Morrison's *The Bluest Eye*, discussed in chapter simply do not have the social power to return the Look. Objectification, with its concomitant potential for alienation, remains firmly unidirectional in many cases.

With respect to race, Frantz Fanon explicitly criticizes Sartre on this point. He writes: "Jean-Paul Sartre had forgotten that the Negro suffers in his body quite differently from the white man. Between the white man and me the connexion was irrevocably one of transcendence."[48] In fact, Sartre's account of the constitution of reflective self-consciousness in *Being and Nothingness* presupposes an egalitarian field of social subjects and social relations. The Other can objectify me with the Look and this Look is didactic, it 'teaches me who I am.' The voyeur realizes he is a sneak or a spy in a flash of shame, but then the shame subsides. In fact, in the realization that there is no one there, he carries on with his activities, the self-evaluative moment of shame a momentary glitch on an otherwise untroubled consciousness. The application of Sartre's dramaturgical renderings of a consciousness experiencing shame, and the resulting self-awareness as a result of an encounter with another, Fanon argues, "proves fallacious" for black consciousness.[49] The inequality of power relations with respect to race and racial identity is significant. Fanon argues: "This is because the white man is not only the Other but also the master, whether real or imaginary."[50] However, it should be noted that Sartre recognized the inequalities in social relations as a result of divergences in social position and inequality. In his essay 'Anti-Semite and Jew,' Sartre explicitly draws attention to the consequences of a subjectivity being treated as an "inferior and pernicious being."[51]

What Fanon's criticism of Sartre's early work makes salient is the fact that shame is by no means a uniform experience across a social group. In fact, as Northrop remarks, shame is "most often experienced by those who occupy positions lacking social authority, those who find themselves in social situations where the parameters of shame are determined, not by themselves, but by a more powerful other."[52] In addition, Cheshire Calhoun notes, "the power to shame is likely to be concentrated in the hands of those whose interpretations are socially authoritative."[53] Essentially, the raced subject, in the context of Euro-American cultural politics, is more "shame–prone," or more likely to feel shame, in the face of his or her more socially authoritative white counterparts, as a result of occupying a less powerful social position in a milieu that designates his identity as inferior.[54] Emily S. Lee quotes Patricia Williams: "[The] cultural domination of blacks by whites means that the black self is placed at a distance even from itself . . . So blacks in a white society are conditioned from infancy to see in themselves only what others, who despise them, see."[55] The same, of course, can be said for most other marginalized groups. However, it is not merely the frequency of the occurrence of shame that is at stake within an imbalanced social relation, but in addition, the phenomenology of shame—or the very structure of a shame experience.

Ullaliina Lehtinen's analysis of shame, employing key insights from Sandra Lee Bartky's discussion of shame and gender in her work *Femininity and Domination: Studies in the Phenomenology of Oppression*, focuses on the differences between the shame experience of those with social privilege and those who are socially subordinated. Those with social power, who constitute and ratify the normative values which carve out the parameters for shame within a social group, are more likely to experience shame as an minor disturbance. In short, for these socially powerful individuals, shame is more often acute, rather than chronic. Like the voyeur in Sartre's example, shame arises as a fleeting disturbance: it is a "blip across the face of an otherwise undisturbed consciousness."[56] She calls this shame of the "aristocrat's kind": "white European or North American, middle-class, academically trained men. The only shame they themselves *knew*, had experienced, was . . . a painful episode, a sudden unexpected change in the state of things, an occasion for moral reaffirmation."[57] This sort of experience of shame has didactic potential. The subject is able to learn from this experience, readjust or regulate their behaviour accordingly and once again reassert his subjectivity within the flow of social relations. As Bartky comments, the "experience of shame *can* be salutary for such a person because he is not systematically impoverished by the moral economy he is compelled to inhabit."[58] In fact, what both Lehtinen and Bartky make clear is that this sort of socially privileged subject (usually white, Western, educated, male) "has escaped the characteristic sorts of psychological oppression on which modern hierarchies of class, race and gender rely so heavily."[59]

The point is that the experience of shame is markedly divergent for the 'shame-prone' socially subordinated subject. Shame experienced by members of subordinated groups is, in fact, different in nature from, and, in addition, more pernicious than, the shame experienced by socially privileged or dominant individuals. In essence, as made clear by thinkers such as Fanon, socially subordinated individuals, such as Pecola, "are not free to resist feeling shame."[60] Instead, chronic shame becomes a permanent possibility as the normative values of the milieu in which this subject is situated render him or her perniciously and permanently disadvantaged within social relations: "the sites of potential shame are literally everywhere."[61] Shame for these individuals is not an acute disturbance, but rather a "pervasive affective attunement to the social environment."[62] This sort of shame does not just affect individuals, but has significance for a whole social group and can be borne across time: "it is inherited, passed on from one generation to the next."[63] Shame becomes deeply embedded and chronic; it is not experienced as an acute disruption to one's situation, but rather as a background of pain and self-consciousness, becoming more acute perhaps in moments of exposure or self-reference. The idea is that even when shame is not felt directly, it is permanently anticipated as one's identity is spoiled in the first instance. The socially marginalized subject can be characterized as a "shame subjectivity" as a result of a set of structural social relations. [64]

Living as a shame subjectivity is not merely having internalized ideas about one's inferior social status. Instead, this inferiority is literally embodied. Gail Weiss notes, referring to the work of Frantz Fanon, that "the invisible social processes at work in the construction of a racially-coded corporeal schema . . . [are] always already operative." She argues that for those designated as 'racial minorities,' "the internalization of this racial epidermal schema . . . results in a (psychophysical) inferiority complex." [65] What this points to is that the consequences of living with chronic shame are not trivial. As Lehtinen points out, the experiences arising from the chronic shame of a socially subordinated individual "often breed a stagnant self-obsession, they are unconstructive and self-destructive; and they function as *confirmations* of what the agent knew all along—that he or she was a person of lesser worth." [66] In fact, the sort of subjectivity that is constituted in light of the experience of chronic shame is one that is politically and socially compromised, leading to a state of profound disempowerment. It does not lead to the sort of transcendental subjectivity as in Sartre's account that has the capacity to judge and constitute their actions freely or the sort of "lucid" agent of moral philosophy, who can supposedly clearly discern between right and wrong. [67]

Perpetually feeling oneself to be a person of lesser worth has concrete consequences in terms of how one views oneself and in terms of one's life chances. In fact, there is substantial empirical research that demonstrates that shame-proneness, in particular shame about the body, directly correlates with the propensity for depression. [68] Even if chronic shame doesn't result in pathological states as serious as depression, in its ongoing landscape of self-reference and self-consciousness, body shame can lead to a psychic confusion which is not only emotional but cognitive as well, and this is profoundly disempowering. Empirical research has demonstrated this over and over again, performance in cognitive tasks, such as mathematics, diminishes when one is made to feel self-conscious or ashamed, especially when these experiences are centred on the body and attention is directed to appearance management. [69]

There are several things to note about shame as an experience that is more likely to affect a marginal group. First of all, this shame is political. It can be and has been employed to systematically disadvantage a social group. This is well documented in the oppression and subordination of racial or religious minorities and individuals with 'deviant' sexuality or disability. These groups are, or historically have been, systematically at the receiving end of public derision, aggression and legal and illegal discrimination. Political strategies of oppression use shame as a means to disempower a group of people. Usually this group is shamed because they embody some moral failing: they do not live up to the normative expectations of the social milieu in which they are embedded: they are greedy, lazy, promiscuous, worthless, untrustworthy, and so forth. However, this brings us to the second point, that the political shame of a subordinated group, and their concomitant moral failing, is usually linked to the body. In short, political shame is often body shame: a public or visible feature of a person, such as his or her skin colour, race, gender, ethnicity, disability, sexual preferences, obesity, or other physical features, becomes correlated to some sort of undesirable or immoral character trait and, as a result, this physical aspect becomes a stigma. Considering the historical link between shame and nudity, and Elias's discussion of the lowering thresholds for shame as directly related to the management of corporeality, it is not surprising that social sanctions are so intimately linked to the body.

Human beings have a long history of linking physical features with personality or character traits and, furthermore, doing so in order to marginalize certain social groups. For instance, in Victorian times, acne and skin blemishes were considered to be the result of moral failure and frequently associated with sexual deviancy. For the Victorians, physical beauty was thought to derive from pure inner qualities, such as morality and spirituality.[70] Hence, social and moral worth were conflated with the physical appearance of the body, an idea that resonates strongly in the present day. Discussing the early twentieth century, Sander Gilman notes how racial features are dubiously linked with character traits in North American and European culture. For instance, 'Jewish' or 'Irish' noses signified criminality or greed. Being overweight, although a sign of prosperity in some cultures and at certain times in our own culture, was, and still is, frequently linked to slovenliness or laziness. Black skin evokes "undesirability" and "criminal inclinations" within the dominant white social order.[71] Gilman discusses how social groups are historically defined by physicality and that the physical characteristics of one social group "must be so constructed that it has a clearly defined, unambiguous antithesis (hairy/bald, fat/thin, . . . large nose/small nose, male/female)." He notes that these binary categories "are all socially defined so as to make belonging to the positive category more advantageous than belonging to the negative category."[72]

Historically, categories of "inclusion/includability" and "exclusion/excludability" have been determined in terms of 'pariah' groups focusing on physical features that signify one's belonging to categories determined by gender, race, sexuality and class.[73] The idea is that at any given moment we know which group we belong to, because we either do or do not bear the physical feature associated with that group. Ensuring a sense of belonging, recognition and social inclusion becomes a constant quest to have the physical body "pass" as "normal," or to achieve (in)visibility and recognition according to the standards of the dominant, or more powerful, social group.[74] Those who actually bear the stigmatized physical feature in question see it as a negative and defining feature of the self. Identity is spoiled not because of some idea, action or principle, but because of the very core of the self: the body bears or *is* your moral failing. Pecola stands no chance: "It is not a matter of what one *does* but what one *is:* black in white America."[75] Shame, as chronic, becomes a permanent possibility.

What is important to note is that when shame is deployed as a strategy of social exclusion, as a means to oppress a particular social group, this shame is often invisible, unacknowledged or individually and collectively bypassed. As Northrop notes, we have a "collective reticence" to confront our failings as social subjects; she writes: "Our collective aversion to facing shame obscures how shame informs the shaping of wider cultural prescriptions and, consequently, the way these prescriptions inform self-experience."[76] This has consequences on two levels. First, shaming strategies are so implicit, that we may fail to notice them. Bartky aruges, the "biases that invade consciousness are so pervasive and so little available to consciousness that they can sabotage good intentions—or even good politics."[77] What gets communicated through the social milieu and social structures about one's spoiled identity or excludability often does not take the form of "propositional meaning" and is both "sent and received below the level of explicit awareness."[78] As a result, it is easy to overlook shame as an aspect of one's own political marginalization. In particular this occurs because the person who is on the receiving end of shame lacks social authority and comes to agree with the parameters determined by a more powerful Other. Internalization, as we saw in Foucault's account, is frequently the result of imbalanced power relations in punitive regimes. Secondly, oppressed individuals become "stigma schematic,"[79] internalizing the beliefs that are associated with their stigma: the homosexual comes to believe that he should be ashamed of his deviant sexuality; the obese person ashamed of their laziness, the African-American slave so ashamed of his physicality that he believes he deserves an inferior social position, and so on.

In addition, shame is often overlooked because, as Lauren Berlant emphasizes, the "*structure* of shame . . . isn't necessary aligned with the *experience* of shame."[80] The emotional experience of shame may be bypassed (for anger, for example) or repressed altogether. It might simply be too devastating or world-destroying to allow shame to enter conscious experience. Berlant emphasizes this point in her discussion of the cultural politics of shame, discussing "the broken circuit," or the "emotional disconnection," that systematically shamed subjects of marginalized groups regularly experience.[81] In these cases, shame is bypassed for another experience, anger, depression or numbness, for example. In addition, it may be that the subject is so adept at creating strategies to avoid shame that it is effectively circumvented most of the time: subjectivity is tightly structured within the parameters of acceptable behaviour, appearance and comportment. Certain behaviours, so thoroughly internalized, come to seem natural, normal or necessary. In this case, one may not even realize that shame, or strategies to avoid shame, are a powerful feature of one's lived experience. Despite not necessarily entering conscious experience, it is important to discern that when the structure of shame is a framing feature of one's subjectivity—bearing a stigma, judgement by the Other, recognition of one's lesser social worth, social inferiority—then this has concrete consequences with respect to creating marginalized identity categories.

However, it is possible for marginalized or oppressed groups to raise "stigma consciousness" and to become aware of the shaming structures within which they are operating and the fallacious nature of the social stigmas that are usually attributed to them.[82] Having stigma consciousness entails that one does not "regard the stereotypes about [one's] group as self-descriptive."[83] Despite this, it is important to note that even with a very developed sense of stigma consciousness, this by no means ensures that one is immune to feelings of inferiority or shame. It is, of course, still possible to feel shame when one enters a social or political space where the sedimented and dominating norms render your marginal identity as inferior or spoiled. The point is that even if these subjects are aware that they are wrongfully shamed, they may not be in a position—socially, politically, personally—to resist it.

Being excluded from the dominant social group entails that one is, as noted above, 'invisible' in the social order. Emily S. Lee relays Patricia William's account of precisely this phenomena. Williams, a middle-aged, black law professor is refused entry into a store in New York by a sullen white teenage shopkeeper: "The saleschild does not perceive Williams in her entirety; he sees an anonymous black woman."[84] Seeing a black woman, however, is not a neutral seeing, but instead a value-laden *Looking*, to use Sartre's terminology. Due to the sedimented cultural history of racial meanings associated with raced corporeality, the "salechild's perception of William's body—brown, round-faced, kinky-haired, together with the cultural implements, the clothes Williams is wearing—sums up to a type of body associated with undesirability, a type of body associated with the likelihood of committing a theft."[85] Williams is not recognized as a full co-subjectivity or co-agent, entitled to the same treatment, rights and privileges as the white-skinned child. Instead the saleschild sees her merely as "a black woman" and this particular category of 'seen body' is loaded with social meanings signalling inferiority, undesirability and even criminality.

This sort of lack of recognition as a full co-subjectivity induces social bodily invisibility. This invisibility arises when a marginalized subjectivity is not given full credit as a social agent within the dominant social order. Axel

Honneth discusses this phenomena as not a "physical non-presence, but rather non-existence in a social sense."[86] To illustrate this species of invisibility he discusses the experience of the protagonist in Ralph Ellison's classic novel *The Invsibile Man:* "Ralph Ellison's first-person narrator tells of his 'invisibility': as this ever anonymous 'I' reports, he is, indeed, a real 'flesh and blood' man, but 'one' simply wishes not to see him, 'one' looks straight through him; he is quite simply 'invisible' to everyone else."[87] The experience is of being 'looked through,' being seen but not being acknowledged as a full social agent is common to the experience of raced subjects in the white dominant social order. This sense of social invisibility is effected through intercorporeal interactions. The white slave master, as Honneth notes, can undress unselfconsciously in front of his or her black slaves, because those slaves do not have any power to Look: "the white masters, intentionally seek to make clear to the blacks, who are physically present, that they (the blacks) are not visible to them."[88] The absence of recognition, achieved through bodily movements, gestures and facial expressions which fail to acknowledge the individual, is not only disrespectful but a potent source of shame. This "overlooking or ignoring," as Honneth notes, "is of a humiliating kind."[89]

Lack of recognition, or social invisibility, is shameful because it signals one's disempowerment: "Pecola's *not being seen*—that is, not being acknowledged as a member of a community—produces shame."[90] Even if Pecola knows the shopkeeper is racist and is entirely in the wrong in believing her to be of lesser social worth, in the moment of her encounter with him, she may not be able to resist his judgemental glare: her youth, skin colour, shame-proneness, social inferiority, coupled with the implicit threat of violence or social sanctions, structurally, if not personally, limit her ability to return his objectifying and alienating Look. She may return his gaze, but, because she is effectively invisible and, as a result, disempowered in his social realm, he will not see it, nor feel its sanctions. Ultimately, he is unable to learn anything about himself from her Look.

As a result of the difficulties of individual resistance, when shame becomes a structural feature of cultural politics, it is not enough to overcome shame individually, but it must be done collectively. Theorists of race and gender have long noted that discrimination is effected not just through legislation, but on two strata: "structural/institutional" and "prejudicial/discriminatory."[91] Institutions can generate and propagate discrimination, but it also proliferates through the sedimented cultural structures and ideas that frame interpersonal and social relations. It is no accident that getting groups out of subordination requires more than changes in legislation to ensure legal equality. Bartky notes that, "black empowerment called not only for black civil rights and economic advancement, but for 'black pride.' Nor should we forget that this was the movement that needed to invent the slogan 'Black is

Beautiful.'"[92] The idea is that in order to overcome oppression, marginalized groups have to equip themselves with self-conceptions and self-representations that enable them to take pride in their identities. We see this with other social movements such as 'Gay Pride,' 'Fat Power' or events such as the Special Olympics. The impetus behind these movements is that socially inferior groups must invert chronic shame—a structural feature of their subjectivities—into pride in order to achieve collective and personal liberation. The struggle to overcome social invisibility, is a struggle to achieve (in)visibility, the body and self are visible in social relations, but not objectified or hypervisible.

These movements make aspects of a collective identity—that may be hidden, erased, non-compliant and, as a result, invisible in the social order—highly visible, demanding recognition and validation. While this process is by no means unproblematic, and the idea that shame can itself be isolated to "distinct 'toxic' parts of a group or individual identity," as Eve Sedgwick notes, is a problematic one,[93] what is apparent is that shame, and overcoming shame (which is often centred on the body), has a central role to play in terms of the validation of subjectivity, both personally and politically. Hence, as Bartky makes clear, when outlining a phenomenology of oppression, or the lived experience of oppression, an account of shame is central. I would further stress that this account must make body shame central.

CONCLUSION

As we have seen, body shame is intimately linked to the powerful fear of stigma and social exclusion. It acts as a mechanism of sorts that ensures one's recognition and belongingness within a social group. When it is mobilized in order to disadvantage a marginalized group, body shame can have political consequences. Overcoming shame is central to the struggle for recognition, both in terms of interpersonal relations, and also in terms of the struggle for rights and social standing within one's social group. As a result, concerns around self-presentation and avoiding body shame, especially with regard to normalized standards, are far from trivial. In fact, what all this tells us is that, when it comes to the body within social relations, looks and appearances are crucial. Flawed or failed self-presentation can have devastating consequences. Hence, subjects are continuously sensitive to how 'attractive' and 'normal' they appear to others, as this has concrete consequences for one's social interaction, social standing, sense of self and embodied identity.[94] Hence, the phenomenological characteristics of body shame coupled with its peculiar social nature, play an important role in understanding how the subject is 'shaped' by the cultural, institutional and social milieu of which it is a part. The avoidance of acute body shame, more commonly manifested as 'milder' self-other-conscious emotions such as embarrassment or social anxiety, leads us to cultivate meticulous control of comportment and appearance, such as the micro movements employed in interpersonal interaction. Avoiding chronic body shame, on the other hand, leads us to more long-term body projects, such as Michelle's decision to undergo rhinoplasty or the internalization of disempowering cultural beliefs regarding one's identity, as we saw in the discussion of race politics.

As a result, what is interesting about body shame, and here we must consider its manifestation as a whole range of negative self-conscious emotions, is that it can tell us something about how the individual body is connected to and ultimately shaped by prevailing norms and mores without reducing the description of the body subject to one of social determinism where the subject is inscribed by external forces, lacking autonomy and agency. The body is by no means passively shaped by external forces, as is sometimes implied in Foucault's social constructionist account; instead, the body subject is constantly interacting with and negotiating the influences of intersubjectivity and the structures of the social, cultural and political fields. In attempting to master prevailing social codes and normative standards regarding body management, the subject is instructed by body shame.

As such, body shame is a fundamental process in the constitution of embodied subjectivity and one's social identity. Body shame is a wholly necessary component of embodied subjectivity—it guides the formation of the habit body and skill acquisition—and, furthermore, it is integral to the order and coherence of social relations; it ensures the uniformity of social norms. Although an unpleasant experience which we are at pains to avoid, body shame is not only normal, it is inevitable and necessary. Self-presentation, as a fundamental part of embodied phenomenology, is essentially about avoiding shame and securing belonging.

However, as noted above, shame can become chronic and can be employed to disadvantage a marginalized group. Although I have used the example of race in this chapter to explore the cultural politics of shame, I will now shift my focus. In chapters 5 and 6, I will explore body shame as an oppressive experience with respect to concerns around appearance production within the experience of female embodiment. The ideas of surveillance, normalization, internalization, objectification and alienation which function in experiences of body shame and which were examined in the chapters above, will be explored with respect to oppressive experiences of body shame. In particular, my focus will be on the experience of Western women, regarding appearance management and beauty norms, within the neoliberal patriarchal structures of late modernity. While chapter 5 is an analysis of shame production within social structures in the case of female embodiment, chapter 6 explores cosmetic surgery in particular. As an overwhelmingly female practice, cosmetic surgery will be used as a case study to understand how the body can be literally 'shaped' by shame.

NOTES

1. Mark R. Leary, *Self-Presentation: Impression Management and Interpersonal Behaviour* (Madison: Brown & Benchmark, 1995), 2.

2. Sander L. Gilman, *Making the Body Beautiful: A Cultural History of Aesthetic Surgery* (Princeton: Princeton University Press, 1999), 26. Emphasis in original.

3. Ibid., xxi.

4. Ibid., 42. See also: Luna Dolezal, "The (In)visible Body: Feminism, Phenomenology and the Case of Cosmetic Surgery," *Hypatia* 25, no. 2 (2010).

5. Bourdieu, *Distinction,* 166.

6. Pierre Bourdieu, *Outline of a Theory of Practice*, trans. Richard Nice (Cambridge: Cambridge University Press, 1977), 214. Emphasis in original.

7. Pierre Bourdieu and Loic Wacquant, *An Invitation to Reflexive Sociology*, trans. Loic Wacquant (Cambridge: Polity, 1992), 128.

8. Merleau-Ponty, *Phenomenology of Perception*, 137.

9. Merleau-Ponty recognizes this aspect of subjective life. He writes: "Each of us sees himself [sic] as it were through an inner eye which from a few yards away is looking at us from the head to the knees." Merleau-Ponty, *Phenomenology of Perception*, 173.

10. Martin C. Dillon, *Merleau-Ponty's Ontology* (Evanston: Northwestern University Press, 1962), 123.

11. Merleau-Ponty, *Phenomenology of Perception*, 420

12. Maurice Merleau-Ponty, *Nature: Course Notes from the Collège de France* trans. Robert Vallier (Evanston: Northwestern University Press, 2003), 28.

13. Marjorie Grene, *Sartre* (Lanham, MD: University Press of America, 1983), 154.

14. Leder, *The Absent Body*, 94.

15. Ibid., 96. Emphasis in original.

16. J. H. van den Berg, "The Human Body and the Significance of Human Movement: A Phenomenological Study," *Philosophy and Phenomenological Research* vol. 13, no. 2 (1952): 182.

17. Quoted in: Michael Schudson, "Embarrassment and Erving Goffman's Idea of Human Nature," *Theory and Society* vol. 13 (1984): 641.

18. Goffman, *Strategic Interaction*, 11.

19. See, for example: Emmanuel Levinas, *Totality and Infinity: An Essay on Exteriority* trans. Alfonso Lingus (The Hague: Nijhoff, 1979).

20. Rosalyn Diprose, *Corporeal Generosity: On Giving with Nietzsche, Merleau-Ponty, and Levinas* (Albany: SUNY Press, 2002), 5.

21. Erving Goffman, *Behaviour in Public Places: Notes on the Social Organization of Gatherings* (New York: The Free Press, 1963), 35.

22. Ibid.

23. Goffman, *Interaction Ritual*, 105.

24. Goffman, *The Presentation of Self in Everyday Life*, 12.

25. Goffman, *Interaction Ritual*, 109, 111.

26. Erwin W. Straus, "Shame as a Historiological Problem," in *Phenomenological Psychology* (London: Tavistock, 1966), 221.

27. Ibid.

28. Erving Goffman, *Stigma: Notes on the Management of Spoiled Identity* (London: Penguin Books, 1990), 9, 11.

29. Ibid., 11

30. Ibid., 12.

31. Ibid., 18.

32. Ibid., 15.

33. Ibid., 18.

34. Evolutionary psychologists suggest that stigma-based exclusion derives from evolutionary adaptations which cause people to avoid interactions which may compromise their standing within the social group, hence imposing 'fitness' costs. See, for example: Robert Kurzban, "Evolutionary Origins of Stigmatization: The Functions of Social Exclusion," *Psychological Bulletin* vol. 127, no. 2 (2001).

35. It seems that some people are more likely than others to take on stigma and accept a diminished and stereotyped status depending on the extent to which they expect to be stereotyped. See: Elizabeth C. Pinel, "Stigma Consciousness: The Psychological Legacy of Social Stereotypes," *Journal of Personality and Social Psychology* vol. 76, no. 1 (1999).

36. Axel Honneth, "Invisibility: On the Epistemology of 'Recognition,'" *Aristotelian Society Supplementary Volume* 75, no. 1 (2001).

37. Goffman, *Stigma*, 19.

38. Roy F. Baumeister and Mark R. Leary, "The Need to Belong: Desire for Interpersonal Attachments as a Fundamental Human Motivation," *Psychological Bulletin* 117, no. 3 (1995): 497, 520.

39. Ibid., 497.

40. Rosalyn Diprose, "'Where' Your People from, Girl?': Belonging to Race, Gender, and Place *beneath Clouds*." *differences: A Journal of Feminist Cultural Studies* 19.3 (2008): 28–29.

41. Ibid., 47.

42. Axel Honneth, *The Struggle for Recognition: The Moral Grammar of Social Conflicts*, trans. Joel Anderson (Cambridge, UK: Polity, 1995).

43. Honneth, "Invisibility: On the Epistemology of 'Recognition,'" 115.

44. Ibid., 119.

45. Gerhart Piers, "Shame and Guilt: Part I," in *Shame and Guilt: A Psychoanalytic Study*, eds. Gerhart Piers and M. B. Singer (Springfield, IL: Charles C. Thomas, 1953), 16. As quoted in: Elspeth Probyn, *Blush: The Faces of Shame* (Minneapolis: University of Minnesota Press, 2005), 3. Emphasis in original.

46. Goffman, *Stigma*, 7.

47. Jane Megan Northrop, *Reflecting on Cosmetic Surgery: Body Image, Shame and Narcissism* (London: Routledge, 2012), 105.

48. Fanon, *Black Skin, White Masks*, 98.

49. Ibid.

50. Ibid.

51. Jean-Paul Sartre, *Anti-Semite and Jew: An Exploration of the Etiology of Hate*, (New York: Schocken Press, 1995), 27.

52. Northrop, *Reflecting on Cosmetic Surgery*: 128.

53. Cheshire Calhoun, "An Apology for Moral Shame," *The Journal of Political Philosophy* 12, no. 2 (2004), 143.

54. Ullaliina Lehtinen, "How Does One Know What Shame Is? Epistemology, Emotions and Forms of Life in Juxtaposition," *Hypatia* 13, no. 1 (1998), 60.

55. Emily S. Lee, "Madness and Judiciousness: A Phenomenological Reading of a Black Woman's Encounter with a Saleschild," in *Covergences: Black Feminism and Continental Philosophy*, eds. Maria del Guadalupe Davidson, Kathryn T. Gines, and Donna-Dale L. Marcano (Albany: SUNY Press, 2010), 193.

56. Sandra Lee Bartky, *Femininity and Domination: Studies in the Phenomenology of Oppression* (London: Routledge, 1990), 97.

57. Lehtinen, "How Does One Know What Shame Is?," 63.

58. Bartky, *Femininity and Domination*: 97.

59. Ibid.

60. Deonna, et al., *In Defense of Shame*, 227.

61. Kathleen Woodward, "Traumatic Shame: Toni Morrison, Televisual Culture, and the Cultural Politics of Emotions," *Cultural Critique* vol. 46 (2000), 218.

62. Bartky, *Femininity and Domination*: 85.

63. Woodward, "Traumatic Shame," 227.

64. Berlant, et al., "The Broken Circuit."

65. Gail Weiss, *Body Images: Embodiment as Intercorporeality* (New York: Routledge, 1999), 27–28.

66. Lehtinen, "How Does One Know What Shame Is?," 62.Emphasis in original.

67. Woodward, "Traumatic Shame," 225.

68. Marcela Matos and Jose Pinto-Gouveia, "Shame as Traumatic Memory," *Clinical Psychology and Psychotherapy* vol. 17 (2010): 300; and Bernice Andrews, "Bodily Shame as a Mediator Between Abusive Experiences and Depression," *Journal of Abnormal Psychology* vol. 104 (1995).

69. See, for example: Fredrickson et al., "That Swimsuit Becomes You."

70. Joan Jacobs Brumberg, *The Body Project: An Intimate History of American Girls* (New York: Random House, 1997), 64, 70.

71. Lee, "Madness and Judiciousness," 195.

72. Gilman, *Making the Body Beautiful*, 22–23.

73. Ibid., 23.

74. Ibid.

75. Woodward, "Traumatic Shame," 222.

76. Northrop, *Reflecting on Cosmetic Surgery*, 111.

77. Bartky, *Femininity and Domination*, 93.

78. Ibid., 94.

79. Pinel, "Stigma Consciousness," 115.

80. Berlant, et al., "The Broken Circuit."

81. Ibid.

82. Pinel, "Stigma Consciousness," 115.

83. Ibid.

84. Lee, "Madness and Judiciousness," 189.

85. Ibid., 190.

86. Honneth, "Invisibility: On the Epistemology of 'Recognition,'" 111.

87. Ibid.

88. Ibid., 112.

89. Ibid., 115.

90. Woodward, "Traumatic Shame," 222.

91. Lee, "Madness and Judiciousness," 191.

92. Bartky, *Femininity and Domination*, 97.

93. Eve Kosofsky Sedgwick, *Touching Feeling: Affect, Pedagogy, Performativity* (Durham and London: Duke University Press, 2003), 63.

94. See: Paul Gilbert, "Body Shame: A Biopsychological Conceptualisation and Overview, with Treatment Implications," in *Body Shame: Conceptualisation, Research and Treatment*, ed. Paul Gilbert and Jeremy Miles (New York: Brunner-Routledge, 2002), 8.

Chapter Five

Body Shame and Female Experience

Sartre's existential reflections on the role of emotions can provide some context through which to further explore shame as constitutive of experience, particularly the experience of a socially marginalized individual. Sartre reflects on how emotions are not merely cognitive events, but instead are embodied experiences which create a context or situation in which meaning, sense and one's lived experience are shaped. As such, an emotion is an active and embodied response to a situation and discloses not only the self, but, in addition, the quality of one's life-world. An emotion, such as anger, guilt, jealousy or shame, can evoke, as Sartre argues, a "total alteration of the world."[1] Consider, for example, the voyeur's jealousy; it organizes his world, shaping his actions, responses and experience within a particular situation. Jealousy is not merely a cognitive event that can be contemplated; instead, "I *am* this jealousy; I do not *know* it."[2] The world constituted by jealousy is one of suspicion and anger. The door and the keyhole that the voyeur encounters are not merely objective objects in a neutral space, but a landscape of betrayal, obstacle and embittered curiosity. Jealousy not only colours his intentional relation to the physical realm, but also shrinks his world. The voyeur's preoccupations, attentions and desires spiral in a tight circle around his jealousy.

Emotions have this world-forming character because, as Matthew Ratcliffe argues, the existential feelings accompanying an emotional state are not merely a set of bodily sensations, but rather constitute a "way of inhabiting the world."[3] Ratcliffe cites Sartre's example of nausea, the particular existential feeling that plagues Antoine, the protagonist in Sartre's similarly-titled novel: "The Nausea isn't inside me: I can feel it *over* there on the wall, on the braces, everywhere around me. It is one with the café, it is I who am inside it."[4]

Sartre's insights on the world-organizing nature of emotions provide an important framework through which we can articulate the affects and consequences of shame experiences, especially when considering chronic or recurring shame of certain marginalized groups, as discussed in chapter 4. Instead of a discrete disturbance of an otherwise untroubled consciousness, living with chronic shame has profound and ongoing consequences for one's subjectivity, both personally and politically, especially when this shame is centred on the body. Shame becomes, to use Sara Ahmed's formulation of emotions as social and cultural practices, a "form of cultural politics" that is "world making."[5]

Body shame, as we have seen, plays an important role in social relations. It establishes the coherence of social interactions and helps social agents enter successfully into the intersubjective realm. Body shame links individuals to a set of normative values which make salient the parameters of acceptance, belonging and recognition. As a result, being a successful social agent entails having a healthy and developed sense of shame. Shame, hence, is not only normal, it is necessary. Although acute body shame is necessary and an inevitable part of human and social existence, there are also times when shame can be limiting, where *chronic* shame can become restricting and must be overcome for life to have the possibility of autonomy, dignity and fulfillment. In this chapter, I will, in part, utilize the approach of feminist phenomenology to elucidate some of the characteristics of 'typical' female bodily experience with respect to shame, looking at not only the characteristics of that experience but the discursive structures which frame and shape it. Feminist phenomenology is a particularly powerful tool which has been used to advance more comprehensive analyses of issues such as bodily self-experience, alienation, objectification, difference and vulnerability.[6] Hence, in this chapter, I will utlize this approach to analyse female embodied experience of beauty and body norms, examining the crippling insecurities and anxieties that plague many women with respect to standards of appearance and attractiveness. Hence, this chapter will continue to explore the cultural politics of body shame, in particular examining chronic shame that is centred upon the female body.

I must stress that this discussion of female embodiment is culturally specific and its applicability is perhaps limited to certain cultural contexts, namely Western, neoliberal consumer societies.[7] When discussing the categories 'female' or 'woman,' I by no means intend to limit gender to the binary categories of male and female. However, for the purposes of this argument my discussion will centre around 'female' bodies and 'women,' where 'female' and 'woman' do not imply essential or natural categories based on biological features, but rather can be considered lived relations between self and world produced, in part, through the self-presentation of a gendered identity.[8] Naturally, I cannot speak for all women, nor do I intend my argument to be applicable to all persons that identify as female. As such, my discussion, or parts thereof, may be applicable to other types of body subjects whether they identify as male, intersex, genderqueer or transsexual. Furthermore, it must be acknowledged that the intersections of sexual abuse, class, race, and sexuality, among others, can further shape the experience and intensity of body shame for a female subjectivity.[9]

Despite these qualifications, it is important to be able to generalize without necessarily universalizing. Ultimately, there are tangible and important differences in the manner that many women live and experience their bodies. Women, compared with men, spend more time, energy and material resources in trying to achieve a socially pleasing body that conforms to prevailing normative standards. Women far outnumber men in incidents of eating disorders, chronic dieting and cases of cosmetic surgery. Young women are disproportionately affected by poor self-esteem, self-harming behaviour and other mental health problems. As we shall see, women are more frequently, if not constantly, hindered by disruptions as a result of experiences of 'dys-appearance' or 'the Look' as discussed in the chapters above. In fact, women's bodies struggle constantly with visibility, invisibility and (in)visibility. While often feeling threatened with invisibility in social relations due to a diminished social status, women's bodies enjoy a hyper-visibility in the social realm; they are objectified and on constant display. As a result, for women, more so than men, the body is an abiding presence in life; it is a source of anxiety in the ongoing projects of self-presentation and impression management to ensure a sense of belonging and recognition. Oppressive—and world-organizing—experiences of body shame, I will argue, figure centrally in this drama of female embodiment.

Bartky's account of the phenomenology of oppression as centred on living with shame as an affective attunement, explored in the previous chapter, is in fact an account of gender. Bartky's central thesis is that femininity is characterized by shame, and the feelings of inferiority and inadequacy that arise as a result of this enduring shame have profound political consequences with respect to the position of women in society: "women are not just situated differently than men within the social ensemble, but are actively subordinated to them within it."[10] This subordination is intimately linked to women's embodiment and a cultural politics of shame.

My focus for the remainder of this chapter will be to utilize the cultural politics of shame to analyse the contemporary situation of women, particularly with respect to appearance management and a phenomenology of self-presentation under the framework of the contemporary Euro-American Western "market-political rationality" of neoliberalism.[11] In doing so, I will go through some well-rehearsed ideas in the tradition of "corporeal feminism"[12] which theorizes the effect of patriarchal power structures on the female body, and hence on women's subjectivity. My aim is to demonstrate that women's bodies are lived, experienced, objectified and alienated differently to their male counterparts as a result of oppressive social structures that position women's bodies as a constant site for body shame. I will further argue that these structures are amplified within contemporary neoliberal culture. In short, I want to explore the central role that body shame plays in the constitution and development of women's identity and examine the consequences of a body, and hence subjectivity, that is essentially 'shaped by shame.'

BODY SHAME AND FEMALE EXPERIENCE

Bartky is not the first to theorize the link between the social oppression of women and shame. In fact, we see a long association historically, sociologically and philosophically between women, shame and the body. In *The Second Sex*, Simone de Beauvoir, drawing on insights from biology, social and economic history and sociology, gives a philosophical account of the process of becoming a woman, essentially characterizing this process as "an extended lesson in shame."[13] She discusses how many ordinary female anatomical differences, such as the onset of menstruation, sexual maturation and breast development, have long been occasions for body shame for young girls.[14] These bodily changes, deviating from an imagined norm of male bodily stasis, are seen as shameful and of needing concealment, and this has a long history in many cultures and traditions. Menstruation, in particular, is a source of anxiety. The "disgrace"[15] of menstruation, and subsequent inferiorization of the female body, is embedded within cultural and religious structures which designate menstruation as impure or unclean and exclude women from certain rituals or activities while they are bleeding.[16] Beyond menstruation, shame accompanies women throughout their sexual development where desire and a sexual appetite are deemed shameful and 'unfeminine.' Furthermore, until recently, pregnant bodies were objects of social taboos, to be hidden and concealed. However, in current times, as motherhood has become fashionable,[17] the post-pregnant body must not show any marks of pregnancy or signs that it has given birth.[18] The experience of becoming and being a woman, as de Beauvoir and many others feminist thinkers argue, historically involves a process of learning to interpret the body as a site of shame.

Lacking a sustained account of gendered differences within the civilizing process, even Elias's account of the changing modes of body management makes salient how, through "a general disgust of embodied feminine sexuality, and an implicit denial of its pleasures, we see repression enacted upon the female body through the modality of shame."[19] Shame about the body, it seems, "is a cultural inheritance of women."[20] In the present day this association continues, both implicitly and explicitly. Northrop offers the extreme example of the practice of the 'honour killing,' where a young female rela-

Erica's family has reclaimed womanhood.

tive is punished by death for bringing shame to her family due to a liaison with a man of which they do not approve. Shame—for an entire group of people—is literally embodied in the young woman, "who is eradicated to restore 'honour' to the family."[21] In patriarchal systems, a great deal of male honour is dependent on women's conduct. As a result, great efforts are made to control the female body and its behaviour through shaming strategies that have the twofold effect of disciplining women's bodies and also appointing the behaviours that are appropriate for them.[22]

The strong relation and association, historically and culturally, between women's bodies, women's sexuality and shame, both personally and politically, is far from trivial. While the male body is the standard for the 'normal' or 'neutral' body in accounts of experience and subjectivity—and there is a long tradition of feminist writing criticizing thinkers such as Merleau-Ponty, Sartre and Foucault for this implicit bias in their work—women's bodies and female experience are positioned as essentially deviant or, in some cases, pathological. This bias whereby male bodies set the standard for what is considered gender 'neutral' and, hence, 'normal' or 'natural' is not just evident in philosophy, but across most disciplines. It is, in fact, well documented that this is a bias which has seeped into everyday understandings of, and attitudes toward, female bodies. Inevitable events in female embodiment such as pregnancy, menstruation and menopause are positioned as anomalies of 'normal' experience, which are not only stigmatized, but also pathologized, requiring professional medical attention (traditionally from male doctors).

APPEARANCE MANAGEMENT AND BODY SHAME

A significant site for body shame for women is in the realm of the seemingly 'trivial' concerns of appearance and physical attractiveness. Seen as a backlash to the modern feminist movement, the control of women's bodies through oppressive beauty norms has been an explicit focus of the feminist critique of the patriarchal framework of consumer capitalism and neoliberalism for several decades. It is widely acknowledged by feminist thinkers that appearances cannot be considered a trivial concern for women and that body dissatisfaction is not merely an individual—and hence marginal—pathology for women, but rather part of a systematic (and oppressive) social phenomenon.[23] Appearances, as we have seen, are much "more than just surfaces."[24] They are intimately linked to how one values and sees oneself, and furthermore to one's social worth and position within a social group. This is especially the case for women, as how they look and present themselves affects how they are treated and their chances for success in various aspects of their lives. In fact, social invisibility is a constant threat for women who feel they

The Body as a central cog in Capitalism

are often ignored and looked through in educational, familial and profession-al settings. Staying in 'the game,' and securing recognition as a full social agent, is an abiding concern for women.[25] Cultural messages emphasize that visibility and inclusion in the social sphere can be achieved through high levels of youthful attractiveness.

As a result, concerns about appearance management have been amplified for women (and increasingly men) under the structures of neoliberalism which promote an endless culture of restyling and self-improvement, centred on the body, within an image-saturated milieu. Under the structures of con-temporary neoliberal consumer culture, bodies are seen as potentially unfin-ished products, the site of projects of self-care, self-transformation and self-reflexive concern.[26] The idea is that changing or transforming the body will yield an improved or more acceptable self. As such, the body is the primary symbol of value and of identity within social relations and as Alison Phipps notes, in her recent book *The Politics of the Body*, the "drive to consume in order to both express and 'add value' to oneself . . . feeds markets that rely upon idealized representations of the body and the elevation of particular prestigious bodily forms through advertising."[27] Hence, the body—an end-lessly unfinished project—is a central cog in the machinery of neoliberal consumer capitalism.

More specifically, it is, in fact, the female body that occupies this central place in the machinations of neoliberalism. Sustaining a multi-billion dollar set of global industries that centre around body grooming, fashion, well-being, medicine, fitness and cosmetics, the female body is positioned as perpetually unfinished and imperfect, needing endless restyling and improve-ment (and hence consumption). Women's bodies are subject to an endless litany of social pressures to emulate the 'prestigious bodily forms' promoted through advertising. These bodily forms, as a result of the routine digital enhancement of images, emphasize an increasingly unrealistic body ideal. The "rhetoric of body perfection" has come to dominate social hierarchies, and what is considered a 'normal' and allegedly attainable standard of attrac-tiveness is in fact an ever-shifting and unattainable body ideal.[28] Body shame is central to this process. As Northrop notes, "grooming industries attempt to access and invigorate the shame associated with the body because it is com-monly acculturated in childhood and readily recalled in adult experience."[29] She notes that these industries "recognize the infinite wealth to be made in exploiting the appearance dissatisfactions of women."[30] As a result, in main-stream Western neoliberal culture, minor variations in appearance on fairly ordinary bodies are cast as major 'defects,' signalling a spoiled identity, and sit on the side of the 'before' in the commonly employed before-and-after photo set. The normalized, perfected body, implicitly standing in for what we *should* look like, comes 'after.' In general, this body is characterized by a white, Western aesthetic of feminine beauty.[31] It is a body that is "neutral" and "unmarked" and does "*not* look disabled, queer, ugly, fat, ethnic or raced."[32]

In this regard, female bodies increasingly aim to converge on what Rosemarie Garland Thomson has termed the "normate," which is "the corporeal incarnation of culture's collective, unmarked, normative characteristics."[33] The normate has a certain "corporeal configuration" that yields "cultural capital."[34] In our contemporary, image-saturated milieu, it is easy to discern that the female normate is young, heterosexual, Anglo-Saxon, slim, toned, able-bodied, with symmetrically proportioned features and smooth, unmarked skin. Furthermore, she is confident, well-coiffed, sexy, wealthy and fashion savvy. Although there are still choices and variations around the details of appearance based on ethnicity, age, fashion, subculture and so on, the normate embodies the pervasive norms that underscore all of these variations. Despite the paucity of real bodies that meet the normate's standards, just a cursory glance at a wide spectrum of fashion and gossip magazines, films and television shows demonstrates the disproportionate ubiquity of the normate in the images of celebrities, models, and other public figures. Normalization very quickly yields homogenization. These homogenized faultless images have become emblematic of the dominant reality, setting the standards for ordinary bodies.

As a result, women understand that it is those who emulate the normate and strive to achieve the 'ideal' body who garner recognition and enjoy social, personal and professional success and fulfillment. This ideal body is characterized by the enduring physical features of the normate coupled with the constantly shifting variations of appearance and style based on the whims of fashion. What is considered 'normal' is actually based on illusory ideals that are extremely difficult, if not impossible, to achieve. As virtually every commercial or media image we encounter has been digitally enhanced or modified, and furthermore these images are sometimes of people who have undergone cosmetic surgical enhancement anyway, the real expectations that women have for their own bodies are increasingly "*un*real."[35]

What we find is that the continuous comparison a woman may make between her actual body and versions of the socially constructed 'ideal' body represented in media images is a potent source of body shame. Women's bodies, already shame-prone as a result of their cultural inheritance, are continuously positioned as inadequate or inferior when compared to these elusive body ideals; shame, and body shame in particular, becomes a permanent possibility. Northrop notes that the "potential for women to feel shame is ubiquitous and potentially overwhelming."[36] As a result, women are already attuned to the feelings and contours of body shame; they expect their bodies to betray them and to deviate from the diffuse and invisible cultural standards of what a body 'ought' to be. Failing to achieve the ideal body signals a deeper failed mastery of the body and corporeal control. This attunement to shame is so pervasive and indeterminate that it is often beyond the reach of reflective consciousness. As noted above, normative values are so thoroughly internalized to ensure one's sense of recognition and belonging in a social group that shame is often collectively and personally bypassed. Women may not even realize that they are experiencing body shame or that they are exerting inordinate efforts to avoid it. Instead they become preoccupied with cultivating pride which hinges on the other side of the emotional dialectic which accompanies the narcissistic concern of the body as spectacle.[37] Or, if shame does in fact enter conscious awareness, it is seen as a result of one's own inadequacies and, in particular, as one's own fault. Personal efforts must be made (shopping, exercise, dieting, surgery) in order to eliminate it.

As physical inadequacies are recurrent, difficult to alleviate and ever-shifting, body shame becomes part of a 'normal' landscape of experience, this is what Courtney E. Martin terms the "frightening new normality of hating your body."[38] Furthermore, shame about the body often produces iterated shame, not only because the physical symptoms of shame are themselves shameful, as discussed in chapter 1, but also because shame about narcissism (especially for feminist women who 'know' appearances *really* don't matter) or certain strategies to maintain appearance (for example, dieting, eating disorders or cosmetic surgery, which are often shameful secrets needing to be concealed) become new sources of shame.[39]

LIVING WITH CHRONIC SHAME

Increased self-consciousness and shame about the body in women are not solely a result of the cultural positioning of anatomical differences, appearance management and sexuality, but in addition are significantly rooted in power discrepancies within gender roles. Women are already prone to body shame, as a result of their subordinated position within social relations, and as a result they are highly susceptible to bodily visibility through the objectifying Look of the Other. This is reflected in the imbalances regarding gendered experiences of the 'seen body' in the social sphere. In general, due to imbalances in power relations, women's bodies are rendered hyper-visible in our contemporary milieu and this has concrete consequences in terms of shame-proneness and its concomitant lived experience.

It is well-documented that a woman's subjectivity is structured by the self-consciousness of being constantly under surveillance and,as a result, visible as a result of objectification. Simone de Beauvoir's experience is illustrative: "A man, sniggering, made a comment about my fat calves. The next day my mother made me wear stockings and lengthen my skirt, but I will never forget the shock I suddenly felt in seeing myself *seen*."[40] As a result, as Simone de Beauvoir notes, women are encouraged to apprehend their own bodies as "object[s] destined for an other."[41] Echoing Fanon's concerns regarding race, de Beauvoir draws attention to the fact that gender has important consequences for objectification, especially with respect to the body. Although Sartre discusses the Look as though it were indifferent to gender, it is, in fact, the gaze and vantage point of (white, educated, Western) men that is cultural definitive and in which social power is situated. As a result, women are implicitly regarded as 'the second' sex and assume the social role of the Other. While man actively ratifies and constitutes the world, it is defined without reference to woman: "she can take in society only a place already made for her."[42]

The point that de Beauvoir is making is that while the male body coincides with his status as a sovereign subject, the female body is frequently overshadowed by the male ego and is more readily reduced to an object for his gaze: "what peculiarly signalizes the situation of woman is that she . . . finds herself living in a world where men . . . propose to stabilize her as object and to doom her to immanence."[43] Being objectified, and subsequently alienated, by the male gaze is an ongoing and often compromising situation for women, and obviously a key source of body shame. Bartky describes this experience of the female body being objectified, and subsequently alienated, due to the antagonizing and objectifying Look of the (male) other:

> It is a fine spring day, and with an utter lack of self-consciousness, I am bouncing down the street. Suddenly I hear men's voices. Catcalls and whistles fill the air. These noises are clearly sexual in intent and they are meant for me; they come from across the street. I freeze. As Sartre would say, I have been petrified by the gaze of the Other. My face flushes and my motions become stiff and self-conscious. The body which only a moment before I inhabited with such ease now floods my consciousness. I have been made into an object . . . in this being-made-to-be-aware of one's own flesh.[44] → *I feel that so often*

The invisibility of the body ('an utter lack of self-consciousness'), as demonstrated by this example, is disrupted through the objectifying and, ultimately, alienating, gaze of the Other. To return to Leder's characterization of social dys-appearance: "one incorporates an alien gaze, away, apart, asunder, from one's own, which provokes an explicit thematization of the body."[45] In this example, the female body is objectified as an object of male desire: she is reduced to a sexual object; or, as Bartky puts it: "a nice piece of ass."[46]

In his discussion of social dys-appearance, Leder recognizes this imbalance in ocular gender relations, commenting that "women are not full cosubjectivities, free to experience from a tacit body."[47] He concedes that, unlike men, women "must maintain a constant awareness of how they appear to men in terms of physical attractiveness and other forms of acceptability."[48] He writes: "For example, while a woman may become self-conscious walk-

ing in front of whistling longshoremen, they do not experience similar objectification in the face of her angry look back. As she is largely powerless in
the situation, her perspective need not be incorporated; it can safely be
laughed away or ignored."[49] In fact, when a woman attempts to return the
Look, she is often, as Phyllis Sutton Morris notes, "not contributing to the
man's capacity for reflective self-knowledge, but rather is taken to be wan-
ton." [50] Mirroring the power discrepancies we see in race relations, women
often do not have the social power to effectively return the Look of their
objectifying male counterparts.

Despite Leder's acknowledgments that objectification and the ability to
experience the body as 'invisible' are in part determined by gender and
power relations, he does not at all consider the effect or significance of social
dys-appearance for women. In contrast, Bartky's analysis reveals the implicit
power relations at play with respect to gender in her particular encounter:

> They could, after all, have enjoyed me in silence. Blissfully unaware, breasts
> bouncing, eyes on the birds in the trees, I could have passed by without having
> been turned into stone. But I must be *made* to know that I am a 'nice piece of
> ass': I must be made to see myself as they see me. [51]

A profound effect of this sort of alienating objectification is that it encourages women and girls to treat themselves as objects to be looked at and
evaluated, and avoiding the concomitant shame that can arise from objectification depends on conforming to and *internalizing* the standards implicit in
the gaze of the (more socially powerful) Other.

Women, accustomed to the visual paradigm of being 'seen,' often experience their bodies in a permanent state of visibility, where the body's appearance and comportment is self-consciously objectified and regarded as an
object for a present or imagined third-person spectator.[52] Femininity, as such,
becomes a constant and ongoing public performance where the female subject has a continuous self-conscious regard for how the body looks to others
within the framework of the restrictive standards regarding appearance and
comportment. This is an analysis of female subjectivity that has endured for
several decades, arguably intensified in the present day. Writing in the 1970s,
the social critic John Berger makes this point arguing: "A woman must
continually watch herself. She is almost continuously accompanied by her
own image of herself . . . Her own sense of being in herself is supplanted by a
sense of being appreciated as herself by another."[53] Likewise, de Beauvoir,
writing in the 1940s, argues that when a girl becomes a women she is "doubled; instead of coinciding exactly with herself, she now begins to exist
outside."[54]

Foucault's omnipresent panoptic gaze becomes an apt illustration for the
visibility of female bodies and their concomitant ongoing projects to avoid

why it can't be related to the
only imbrushing male

body shame. Bartky employs the Foucauldian paradigm of panopticism in her well-known feminist analysis of shame and female embodiment. She argues that in contemporary patriarchal culture "a panoptical male connoisseur resides within the consciousness of most women: they stand perpetually before his gaze and under his judgement."[55] A woman learns to appraise and judge herself and her appearance according to the gaze of this omnipresent "male connoisseur."[56] Women, in the patriarchal order, identify with men and learn to see themselves through their eyes. Having internalized the gaze of the (male) Other, Bartky argues, women begin to regulate themselves according to 'his' standards. Naturally, these standards do not emanate from any particular male person or group of persons, but rather are dictated by mass standards emanating from our socio-cultural milieu, namely the patriarchal framework of late modernity and neoliberal consumer capitalism.

As such, to varying degrees, women become used to experiencing their bodies from a distanced perspective, in terms of how they look to others, rather than in terms of non-observable attributes such as how they feel or in terms of their body's capacities or abilities. As a result, the female body feels itself to be constantly under "surveillance"[57] and is more frequently rendered an objectified 'seen' body. A woman's phenomenology of self-presentation becomes dominated with conscious strategies to manage physical appearance. This of course, as we have seen, is intimately linked to one's propensity to feel body shame.

There are concrete consequences, in terms of the phenomenology of embodied experience, as result of living with sense of bodily visibility and constant self-consciousness regarding the seen body. When one maintains an observer's or externalized perspective on one's own body, one experiences the body simultaneously as an object (to be watched) and as a capacity (an *I can*). Similar to the inferior corporeal schema of the raced subject discussed in chapter 4, this division of attention, as Iris Marion Young notes in her well-known article 'Throwing Like a Girl,' can alter comportment, disrupting flow and a smooth intentional relation to the world, making movements uncertain, unconfident and limited.[58]

Employing the methodology of feminist phenomenology, combining insights regarding the phenomenology of embodied experience with reflections about the discursive structures which frame that experience, Young comments on Erwin Straus's discussion of the differences in movement and the use of lateral space among young boys and girls when engaged in the act of throwing a ball. Young girls, in Straus's analysis, do not make use of lateral space—they do not twist, turn or move their legs—and throw the ball without force. Boys, on the other hand, extend, stretch and twist using the space around them freely in order to project the ball with considerable confidence, force and aim. Straus suggests that this significant difference in bodily com-

Same for gay men? These bad at sports?

114   Chapter 5

portment results from a 'feminine attitude' toward the world and space and has biological, but not necessarily anatomical, origins.[59]

Young takes issue with Straus's interpretation of this gendered difference and argues that female bodily comportment is not essentially or biologically different to that of male bodies, as Straus suggests, but rather is characterized by self-consciousness and a hindered motor intentionality as a result of pre-existing cultural expectations and conditions. While acknowledging that, on average, there are real physical differences between men and women in terms of size, strength and physical capacity, Young argues that it is not due to biological difference that male and female body comportment may differ, but rather as a result of the way one uses the body due to internalized ideas about one's social place and role. This inhibited intentionality, as Young describes it, results from the fact that, as a result of certain conditions in place in patriarchal society, woman, as Straus concedes, "lives her body as *object* as well as subject."[60] A woman moves her body, but at the same time watches and monitors herself, and sees her action as that which is 'looked at,' so in general, female bodily comportment does not achieve open, free and unselfconscious movement. Objectified bodily existence, or bodily visibility, leads to an obtrusive self-consciousness and resulting discontinuity with respect to the body and its actions.

Young contrasts this typical female embodiment to the implicitly male body she sees as described by Merleau-Ponty in the *Phenomenology of Perception*. The body described by Merleau-Ponty, according to Young, is a socially uninhibited body which has a confident and unhindered relation to the world.[61] Moreover, it has a confident attitude in terms of body movement where "free motion" and "open reach" typically characterize a male approach to sport and other physical tasks.[62] Young argues that Merleau-Ponty implicitly describes male bodily comportment in his discussion of motor intentionality; it is comportment that is, in general, confident, uninhibited and maximizes its bodily potentialities, moving "out from the body in its immanence in an open and unbroken directedness upon the world in action."[63]

Although Young's analysis of female comportment as self-conscious and inhibited is valid and of interest, it is worth commenting on Young's understanding and critique of Merleau-Ponty's conception of motor intentionality. Merleau-Ponty's description of the lived body, as Young sees it, is expressed in the affirmative expression, '*I can*,' which Merleau-Ponty borrows from Husserl to describe the structure of bodily intention and fulfillment. In her critique of Merleau-Ponty, Young mistakenly assumes that Merleau-Ponty intends the 'I can' to in some way indicate capability, skill, or the range, size and scope of movement—namely, a certain masculine quality of bodily comportment. In fact, the 'I can,' for both Husserl and Merleau-Ponty, simply describes the faculty subtending the ego which allows it to freely move the body and to perceive in an active, engaged manner. 'I can' illustrates how movement is not "thought about movement"[64] but rather is a bodily structure of intention and fulfillment. This formulation of intention and fulfillment does not carry qualitative claims, as Young suggests. Indeed, Merleau-Ponty uses the blind man—someone whose movement would surely be character-ized as hesitant, hindered and overly self-conscious—as an example of suc-cessful motor intentionality.[65]

Furthermore, Young's analysis does not consider how certain activities and body practices are gendered and, furthermore, performed in particular social spaces. While women may lack confidence and skill when it comes to throwing a ball on a football field or performing martial arts, they might display open, free and confident movements performing certain typically 'female' practices such as dance or gymnastics, or in certain 'female' social spaces such as an aerobics studio.[66] As such, Jean Grimshaw critiques Young for idealizing 'masculine' embodiment, while ignoring the specificities of its expression. When comparing throwing like a girl with men's participation in an aerobics class, she writes: "Commonly . . . men are ill at ease, inhibited in their movements, and above all stiff and rigid; they often find it very hard to engage in . . . co-ordinated or flowing movements."[67]

Naturally, this qualification does not override the fact that typically fe-male practices and typically male practices come with their own prejudices regarding the abilities and social roles of girls, boys, men and women. How-ever, it does point to a shortcoming in Young's analysis. The inhibited 'fe-male' body that Young describes cannot be put into neat opposition with a completely free and uninhibited 'male' body. It is rather the gender coding of certain practices, along with the intersection of a multitude of other factors such as class, race, experience, circumstance, health, and so on, which may determine this qualitative aspect of one's motor intentionality.

Despite these qualifications, Young's analysis of female movement as inhibited remains of interest. What Young does successfully highlight in her discussion—beyond the lack of consideration of gender in Merleau-Ponty's account—is how women are more likely to see their bodies as objects and how female comportment is likely to be coloured by experiences of self-consciousness in many, if not most settings. In general, women are more likely to feel under large- and small-scale surveillance, and this has real qualitative consequences for motility, performance and action.

As a result, inhibited and self-conscious bodily comportment, arising from the habit of self-conscious appearance management driven by body shame, has implications that extend far beyond merely the manner through which one moves or carries one's body. As noted above in the discussion of the cultural politics of shame, bodily self-consciousness arising from imbal-anced power relations within the social field breeds insecurity, lack of confi-dence and an affective attunement to body shame. Women who are constant-ly self-conscious about physical appearance, consumed with conscious strat-

effects extend beyond comportment.

egies of self-presentation, may not be attuned to the possibilities of creativity, transcendence and fulfillment which may otherwise be possibilities for them. An over-developed concern with physical appearance can, as Andrea Dworkin points out:

> [P]rescribe her motility, spontaneity, posture, gait, the uses to which she can put her body. *They define precisely the dimensions of her physical freedom.* And of course, the relationship between physical freedom and psychological development, intellectual possibility, and creative potential is an umbilical one.[68]

Hence, it is no surprise that psychology confirms that women generally have lower self-esteem, less confidence and poorer self-concepts than men, while at the same time being less assertive.[69] Nor is it surprising that women are more likely to suffer from body issues with a shame component, such as eating disorders. The timidity and sense of inadequacy that comes with chronic body shame can shrink one's world and possibilities. As a result, shame may not only be a part of female embodied experience, but may come to shape, dictate and dominate that experience. While experiencing body shame, one's consciousness spirals tightly around concerns regarding the body and appearance.

Women are used to compulsively checking themselves in mirrors and worrying about flaws in clothes, make-up and appearance while engaged in other projects. Dinah Shore's remark is telling: "One of the many things men don't understand about women is the extent to which our self-esteem depends on how we feel we look at any given moment . . . If I had just won the Nobel Peace Prize but felt my hair looked awful, I would not be glowing with self-assurance when I entered the room."[70] Michelle worries about her nose instead of enjoying a meal with her boyfriend. Or consider Jennifer, whose obsessive shame-driven concern about her skin continuously involuted attention to her body, disrupting other activities:

> *I couldn't stop thinking about my face, and I had to check it.* I *had* to make sure I looked okay, but I usually thought it looked bad. When I looked in the mirror I felt totally panicked seeing all those pimples and marks. Sometimes I even had to leave work and go to bed for the rest of the day.[71]

Although Jennifer was eventually diagnosed with Body Dysmorphic Disorder (BDD), which is, as discussed above, a pathological condition of which body shame is a core aspect and which is treated with medication and therapy, her compulsive body checking and concern with appearance is reminiscent of 'normal' and mentally healthy female embodiment which involves a preoccupation with bodily faults and constant feelings of surveillance and self-consciousness.[72] As Cressida Heyes contends: "Constant intrusive thoughts of one's own embodied ugliness, or the aesthetic failure of a particular body part or parts, or constant comparative and unfavourable evaluation of one's own body with others, seem quite typical of a lived experience of femininity in Western countries."[73] Although most women do not suffer from BDD, it is interesting to note that contemporary neoliberal consumer culture encourages and expects women to maintain a "BDD-like relation" to their own embodied selves.[74] As a result, the body becomes a primary concern, it consumes one's attention and resources. For some women it may become like a hobby, creative outlet, occupation or even primary relationship. Indeed, a woman whose life centres around her body and self-presentation in this BDD-like manner, who invests her energy and resources into her body, and who feels constantly dissatisfied with her appearance is the ideal neoliberal subject.

CONCLUSION

It is important to remember that a concern with appearance or 'doing looks' is not optional, since we are always, and *necessarily*, engaged in self-presentation and body management. Self-presentation, as we have seen, is in fact constitutive of subjectivity. As such, it is certainly not the case that self-presentation concerns about appearance or the publicly seen body are inherently oppressive nor that women will ever be free of them. At times, appearance management may even be a potential source of pleasure and creative expression for women.[75] However, when appearance management comes to be dominated by chronic feelings of body shame, then concerns around appearance can become compromising and oppressive. The lived experience of constant and recurring shame is world-making, as we have seen. Chronic body shame can shrink one's world, disrupting ongoing activities and life projects as the self turns attention inwards on itself. This may result in a state of confusion or inaction, and perhaps an inability to engage meaningfully with projects in the world. Or perhaps it evokes an inhibited style of bodily movement, rendering one fragile, insecure, timid and emotionally vulnerable. To alleviate this shame and reclaim a sense of belonging and acceptance, women will go to inordinate lengths to instill a sense of (in)visibility.

However, compared to other marginalized groups, women find themselves in a unique position. As Simone de Beauvoir notes in the introduction to *The Second Sex*, the position of women is constituted by the fact that they are positioned as Other. Defined in essential opposition to man, woman is incomplete, inessential, mutilated, however at the same time she is necessarily bound to man; she lives "dispersed among the males, attached through residence, economic condition, and social standing to certain men."[76] Unlike other subordinated groups—the "ghetto Jews," the "American Negroes," the "proletariat"—de Beauvoir argues that women lack a common past, tradition, religion or culture. The bond that unites women to her oppressors is "not comparable to any other . . . she is the Other in a totality of which the two components are necessary to one another."[77] As a result, women "lack concrete means for organizing themselves into a unit which can stand face to face with the correlative unit."[78]

Simone de Beauvoir was, of course, writing in the 1940s, a time when the legal status of women was almost nowhere equal to that of men. However, her insight into the status of women, as the objectified Other and as subordinated in social relations due to shame about the body, resonates profoundly in the present day. However, unlike other marginalized groups, women have not organized collectively to name and subvert the shame that oppresses them. Instead of organizing a collective 'pride' movement, where shame about women's bodies might be overturned and women may start to reclaim a fundamental sense of self-esteem and recognition, women are increasingly isolated from each other in a disempowering self-obsessing narcissism that centres tightly around concerns about the appearance of the body. The reasons for this are multiple. Concerns about appearance and the body are positioned as trivial in our cultural discourse, and women as vain and superficial for being affected by them. In some sense, this has an appealing logic, as beauty pressures are in many ways not politically comparable to the oppressive discrimination and social injustices arising from racism or homophobia, for instance. However, this trivialization is precisely why the control of women bodies through body norms is so pernicious and complete. Because concerns about appearance are seen as marginal to one's social and political identity, tackled recreationally in one's private sphere, women are isolated from each other and, as a result, body shame remains, for the most part, acutely personal, rather than a collective or political concern. Furthermore, as shame is such an integrated part of female identity and preying on this shame such a central part of our cultural discourse and the machinations of neoliberal consumerism, it is easily overlooked or ignored. Tackling body shame as a serious political problem facing women would involve the dismantling of many cumbersome commercial, social and political structures which have a vested interest in encouraging insecurity, and hence consumption, among women (and increasingly men) through engaging in self-improvement body projects.

As a result, there is an abiding cultural reluctance to confront the pernicious and ubiquitous shame that infects women's day-to-day lived experience. It has become so thoroughly integrated into our social, cultural and political landscape as to be rendered invisible. It is precisely for this reason that any useful account of body shame must look at its phenomenology, how it is experienced or, in the case of the 'broken circuit,' *not* experienced, alongside the broader social structures which cause it to arise. In short, a subjectivity can be structured by shame, or the ongoing strategies of self-presentation to avoid shame, without shame necessarily entering into conscious awareness or being an explicit part of the way one self-identifies one's experience. It is for this reason that any account of affect or emotion must be more than a cognitive or analytic account. As we have seen, shame is not merely an event that occurs in consciousness, but part of a whole complex nexus of body, self, others and world. Shame has the power to subtend all of our experience and to form our world and this can have profound consequences.

The power of shame is beyond reproach and body shame has come to have a powerful hold over women. Women are depleted physically and psychologically through an incessant and obsessive concern over the physical body. Inducing and amplifying body shame has become a key marketing strategy for the industries which stand to profit from women investing in their bodies and appearance. In the present day, instead of any legislative, social or political movements to dismantle the oppressive social structures that induce shame, what we are seeing is an intensification of these structures. Beauty regimes are becoming more punishing, more painful, more expensive, more intrusive, more extreme and, as a result, more disempowering. Shame challenges rationality, rendering one desperate and fearful. When acting from a place of body shame, women are willing to take risks, pay anything, even harm themselves. As a result, women may feel compelled to invest in expensive, unnecessary cosmetic products and fashions, experiment with risky diets, exercise obsessively and, as a result of recent developments in biomedicine, perhaps even turn to invasive procedures such as cosmetic surgery. Hence, in the next chapter, I will discuss at length the case of cosmetic surgery, a beauty practice which has become ever more accessible and acceptable and which is intimately linked to the oppressive experience of chronic body shame. Cosmetic surgery is a means through which we can see the body literally *shaped by shame.*

NOTES

1. Jean-Paul Sartre, *Sketch for a Theory of the Emotions*, trans. Philip Mairet (London: Methuen & Co Ltd, 1971), 47.
2. Sartre, *Being and Nothingness*, 283.
3. Ratcliffe, *Feelings of Being*, 112.
4. Quoted in: Ibid.
5. Ahmed, *The Cultural Politics of Emotion*, 9, 12.
6. See: Lisa Folkmarson Käll and Kristin Zeiler, "Why Feminist Phenomenology and Medicine?" *Feminist Phenomenology and Medicine*, eds. Lisa Käll Folkmarson and Kristin Zeiler. (Albany: SUNY Press, 2014), 1–25.
7. However, as the Western, consumer, neoliberal capitalist social structure is a cultural framework that is increasingly infusing other societies, the relevance of this discussion may be

more extensive. As we shall see, Western normative standards regarding appearance and attractiveness are increasingly adopted by Asian, African and other cultural and ethnic groups.

8. Judith Butler, *Gender Trouble: Feminism and the Subversion of Identity* (London: Routledge, 1990).

9. See J. Brooks Bouson's *Embodied Shame: Uncovering Female Shame in Contemporary Women's Writing* (Albany: SUNY Press, 2009) for an analysis through several literary examples of how sexual, racial and cultural denigration affects women's perceptions of themselves and their bodies, particularly in terms of spoiled or stigmatized identity.

10. Bartky, *Femininity and Domination*, 84.

11. Alison Phipps, *The Politics of the Body* (Cambridge, UK: Polity Press, 2014), 11.

12. Liz Frost, "Theorizing the Young Woman in the Body," *Body and Society* vol. 11, no. 1 (2005): 65.

13. Lisa Guenther, "Shame and the Temporality of Social Life," *Continental Philosophy Review* 44, no. 1 (2011): 11.

14. de Beauvoir, *The Second Sex*, 355.

15. Ibid., 356.

16. J. Lee, "Menarche and the (Hetero)Sexualization of the Female Body," in *The Politics of Women's Bodies: Sexuality, Appearance and Behaviour*, ed. Rose Weitz (Oxford: Oxford University Press, 1998).

17. Until very recent times, the pregnant body seemed to be exempt, excused or outside beauty and social pressures. Pregnancy traditionally was seen as a 'grace period' for women, who were de-sexualized and de-objectified as their bodies became functional objects within the institution of motherhood. This was overturned dramatically by the August 1991 issue of *Vanity Fair* magazine which featured Annie Leibovitz's photograph of the very nude and very pregnant actress Demi Moore on its cover. The photograph was extremely controversial as it sexualized and publicized the pregnant body at a time when societal conventions dictated that the pregnant body should be concealed. Since the unveiling of the pregnant body in the Moore picture there has been a dramatic shift in the way pregnant bodies are portrayed in mainstream media. See, for example: Imogen Tyler, "Skin-Tight: Celebrity, Pregnancy and Subjectivity," in *Thinking through the Skin*, ed. Sara Ahmed and Jackie Stacey (London: Routledge, 2001); Susan Dobscha, "The Changing Image of Women in American Society: What Do Pregnant Women Represent in Advertising?," *Advertising and Society Review* vol. 7, no. 3 (2006); and Sarah Earle, "'Boobs and Bumps': Fatness and Women's Experience of Pregnancy," *Women's Studies International Forum* vol. 26, no. 3 (2003), 250.

18. See: Stephanie O'Donohoe, "Yummy Mummies: The Clamor of Glamour in Advertising to Mothers," *Advertising and Society Review* vol. 7, no. 3 (2006).

19. Northrop, *Reflecting on Cosmetic Surgery*, 87.

20. Bouson, *Embodied Shame*, 1.

21. Northrop, *Reflecting on Cosmetic Surgery*, 122.

22. Stepien, "Understanding Male Shame," 11–12.

23. The consequences of beauty norms and pressures on women's bodies have been explored in countless feminist academic and populist works. Notably: Naomi Wolf, *The Beauty Myth* (London: Vintage, 1990); Susan Bordo, *Unbearable Weight: Feminism, Western Culture and the Body* (Berkeley: University of California Press, 1993); and Susie Orbach, *Fat Is A Feminist Issue* (London: Arrow Books, 2006). More recently, see: Natasha Walter, *Living Dolls: The Return of Sexism* (London: Virago, 2010) and Deborah Harris-Moore, *Media and the Rhetoric of Body Perfection: Cosmetic Surgery, Weight Loss and Beauty in Popular Culture* (Ashgate, 2014).

24. Beverly Skeggs, "Ambivalent Femininities," in *Gender: A Sociological Reader*, ed. Stevi Jackson (London: Routledge, 2002), 317.

25. Northrop, *Reflecting on Cosmetic Surgery*, 113.

26. Although this self-reflexive concern is habitual for those who work on the body, such as athletes and dancers, it has in recent times become a more general concern. See, for example: Nick Crossley, *Reflexive Embodiment in Contemporary Society*, eds. Alan Warde and Nick Crossley, Sociology and Social Change (New York: Open University Press, 2006). Some thinkers argue that this excessive concern with controlling the body and the personal sphere is

an attempt to cope with insecurities that arise in an increasingly complex, dynamic and global world which feels out of one's control. Self-control and controlling the body become ways to deal with the confusion of modern life. Also see, for example: Frost, "Theorizing the Young Woman in the Body," 67–68.

27. Phipps, *The Politics of the Body*, 10.

28. Harris-Moore, *Media and the Rhetoric of Body Perfection.*

29. Northrop, *Reflecting on Cosmetic Surgery*, 179.

30. Ibid.

31. Llewellyn Negrin, "Cosmetic Surgery and the Eclipse of Identity," *Body and Society* vol. 8, no. 4 (2002), 27.

32. Rosemarie Garland Thomson, "Integrating Disability, Transforming Feminist Theory," *NWSA Journal* vol. 14, no. 3 (2004), 8.

33. Ibid.

34. Rosemarie Garland Thomson, *Extraordinary Bodies: Figuring Physical Disability in American Culture and Literature* (New York: Columbia University Press, 1997), 8.

35. Susan Bordo, *Twilight Zones: The Hidden Life of Cultural Images from Plato to O.J.* (Berkeley: University of California Press, 1997), 3.

36. Northrop, *Reflecting on Cosmetic Surgery*, 179.

37. Bartky, *Femininity and Domination*, 84.

38. Courtney E. Martin, *Perfect Girls, Starving Daughters: The Frightening New Normality of Hating Your Body* (London: Piatkus Books, 2007).

39. See, for example: Northrop, *Reflecting on Cosmetic Surgery*, 162–164; see also: Martin, *Perfect Girls, Starving Daughters*, 223.

40. As quoted in: Guenther, "Shame and the Temporality of Social Life," 11.

41. As quoted in: Bartky, *Femininity and Domination*, 38.

42. de Beauvoir, *The Second Sex*, 355.

43. Ibid., 29.

44. Bartky, *Femininity and Domination*, 27.

45. Leder, *The Absent Body*, 99.

46. Bartky, *Femininity and Domination*, 27.

47. Leder, *The Absent Body*, 99.

48. Ibid.

49. Ibid.

50. Phyllis Sutton Morris, "Sartre on Objectification: A Feminist Perspective," in *Feminist Interpretations of Jean-Paul Sartre*, ed. Julien S. Murphy (University Park, PA: The Pennsylvania State University Press, 1999), 77.

51. Bartky, *Femininity and Domination*, 27. Emphasis in original.

52. These intuitions have been confirmed in some empirical work. See, for example: Fredrickson et al., "That Swimsuit Becomes You."

53. John Berger, *Ways of Seeing* (London: Penguin, 1972), 46.

54. As quoted in: Bartky, *Femininity and Domination*, 38.

55. Bartky, *Femininity and Domination*, 72.

56. Ibid., 38.

57. Nita Mary McKinley, "Women and Objectified Body Consciousness: Mothers' and Daughters' Body Experience in Cultural, Developmental, and Familial Context," *Developmental Psychology* vol. 35, no. 3 (1999), 760. See also: Nita Mary McKinley, "Feminist Perspectives and Objectified Body Consciousness," in *Body Image: A Handbook of Theory, Research and Clinical Practice*, ed. T. H. Cash and T. Pruzinsky (New York: The Guilford Press, 2002).

58. Iris Marion Young, "Throwing Like a Girl" in *Throwing Like a Girl and Other Essays in Feminist Philosophy and Social Theory* (Indianapolis: Indiana University Press, 1990).

59. See: Erwin W. Straus, "The Upright Posture," in *Phenomenological Psychology* (London: Tavistock Publications, 1966), 156–157.

60. Ibid., 155.

61. In addition, Judith Butler argues that Merleau-Ponty's body subject is not only male, but a heterosexual male. See: Judith Butler, "Sexual Ideology and Phenomenological Description: A Feminist Critique of Merleau-Ponty's *Phenomenology of Perception*," in *The Thinking*

Muse, eds. Jeffner Allen and Iris Marion Young (Bloomington: Indiana University Press, 1989).

62. Young, "Throwing Like a Girl," 146.

63. Ibid., 148.

64. Merleau-Ponty, *Phenomenology of Perception*, 159.

65. Ibid., 175–176.

66. See: Jean Grimshaw, "Working Out With Merleau-Ponty," in *Women's Bodies: Discipline and Transgression*, eds. Jane Arthurs and Jean Grimshaw (London: Cassell, 1999).

67. Ibid., 107.

68. Andrea Dworkin, *Women-Hating* (New York: Dutton, 1974), 113. Emphasis in original.

69. See for example: M. W. Matlin, *The Psychology of Women* (New York: Holt, Rinehart and Winston, 1987), 129–132.

70. Quoted in: Bartky, *Femininity and Domination*, 33.

71. Quoted in: Phillips, *The Broken Mirror*, 9. Emphasis in original.

72. While BDD is not significantly more prevalent for women, it is interesting to note that women who suffer from BDD are more likely to be preoccupied with their hips, weight and skin, and furthermore suffer from eating disorders, while men are more likely to be preoccupied with their build, genitals and thinning hair. These patterns which mirror societal preoccupations suggest an inherently socially constructed aspect of this disorder. See: Katherine A. Phillips and S. F. Diaz, "Gender Differences in Body Dysmorphic Disorder," *Journal of Nervous and Mental Diseases* vol. 185 (1997).

73. Cressida J. Heyes, "Normalisation and the Psychic Life of Cosmetic Surgery," *Australian Feminist Studies* vol. 22, no. 52 (2007): 66.

74. Cressida J. Heyes, "Diagnosing Culture: Body Dysmorphic Disorder and Cosmetic Surgery," *Body and Society* vol. 15, no. 4 (2009): 77. Heyes makes this argument with particular reference to the practices of cosmetic surgery which will be discussed further in chapter 6. It should be noted that a BDD-like relation to oneself is not equivalent to the actual pathological condition of BDD. As such, it could be the case that women are more likely to have a BDD-like relation to their bodies without it being the case that women are more likely to have BDD. The two 'conditions' are not necessarily correlating.

75. See, for example: Frost, "'Doing Looks': Women, Appearance and Mental Health."

76. de Beauvoir, *The Second Sex*, 19.

77. Ibid.

78. Ibid.

Chapter Six

The Case of Cosmetic Surgery

The Body Shaped by Shame

There have been many feminist critiques of cosmetic surgery practices in recent times, however, with the notable exception of Jane Megan Northrop's recent study *Reflecting on Cosmetic Surgery: Body Image, Shame and Narcissism*, there has been little explicit analysis of cosmetic surgery with respect to the experience of body shame. Considered through a framework of body shame, cosmetic surgery is revealed to be a practice where the body is *literally* shaped by shame. When considering cosmetic surgery and the narratives of women who chose to undergo aesthetic surgical interventions, we see the complex intersection of issues related (but not limited) to health, gender, biomedicine, ethics, politics, economics, aesthetic ideologies, pathology, psychology and emerging technologies. As such, cosmetic surgery is a rich ground to explore the personal dynamics, alongside the politically oppressive potential, of body shame.

Unlike other practices on the spectrum of beauty, fashion and grooming, cosmetic surgery is markedly divergent. Not only positioned as a medical intervention, it is a practice that is so extreme and invasive that some thinkers believe "that it can only be interpreted as subjugation."[1] This subjugation is not only about women trying to find their footing within oppressive and shame-inducing patriarchal structures, amplified, in contemporary times, by the logic of neoliberalism; but it is also about the reach of biomedicine and the scope of what we consider women's health and the lengths we should go to in order to achieve it. Inflicting physical harm on the body and penetrating the flesh is a form of social control and punishment that, as Foucault points out, was largely eradicated from Western penal systems by the early nineteenth century.[2] As a result, penetrating the body through invasive surgical practices is not a trivial matter. Far beyond the risks which routinely arise in undergoing serious surgery are existential issues about what it means 'to have' and 'to be' a body. Treating the body as a commodity which can be improved and reworked, in the same manner that we may 'makeover' a house or car, presupposes some sort of Cartesian self, where the body is merely a container for and commodity of the true inner self. However, as we have seen, the body is much more than something we 'have,' but fundamentally is something which we *are*; as the phenomenologists illustrate, it is the ground for being itself. Modifying the body has phenomenological consequences for issues relating to the body schema, body image, motor intentionality and self-presentation. As a practice which penetrates the flesh, modifies the physical body, requires medical consent and involves a relinquishment of autonomy at the hands of medical professionals, the decision to undergo cosmetic surgery is not on par with other decisions regarding self-presentation and beauty practices, such as fashion and cosmetics.

In this chapter, I will discuss cosmetic surgery as a practice that is engaged with in strategies of self-presentation in order to ameliorate psychological dissatisfaction with the 'seen body' and to alleviate chronic body shame. Examining the conflation of beauty and biomedicine, as occurs in cosmetic surgery practices and particularly as it affects women, I will explore the familiar themes of visibility and (in)visibility, normalization, internalization, objectification and alienation. Considering body shame as a key component of women's decisions to undergo surgery will be instrumental in highlighting concerns around pathology and normality in these practices, demonstrating that body shame is often exacerbated, rather than eradicated, by the cosmetic surgery industry. I will consider the arguments that cosmetic surgery offers some sort of psychological cure, demonstrating that when women make decisions about cosmetic surgery from a place of body shame and emotional vulnerability, then any rhetoric of empowerment and personal responsibility used to justify these practices must be critically examined. Finally, I will suggest that cosmetic surgery must be considered a political issue, looking at the complex intersection between beauty, power, medicine, race, shame and women's bodies.

COSMETIC SURGERY AND GENDER

Current cosmetic surgery[3] practices originate from experimental procedures developed as early as the late 1800s and were further refined in the years subsequent to World War I to treat the victims of modern warfare, many of whom suffered from disfiguring war wounds and facial injuries. Initially developed by enterprising doctors to correct stigmatizing physical defects that arose from illness or injury, these reconstructive plastic surgery methods endeavoured to restore a body's 'normal' appearance. The development of these plastic surgery techniques led to the emergence of aesthetic plastic surgery, or cosmetic surgery, where surgeries are performed for purely cosmetic reasons, to enhance, modify or beautify a body with already 'normal' or 'acceptable' levels of appearance. Although cosmetic surgery was initially employed to 'correct' racial features that deviated from the preferred white racial norm, such as 'Jewish,' 'Irish' or 'Negroid' noses, in more recent times, it has proliferated drastically as a beauty practice and means to 'correct' perceived unattractiveness and signs of aging.

It is only very recently that elective cosmetic surgery has entered the mainstream as a routine and socially acceptable way to alter appearance. In the 1950s, for example, aesthetic plastic surgery was a largely marginal and unknown medical practice.[4] Just a few decades later, it is a recognized medical speciality, not to mention a highly lucrative multi-billion dollar global industry. While cosmetic surgery initially targeted salient and visible aspects of the body such as the nose, breasts and belly,[5] modern techniques catalogue an astonishing number of procedures (some even targeting parts of the body largely hidden from view) including face-lifts, thigh-lifts, buttock implants, liposuction, leg extensions, nose jobs, calf implants, tummy tucks, eyelid surgery, female genital surgery and penile enlargement, among many others. As cosmetic surgery has proliferated, it has also become more democratic. No longer the privilege of the wealthy or elite, procedures are increasingly more affordable and cosmetic surgery is now a pursuit of the middle and more affluent lower classes.[6]

In the last decade, elective medical intervention through a variety of invasive and non-invasive surgical procedures has become increasingly economically accessible and, simultaneously, a more socially acceptable means of maintaining the 'normal' body. In the United States alone, over eleven million cosmetic procedures were performed in 2013 (a 279% increase since 1997). Of these eleven million procedures, 1.9 million were surgical interventions such as breast augmentation, liposuction and eyelid surgery. Non-surgical procedures included 'injectables' such as Botox,[7] laser skin resurfacing and chemical peels. Overall, Americans spent almost $12 billion on cosmetic procedures in 2013 alone.[8] These statistics say nothing of the many millions of procedures performed in the U.K., Ireland and mainland Europe, nor in other overseas clinics for reasons such as anonymity, waiting-list avoidance, and most significantly, reduced cost, where the cost of a procedure offered in Brazil, India, South Africa, or Thailand, for example, can be as little as one-tenth of the price of a similar procedure in the United States or Western Europe. As a result, the medical tourism market has grown dramatically in recent years.[9]

Although cosmetic surgery is regularly performed on men, it is by and large a female practice. In 2013, for instance, in the United States, just over

90 percent of surgical and non-surgical cosmetic procedures were performed on women, and only 9 percent on men.[10] (Interestingly, although women are by and large the primary recipients of cosmetic surgery, eight out of every nine cosmetic surgeons are male.[11]) Men who undergo cosmetic surgery have been typically cast as either "neurotic or gay,"[12] reinforcing the idea that constant dissatisfaction with appearance and the pursuit of beauty are natural and inevitable concerns for women, for whom cosmetic surgery is an understandable undertaking. However, a similar preoccupation with appearance for men is considered (especially by male surgeons) to be unnatural and potentially pathological.[13]

THE PSYCHOLOGICAL 'CURE'

As a result of heightened levels of body shame, women, rather than considering cosmetic surgery as a frivolous or 'superficial' aesthetic practice, sometimes see cosmetic surgery as a means to take control of their bodies and lives, exercising their agency in order to alleviate psychological distress as a result of body dissatisfaction. This is an argument made by the sociologist Kathy Davis who interviewed Dutch women who were granted publicly funded cosmetic surgery to alleviate mental suffering, such as low self-esteem and chronic and disruptive body shame, as a result of perceived defects in appearance.[14] (In these cases, the surgery is arguably not merely *cosmetic*, as it was deemed medically or psychologically necessary.) These women saw their decisions to undergo cosmetic surgery as autonomous choices which empowered them to change their lives and improve their psychic well being. They were all too aware of the social pressures that led many women to seek out cosmetic surgery. As Davis notes, "they would make disparaging remarks about other women who were preoccupied with physical attractiveness," and seemed to think that their motivations for undertaking cosmetic surgery were "of another order."[15] Davis ultimately argues that cosmetic surgery allows "the individual woman to re-negotiate her relationship to her body."[16]

Hence, despite the (obvious) focus on the physical body in cosmetic surgery practices and the promise of ameliorating physical flaws, a common justification by doctors for the medical need for cosmetic surgery is not about the physical body, but related to the alleviation of psychological distress—significantly, they argue that cosmetic surgery will alleviate anxiety and suffering arising as a result of perceived flaws in one's body image and the threats to one's social standing that this may incur. This of course, as Northrop makes clear in her analysis, is intimately connected to shame. Women see cosmetic surgery as a means to alleviate or circumvent shame, while ensuring a sense of social acceptance or belonging through impression man-

agency & the body pg. 144

agement. Northrop writes that some of her interviewees, "described their engagement with cosmetic surgery as a pre-emptive act of impression management, undertaken to avert a loss in status or to secure the confidence of others."[17]

As cosmetic surgery sits on somewhat shady ground with respect to medical ethical issues around treatment (versus enhancement), necessity, normalization and allocation of resources, doctors acknowledge that of course women don't *need* face lifts and breasts implants, in the same way one might *need* a kidney transplant, chemotherapy or a coronary by-pass. However, some doctors (who have a vested interest in the continuation of cosmetic surgery practices and who wish to be considered more than merely highly skilled technicians of the beauty industry) argue that women will benefit psychologically from these procedures; surgery will improve self esteem, social functioning and ameliorate negative self-conceptions. Medical advocates of cosmetic surgery argue that as one of medicine's primary goals is to reduce suffering, insofar as cosmetic surgery can offer relief to psychological distress—resulting from perceived threats to one's social bonds—then it should be considered a viable medical treatment.[18] It is by this logic that cosmetic surgery is sometimes seen as medically justified rather than merely an enhancement of already 'normal' functioning, and is sometimes funded by national health services.

This notion of cosmetic surgery as some sort of psychological 'cure' or 'treatment' has become a common sense idea in the industry.[19] The cosmetic "cure," as Thomas Pruzinsky states in an article in *Plastic Surgery Nursing*, changes "patients' perceptions of themselves" in order to "facilitate improvement in the patient's psychological functioning."[20] Suzanne Fraser notes that the notion that cosmetic surgery is "psychology with a scalpel" is a common motif in the literature.[21] In addition, Alexander Edmonds remarks that this idea that the cosmetic surgeon is a "healer of mental affliction" is common in the justification of cosmetic surgeons that he interviewed in Brazil.[22] These surgeons, he writes, "invoke the 'progressive' notion of health defined by the World Health Organization, implying cosmetic surgery is part of a larger effort to treat the psychological and social determinants of disease."[23]

Appealing to the logic of the 'psychological cure' is the strategy that many women employ in order to be granted permission to undergo cosmetic surgery.[24] As Rachel Hurst notes, "a patient who expresses that s/he would like to undergo surgery in order to please or be more acceptable to others is likely to be rejected as a candidate for surgery."[25] This is because doctors would see the patient's motivations as tainted by outside influences. Patients are, as Hurst explains, "well aware of this reality, and structure their stories to fit this narrative expectation."[26] Women have, in short, "absorbed clinical knowledge" and learned to "speak in the psychotherapeutic idiom of the beauty industry."[27]

This view is corroborated by the evidence that many women report that they seek out cosmetic surgery not as a beauty practice to *enhance* their appearance, but instead as a means to alleviate psychological distress and chronic body shame caused by a perceived physical abnormality. In her guarded defence of cosmetic surgery, Davis argues that cosmetic surgery is seen by some women not as "a *luxury*, but a *necessity* for alleviating a specific kind of problem."[28] She writes of the women whom she interviewed: "I learned of their despair, not because their bodies were not beautiful, but because they were not ordinary—'just like everyone else.'"[29] Indeed, "these women insisted that they did not have cosmetic surgery to become more beautiful. They had cosmetic surgery because they did not feel at home in their bodies."[30]

Although it is perhaps not surprising that Davis came to these conclusions, considering that all of the women in her focus group received cosmetic surgery that had been deemed medically necessary,[31] similar findings have been reported by several other researchers examining different demographics. For instance, Rebecca Huss-Ashmore, a medical anthropologist conducting research in a private cosmetic surgery practice in an affluent American suburb, notes: "the primary complaint of many cosmetic surgery patients is less 'I am not beautiful' than 'this is not me.'"[32]

Debra Gimlin comes to comparable conclusions in her research examining British women's motivations for undertaking cosmetic surgery. Employing Drew Leder's framework of bodily dys-appearance in her analysis, Gimlin discovered that cosmetic surgery is not considered a beauty practice for most of the women she interviewed but instead was sought out to eliminate unwanted intrusions of the body in conscious awareness, as experienced in instances of objectification and alienation as discussed in chapter 5. She concludes that:

> [W]omen sometimes have cosmetic surgery in an attempt to lessen or eliminate their experiences of bodily intrusion . . . removing from explicit focus an aspect of the body that causes self-consciousness or discomfort, or draws the attention of the alienating gaze.[33]

Cosmetic surgery, Gimlin argues, is not simply an expression or manifestation of excess vanity in contemporary Western women, but rather it is sometimes utilized as a means to achieve normalization, avoiding body shame and ensuring the social and phenomenological invisibility of the body.[34] This is achieved through the elimination of bodily features or characteristics that deviate from the internalized bodily standards of the normate.

Moreover, Gagné and McGaughey, in their study of American Midwestern women who had undergone elective mammoplasty, come to comparable conclusions. In their study, they discovered that achieving "normalcy," which was "based on their perceptions of who they were as well as what others expected from women in general," was a fundamental concern for women who underwent elective mammoplasty.[35] They cite the example of a woman who felt excluded from 'ordinary' activities, such as buying ready-made clothes, because of her 'abnormal' breast-size. In this case, and in others, "the pre-surgical body [is seen] as an obstacle to participating in mundane activities that are readily available to 'normal' people."[36]

Consider Diana, who reports the positive and desired result of feeling (in)visible after her cosmetic dental surgery:

> What I noticed right away was that no one noticed me. Now, *that* was a great feeling, let me tell you. I realize that more and more. Finally, nobody is there looking at me. Not a single kid who yells something at me. That was the first thing I noticed after the surgery and I was really glad.[37]

Hence, it seems that for some if not many women, cosmetic surgery is not about becoming beautiful or exceptional, but about merely 'passing.' Sought out in response to body shame that can perhaps range from minor to severe to completely unbearable, these women hope cosmetic surgery will help them become, like Diana, "unnoticeable," "invisible," and "ordinary."[38]

The psychological cure hinges on the idea of what Nikki Sullivan terms the "wrong" body problem, where the "surgeon act[s] on the body to ease the pain of the dys/embodied self 'inside.'"[39] This is the experience of having a mis-match between the 'outer' body and the 'inner' self—the common trope of the thin person trapped within a fat body, the women within a man's body, the young person within the aged body, and so on.[40] Increasingly this 'wrong body' phenomena is a concern of medical practice and is treated through procedures such as gender reassignment, cosmetic surgery, anti-aging treatments and even amputations, as in the case of Body Integrity Identity Disorder (BIID).[41] The experience of the 'wrong body' is challenging to theorize when working from a phenomenological framework which repudiates any dualistic conception of the body or any fixed distinction between 'inner' and 'outer.' In the case of transgender, for instance, there seems a clear distinction between one's authentic 'inner' self and one's physical body, seemingly confirming the dualistic paradigm.

To resolve this apparent problem, Lanei Rodemeyer introduces Edmund Husserl's distinction between *Körper* and *Leib* as a means to give a phenomenological reading to the experience of the 'wrong body.'[42] While *Körper* refers to the body as a physical object, *Leib* refers to body of lived, sensory experience. Our experience, as embodied beings, as noted in chapter 2, is an entanglement of both *Körper* and *Leib*. However, *Körper* can be understood and experienced in two distinct ways, as a purely *physical* reality (body, genitals, hormones etc.) or as a *social* reality (the result of social conditioning or discourse).[43] Experiences that seem to confirm some sort of dualism between 'inner' and 'outer' arise, Rodemeyer argues, when the "voice" of the *Leib*—existential feelings, sensations, sensings—do not resonate with the experience of one's *Körper*, in both the physical and social senses.[44] As a result, there is an experienced difference between one's 'inner' self and one's 'outer' body.

As a result, it seems women sometimes partake in cosmetic surgery practices in order to reconcile this difference, closing the gap between the perceived 'inner' and 'outer' bodies. Through undertaking cosmetic surgery under the paradigm of the psychological cure, they hope to facilitate their daily existence by enhancing the experience of physical *and* social bodily (in)visibility, thus facilitating successful intentional action and the flow of social relations. In these contexts, arguably, cosmetic surgery can be seen as something *beneficial* for the subject where exercising one's choice to have surgery can improve one's quality of life, self-esteem and psychological functioning, as indicated (albeit with reservations) by Davis, Northrop, Huss-Ashmore, Gimlin, Gagné and McGaughey.

COSMETIC SURGERY JUSTIFIED?

In the context of the neoliberal imperatives of self-care, self-transformation and self-improvement through an endless restyling of the body, cosmetic surgery has a tidy and appealing logic. It can, quite simply, enhance one's body capital, yielding a more valuable or acceptable self and, as a result, enhancing one's personal and professional success.[45] In some contexts, cosmetic surgery is even considered *necessary* in order to maintain one's social standing or to ensure the continuation of one's career. For example, leg lengthening procedures are undertaken in height-conscious China where height requirements in professional contexts, such as retail jobs, the foreign service and law school admissions, routinely limit opportunities for those who fall short.[46] In a Western context, consider Hollywood actresses who are under enormous pressure to maintain high levels of attractive youthfulness as they age in order to ensure the continuation of their careers.

Although it seems obvious that the problem in these examples lies not with the particular physical 'flaws' of any (short or aging) individual, but rather with the contingent socio-cultural standards which deem otherwise ordinary physical traits to be defective and deficient, some thinkers maintain that it is not only justifiable to utilise cosmetic surgery to enhance or maintain one's social and body capital, but in some cases it is even *necessary*. Consider Stephen Coleman's argument in his chapter 'A Defense of Cosmetic Surgery':

If an actress was to have . . . [face-lift] surgery, and if the surgery was motivated by her desire to continue working as an actress . . . then I would suggest
that face-lift surgery . . . does not qualify as cosmetic surgery under my
definition, since the surgery was not undertaken purely, or even primarily, for
the purpose of appearance, but was rather undertaken as a means to an end,
that of allowing her to resume her career as an actress . . . given the acknowledged fact that there are few, if any, worthwhile roles for older-looking wom-
en, it must be acknowledged that it is indeed *necessary* for most Hollywood
actresses to seek plastic surgery in order to continue to work in their chosen
field.[47]

Beyond the inherently sexist and ageist implications in this passage, Coleman's logic is arguably flawed in that he assumes some sort of objective
necessity within a socio-cultural framework which itself should be put under
question. He seems to be arguing that the way actresses can overcome the
sexism and age-ism inherent to their industry is through engaging in inherently sexist and ageist practices.

Coleman tellingly notes that "male stars certainly do not experience the
same pressures to look youthful that female stars do."[48] As a result, these
male actors will not perceive cosmetic surgery as a necessity in the same
manner as their female peers. That Coleman acknowledges Hollywood's
"sexist stance" in this matter but ultimately accepts this stance as immutable
and takes no issue with this gender imbalance is striking. Coleman goes on to
argue that breast augmentation may also be considered reasonably 'necessary' "if it is true, other things being equal, that directors and casting agen-
cies will offer roles to actresses with larger breasts over actresses with smaller breasts."[49] Ultimately, Coleman justifies cosmetic surgery as a practice
which can bring (short-term and questionable) benefits to a subject, while
ignoring the broader social circumstances in which those benefits are valued.

BEAUTY AND BIOMEDICINE: NORMALIZATION
AND MEDICALIZATION

Looking at the broader social structures and normative values, within which
women's choices to have cosmetic surgery are valued, is central to any
accurate analysis of the practice. Positioning decisions to undergo cosmetic
surgery as empowering is consistent with a cultural logic that ensures that
women are constantly insecure and dissatisfied with their bodies which require endless improving and restyling. Under this logic, engaging with body
projects is a means to success and fulfillment (both professionally and personally). However, when looking at the broader social structures and power
relations which frame individual decisions to undergo surgery, a more worrying picture emerges. We see the structures of biomedicine conflating with
those of neoliberalism, targeting women's bodies with shame-inducing

forces under the spurious legitimation of promoting health and well being. Making women feel insecure by encouraging them to feel they have a spoiled identity and that their personal or professional social bonds are under threat, is key to the continuation of these practices.

What is of particular interest when considering the rise of cosmetic surgery, especially among women, is the conflation of the concerns of beauty and attractiveness with the practices of biomedicine under the broader framework of neoliberalism. This combination has resulted in an unprecedented commodification and medicalization of the female body. If we are to follow the logic of the discourses of the beauty-biomedicine industry, it seems that the (female) body's appearance increasingly requires regular medical expertise and intervention to maintain its 'healthy,' that is, 'normal' state, where health and normality have been neatly conflated with normative standards of attractiveness propagated by commercial advertising. In short, women need doctors to help them manage their bodies. This motif is a familiar one for feminist thinkers who have sharply critiqued patriarchal control through the pathologization of women's bodies and reproductive functions, where, for example, pregnancy, menstruation and the menopause are treated as medical events which need professional attention from (often male) doctors. [50]

As a result, the markers and norms that dictate health and expertise in medical discourse are being conflated with the norms propagated commercially by the various beauty industries. This is not entirely new. The beauty industry has routinely employed scientific discourse and jargon to lend weight to potentially spurious or vacant claims. Creams, cosmetics and beauty treatments are 'clinically tested,' 'dermatologist recommended,' and the result of 'years of groundbreaking DNA research.' Products contain fantastic sounding ingredients such as 'the GF-Volumetry complex,' 'Idebenone and Soy Ferulate-C,' 'advanced antioxidants,' 'new regenerist three point super serum' and 'rice peptides' which do things like 'fight free radicals' or 'DNA damage.' [51] Scientific and diagnostic sounding language is compelling; it carries the weight and professionalism of science, which is authoritarian in so far as it is cast in our culture as the primary means to reason, rationality and truth. Coupled with the "social imaginary of medicine as a modern good," this sort of medicalized scientific discourse has a lot of cultural weight. [52] Medical experts and scientists therefore lend a legitimacy to beauty practices, seemingly confirming what women have felt all along: these pursuits are far from trivial. It has become reasonable and even 'medical' to worry about appearance and beauty concerns.

Kathryn Pauly Morgan noted in 1991 that the beauty industry "is coming to be dominated by a variety of experts . . . cosmetic surgeons, anaesthetists, nurses, aestheticians [etc.]." [53] This trend has become increasingly manifest in contemporary beauty discourse over the last two decades and can be seen explicitly in the recent Irish publication *Rejuvenate*. Launched in 2007, it is

"Ireland's FIRST Cosmetic Enhancement Magazine." The vocabulary employed in this publication, a glossy magazine reminiscent, in its design and presentation, of fashion and women's serials such as *Vogue* and *Elle*, reveals how beauty and biomedicine have converged on the female body. Discussing various beauty practices, women are "patients" who undergo "consultations" by "physicians," "surgeons," and "doctors" in order to go through "procedures" in "hospitals," even though these aesthetic interventions are not at all health-related.[54]

Introducing medical discourse into beauty practices has consequences. As Foucault highlights, clinical medicine and psychiatry provide categories through which individuals can be assessed and classified in terms of health and pathology. As discussed above, these categories hinge around the binary standards of "normal" and "abnormal."[55] Doctors and other health professionals become the arbiters for normality, and employ methods to measure, judge, regulate and ultimately correct any deviance from established medical norms which are based on various methods of scientific classification. The "anatomo-clinical regard," which Foucault explores in his analysis of modern medical techniques in *The Birth of the Clinic*,[56] imposes a scientific structure on each individual and body, neglecting the specificities of lived experience. Conceived in this way, biomedicine becomes the primary means to understand and ameliorate the body. As the body has become subject to this process of medicalization, more and more phenomena in human life are governed by a medical perspective. Essentially, normalization becomes the crux of biomedical practice which is constantly endeavouring to return body subjects to the narrow parameters of 'health.'

Hence, the coupling of biomedicine with the beauty industry has crystallized and legitimized the normalizing tendencies of contemporary grooming industries. It is certainly not the case that *any* body will do. Instead, medical and beauty discourses, by and large, promote the normate and tell us that the marked, aging, overweight, raced, or unattractive body requires medical intervention: it is, in some sense, an unhealthy body. Clearly this association is not *entirely* arbitrary, as old age and excess weight are often associated with health problems, and good health is often indicated by a certain robust external appearance, characterized by features such as a muscular form, good teeth, clear skin and so on. However, these external manifestations of good health do not in any way imply a standardized or normalized appearance as is promoted by the beauty-biomedicine industry.

In fact, the publication *Proportions of the Aesthetic Face*, published by the American Academy of Facial Plastic and Reconstructive Surgery,[57] which is widely used by plastic surgeons and which claims to "document objectively the guidelines for facial symmetry and proportion,"[58] demonstrates the racist, able-ist, ethnocentric and ageist ideologies that largely inform medical discourse in this context and shape conceptions of the normate.

The face presented in this publication is based on a white, youthful, Western aesthetic of feminine beauty, where faces with so-called 'deviant' appearances, such as older faces marked with lines and wrinkles, the features particular to an ethnic group, or facial characteristics as a result of some genetic disorder, such as Down's Syndrome, are aberrant and need 'correction' to conform to this ideal.

Eugenia Kaw explores this phenomenon with respect to Asian-American women who undergo plastic surgery, in particular double-eyelid surgery (blepharoplasty) and nose sculpting, in order to transform their features into those more characteristic of their Caucasian contemporaries.[59] In fact, "ethnic cosmetic surgery"[60] is a frequent phenomenon within cosmetic surgery practices, where individuals with stereotypically 'ethnic' features undergo cosmetic surgery for reasons of beautification, which in fact results in normalization toward a white aesthetic ideal: broad 'African' noses are narrowed, short 'Asian' legs are lengthened, large 'Jewish' noses are made smaller.[61] This tendency toward a 'white' aesthetic is evident both in predominately white cultures where racial and ethnic groups are in the minority, but interestingly also in countries where non-white racial groups are in the majority, such as Brazil and Japan. This probably reflects, as Edmonds notes, the neo-colonial origins of the global economy, and how "white dominance" is implicitly racist.[62]

However, doctors are careful to avoid racist language in talking about cosmetic surgery procedures, arguing that features become more "proportionate" or "suitable" while patients "retain their distinctive ethnic appearance."[63] Despite this, it is evident that the dominant aesthetic standard among cosmetic surgery recipients is inherently racist. However, these racist ideals are not immutable, and, as Cressida Heyes points out, the Western idealized body may "appropriate pieces of 'ethnic' physicality for [its] exoticism and eroticism."[64] Consider buttock implants or collagen lip injections which give white bodies a more 'Latin' (Jennifer Lopez-like) aspect. However, these ethnic embellishments to the normate's form seem to be permissible only within extremely narrow limits.

Cosmetic surgery used to 'correct' disability demonstrates another normalizing tendency within medical discourse, which operates with an able-ist cultural bias conceiving that all disabilities have "uniformly negative consequences."[65] Heyes, in her analysis of the reality television program *Extreme Makeover*, reveals how some rather diverse disabilities—albeit ones that can be corrected to easily conform to prevalent norms of the able-bodied—such as deafness and impaired vision, are considered somehow tantamount to unattractiveness in that they are corrected as part of a 'makeover.' In a more medicalized context, since the 1980s cosmetic surgery procedures have been routinely carried out on children with Down's Syndrome to help them 'fit in.'[66] Doctors argue that, "Elimination of mongoloid features of the face (tongue, lower lip, eyelids, nose) has a positive influence on rehabilitation."[67] Disability advocates, however, argue that these procedures are unnecessary and cause psychological distress. It seems there is ambivalent empirical evidence about whether these procedures are beneficial for Down's Syndrome children, although the operations may make some parents feel better.[68]

Collapsing race, old age, ugliness, and disability into a particular type of aesthetic pathology, a pathology with seemingly only social symptoms, but which, doctors argue, causes psychological distress that can be 'cured' through the use of cosmetic surgery, is the enterprising marketing strategy of the commercial bodies that stand to gain from more women (and increasingly men) going under the knife. As Morgan notes, "women are being pressured to see plainness or being ugly as a form of pathology" that can be fixed through medical intervention.[69] The medical terminology used to describe ordinary bodily features, such as "micromastia"—the term among plastic surgeons for "too small" breasts—denotes them as "disorders," which normally denote dysfunction.[70] Bodily conditions such as "sagging breasts and 'Negroid noses,'" Edmonds argues, "become analogous to the congenital defects and injuries that reconstructive [rather than aesthetic] surgery treats."[71] These so-called "disorders," as Bordo notes, are "entirely aesthetic and socially constructed."[72]

The recent dramatic proliferation of cosmetic surgery demonstrates that Morgan's observations have been confirmed: "Not only is elective surgery moving out of the domain of the sleazy, the suspicious, the secretly deviant, or the pathologically narcissistic, it is *becoming the norm*."[73] In the present day, a variety of elective surgical and non-surgical procedures have become as mainstream, and as financially and materially accessible, as joining a weight-loss program or taking out a gym membership. Popular culture has become saturated with references to cosmetic surgery. It is routinely discussed in women's magazines, on beauty and fashion websites, by celebrities, in films and on television. Several reality television programs such as *The Swan, Plastic Surgery: Before and After, Extreme Makeover* and MTV's *I Want a Famous Face* feature 'ordinary' people undergoing cosmetic surgery, demonstrating the mass consumption of the notion of self-transformation through surgical intervention. In these shows, individuals embark on cosmetic surgery in the same way they may have participated in a fashion makeover just a few years ago. Cosmetic surgery is now on a continuum of beauty practices available to women including dieting, exercise, makeup, fashion, hair colouring, and so forth. Many non-surgical procedures, such as Botox injections and laser skin treatments, are performed in salons by aestheticians and are as commonplace as getting one's hair dyed or legs waxed. As Heyes remarks: "We certainly see more and more *images* of cosmetic surgery that portray it as 'no big deal'; anecdotal evidence (the only kind presently available) suggests that some consumers also see minor procedures as a fairly routine kind of body maintenance that belongs more appropriately in the salon than in the hospital."[74]

In what must be one of the most audacious triumphs in marketing history, cosmetic surgery is now seen by many as something women 'need' and 'deserve.' Cast as a tool of empowerment, cosmetic surgery is often seen to be a means to success and to achieving personal and professional ambition. Serious risks, such as disfigurement or even death, and long, painful recovery times, are for the most part unacknowledged in the popular media about these procedures.[75] In addition, although it is commonly acknowledged that women who seek out cosmetic surgery are emotionally vulnerable and often suffering psychologically from negative 'self-other-conscious' emotions such as chronic body shame and dissatisfaction about appearance, these women are cast as empowered agents who choose cosmetic surgery autonomously as something they are doing wholly for *themselves*. Examining the role of body shame in decisions to undergo cosmetic surgery will be the focus of the next section.

BODY SHAME AND COSMETIC SURGERY

The success of the marketing approach of the beauty-biomedicine industry is corroborated in recent feminist scholarship about cosmetic surgery which reveals that more and more women see cosmetic surgery as something they *need* in order to correct what they perceive as an abnormality in their physical form. Hence, it should not come as any surprise that the desire to undergo cosmetic surgery, like other projects of bodily transformation, is largely driven by strategies to alleviate or avoid body shame in order to assuage the pervasive fear of social exclusion which, as social thinkers such as Anthony Elliott argue, has become increasingly prevalent in contemporary neoliberal society.[76] However, interestingly, shame is frequently invisible in the discourse of cosmetic surgery. Northrop notes that: "Participants only occasionally used the term 'shame' to describe how they felt about themselves, and rarely spoke of feeling ashamed of their appearance."[77] Despite remaining largely unarticulated by both patients and doctors in her interviews, Northrop found shame about the body to be the structure driving not only women's decisions about surgery, but also the entire "transformative arc in which cosmetic surgery is located."[78] Transforming body shame into pride is, in fact, central to the drama of cosmetic surgery: shame drives women to seek out surgeons; surgeons cultivate it in order to acquire and maintain their clients; and, ultimately, surgeries are performed in order to alleviate it.

In a recent study, Katherine J. Morris (citing Kathy Davis's research) draws on the Sartrean concepts of shame, being-for-others and the Look in an analysis of why women undergo cosmetic surgery. Morris notes that shame is a common motif and motivating factor for many individuals who seek out cosmetic surgery to correct a perceived flaw in their appearance.[79] For example, she cites one woman interviewed by Davis who explains: "I always had this deep-rooted feeling of dissatisfaction, of *shame* . . . you look in the mirror and you feel so totally humiliated. And you start thinking, God, if only it could be a little less—just a little less—*shaming*."[80] Davis concludes that many "women were ashamed of how they looked, experiencing their bodies as inherently deficient or faulty. The women I talked with often described their problems as a kind of disgraceful secret."[81] Northrop corroborates; she argues that it is "the 'intolerable' shame of having a body that is 'unlovable' which leads people to surgically alter their appearance."[82]

Doctors prey on this shame and offer diagnostic language and a therapeutic narrative to alleviate the shame cycle that many women feel regarding their concerns with appearance, where the advice and attentions of a medical expert legitimates what might otherwise feel like a shameful preoccupation. As Blum notes:

> The surgeon is in many ways the legitimator of our otherwise embarrassing preoccupation with physical appearance. In the plastic surgeon's office, you are in the place of unsuppressed narcissism—the place where your otherwise absurd concern with the angle of your chin will feel entirely 'normal.' It will feel scientific even, as the surgeon measures and evaluates the arrangement of your features. He will make you feel that all your trivial obsessions are absolutely justifiable.[83]

A reassuring doctor will alleviate your shame, recasting what you feel might be mere vanity or narcissism into a serious medical concern. A perceived physical flaw is no longer a shameful secret or a personal failure, but part of a medical problem.

Diagnostic language is powerful. As critics writing about gender, race, sexual orientation and disability, among other embodied states that carry stigma, have noted, a medical diagnosis can alleviate shame and stigma, empowering and enabling an individual or group. For instance, in the case of transgender, although the diagnosis of Gender Identity Disorder is troubling in that it is inherently pathologizing with reference to an imagined norm of 'healthy' gender expression, this diagnosis can at the same time offer relief to individuals who are suffering in isolation.[84] As against feeling different, ashamed and alone, belonging to a medically classified group can be a positive and even life-changing experience, validating and endowing recognition to a subjectivity that was previously politically or socially marginalized, invisible and ignored. Not only is one's shame alleviated, but often the medical model provides avenues and options for treatment and perhaps even a 'cure.'

However, once these diagnoses or classifications are accepted and perceived as reality, it is difficult to resist the dictates of biomedicine and the normalizing ideology which underpins it. As a result, although doctors are key in alleviating the shame and embarrassment that one might feel about the body, they are also in a prime position to incite them. Surgeons participate in a what Bordo has termed a "pedagogy of defect," where women are taught that their bodies are faulty, unacceptable and in need of remedy.[85] A common motif on the websites and in the publicity of cosmetic surgery clinics is the visual pedagogy of the 'before and after' photo set which instructs viewers to first identify their defects and then to recognize their amelioration.[86] These sorts of comparative images can teach women to regard as defective parts of the body that were not even scrutinized beforehand. For example, Virginia Braun notes how cosmetic surgeons promote female genital cosmetic surgery (labiaplasty) by publishing photographs of 'normal' post-surgical vaginas, generating dissatisfaction and shame in women about body parts that may never have been previously held up to aesthetic regard.[87]

There are numerous accounts in feminist literature on cosmetic surgery of doctors who, in consultation, routinely make women 'see' that parts of their bodies, for which they had not even considered surgery, are in fact also defective and in need of intervention. This has profound consequences for one's self-perception and self-esteem. Bordo cites this example:

> Writing for *New York* magazine, 28-year-old, 5-foot 6-inch, and 118-pound Lily Burana describes how a series of interviews with plastic surgeons—the majority of whom had recommended rhinoplasty, lip augmentation, implants, liposuction and eyelid work—changed her perception of herself from 'a hardy young sapling that could do with some pruning . . . to a gnarled thing that begs to be torn down to the root and rebuilt limb by limb.[88]

In this manner, cosmetic surgeons play out the common formula of neoliberal consumer culture: they cultivate profound anxieties about the body and then present themselves and their services as the only means to eliminate or alleviate the very shame and guilt they have themselves helped to produce.

In addition, within the power dynamic of patriarchy, where women are already infantalized and insecure, the lopsided power relation between the (usually male) doctor, who is an expert and medical authority, and the (usually female) patient is augmented to the extent that it is difficult, if not impossible, for women (who are already vulnerable) to resist the advice (or judgmental Look) of their doctors. The discrepancy in power in the doctor-patient relationship, as Leder points out, means that it is "not a matter of reciprocal exchange of intentions, so much as one body submitting to the intentions of another."[89] Undergoing surgery necessitates a passivity and temporary abnegation of agency and control, where women must relinquish control of their bodies at the hands of surgeons operating within a biomedical system dominated by normalizing, patriarchal principles. Ultimately, it is doctors who hold a monopoly on expertise in cosmetic surgery practices; they make and implement aesthetic judgements and have their own "aesthetic agendas" that are difficult for individual women to resist.[90] Northrop recounts a telling example about one of her interviewees who, in the context of her doctor's clinic was unable to resist the shame-inducing medical gaze: "In their domain the surgeon and his receptionist left her little choice but to accept their version of her. In their presence she felt acutely shamed . . . Away from their gaze she was able to amend her sense of self and dispel their imposed shame by recounting the event to a girlfriend."[91]

Arising from this inherent discrepancy in the power relations between doctors and patients is an endless ground to invent new defects and, correspondingly, new interventions to correct them, inciting further anxieties in already existing clients while simultaneously broadening its markets to younger women, adolescents, men and diverse ethnic groups. As a result, as Heyes notes, we "will never be good enough, no makeover can fix our flaws . . . [as] cosmetic surgery promises a transformation the adequacy of which it will later deny."[92] Hence, what is interesting is that despite numerous testimonials that cosmetic surgery is sought out as a means to alleviate psychological distress caused by perceived flaws in appearance, there is ambivalent evidence on the overall positive psychological and social impact of cosmetic surgery, nor any clear evidence on how long any reported positive impacts will last.[93] In a review of changes in body image following cosmetic surgery, David Sarwer makes these telling remarks:

> Compared to their preoperative assessment of body image, cosmetic surgery patients reported a significant reduction in dissatisfaction with the specific feature altered by surgery . . . These women, however, reported *no significant improvements* in the degree of investment or dissatisfaction with their overall appearance.[94]

It seems that cosmetic surgery may offer a superficial fix targeting a particular instantiation of body shame, while, at the same time, ultimately exacerbating overall body dissatisfaction. A previously minor dissatisfaction with an aspect of one's appearance may become an unbearable flaw after surgery on another part of the body. It is not for no reason at all that multiple surgeries are frequently undertaken and the process of women "becoming surgical," or 'addicted' to cosmetic surgery, is well documented.[95] Considering these ambivalent findings it would seem plausible that if doctors were actually *serious* about improving the psychological health of their clients, they would work closely with psychologists, psychiatrists and other mental health professionals offering sustainable treatments that could potentially alter self-perception and body image,[96] instead of performing expensive, painful, potentially life-threatening and functionally unnecessary surgeries which offer a temporary fix, as all bodies inevitably change and age.

In fact, the argument that cosmetic surgery is psychologically beneficial is extremely problematic and fraught with contradictions. Surgeons are regularly advised not to operate on those who suffer from mental health issues, especially BDD[97] or other disorders which are characterized by chronic body shame and dissatisfaction with appearance or body image.[98] These individuals are unlikely to be satisfied with the results of their surgeries, nor to experience any relief from their psychological suffering, and, moreover, they are the most likely to become litigious. However, as Heyes notes, while rejecting those with BDD as potential candidates for surgery, doctors simultaneously encourage BDD-like behavior in their 'healthy' and 'suitable' patients who turn to surgery as a result of dissatisfaction with minor or even imperceptible flaws in otherwise normal appearance.[99] As a more honest surgeon remarks: "Plastic surgery sharpens your eyesight . . . You get something done, suddenly you're looking in the mirror every five minutes—at imperfections nobody else can see."[100] Indeed, a common mantra for women who undergo these sorts of procedures is: "You might not notice it . . . but *I* do."[101]

This is an interesting observation raised by Kathy Davis in her study of Dutch women. With most of the women Davis interviewed, she found that she could not tell which was the 'offending' body part. She writes:

> I did not necessarily share these women's conviction that they were physically abnormal or different. Their dissatisfaction had, in fact, little to do with inter-subjective standards for acceptable or 'normal' feminine appearance. For example, when I spoke with women who were contemplating having cosmetic surgery, I rarely noticed the 'offending' body part, let alone understood why it required surgical intervention.[102]

That the body part in question was not apparent to Davis demonstrates that the 'problem' these women had with their appearance was not intersubjectively corroborated, but rather was due to a distorted and internalized self-perception, potentially even as a result of mental health problems such as BDD. Similar findings are reported by Northrop in her recent study of Australian women. Many of her interviewees saw cosmetic surgery as a means to 'take control' of their lives through taking control of their bodies. She notes, "when participants spoke of improving their appearance with cosmetic surgery, they were not actually speaking about their bodies; rather they were referring to body image, their own subjective experience of perceiving how their bodies appeared."[103]

Women who are constantly preoccupied and dissatisfied with their bodies, who are willing to invest much time, energy and material resources in maintaining and transforming their bodies, and who believe surgery will make them feel better about themselves, are the ideal candidates for cosmetic surgery. However, when these preoccupations and desires slip beyond an allegedly 'normal' preoccupation with appearance, into the realm of pathology, then these women are eliminated as candidates for cosmetic surgery and encouraged to seek psychological or psychiatric assistance. As Heyes remarks, "the cosmetic surgery industry contributes to the production of a subjectivity that it then pathologizes if enacted too convincingly."[104] This is, she notes, "tremendously paradoxical."[105]

There seems to be a tacit understanding among doctors and health regulators that the rhetoric of psychological benefit in the discourse of cosmetic surgery is mostly just lip-service employed to justify a very lucrative medical practice that often does not improve psychological or physical health in any tangible way. As Alex Kuczynski notes, cosmetic surgery has become an "an industry governed not just by money but by psychology, a conspiracy between patients who don't want to hear what they really need and doctors who won't tell them."[106] In fact, counter to the classical feminist critique of cosmetic surgery which argues that women are making false decisions under an oppressive patriarchal regime when they 'choose' cosmetic surgery, positioning women as "cultural dope[s]"[107] or "misguided or deluded victims,"[108] what we find is that many women who engage in cosmetic surgery have highly elevated consciousnesses about the patriarchal origins of beauty norms.

However, even women that have extensively researched and reflected on these matters still experience body dissatisfaction and engage in beauty practices. These women may have awareness that their desires to not heed or place value on oppressive beauty norms are in conflict with their desires to be attractive and amass body capital; however, as a result of constantly negotiating body shame, they may not have the strength, self-esteem or merely the desire to resist socio-cultural dictates, even when they know these dictates to be against their best interests. Or, quite simply, operating within a sexist, ageist, patriarchal framework, perhaps these women know that it is too socially costly to resist beauty norms. In addition, in a cultural milieu that positions cosmetic surgery as 'no big deal' and continuously conflates female health with beauty norms, it seems increasingly reasonable to turn to medical practices when dealing with aesthetic concerns.

AESTHETIC HEALTH?

It is not at all straightforward to determine how far medicine should encroach on aesthetic matters or to what extent we should be concerned with "aesthetic health."[109] We regularly—and uncontroversially—seek out orthodontists and dermatologists to 'correct' crooked teeth or flawed skin even though these

conditions often have no consequences for overall health and are often merely aesthetic concerns. Cultural expectations regarding straight teeth and clear
skin have become so normalized as to render these orthodontic and dermatological practices medically reasonable, if not medically necessary. However,
aesthetic standards are culturally malleable, where various cultures have lower or differing thresholds for 'acceptable' appearance. The trans-cultural experience of a victim of disfiguring facial burns is telling:

> A few years after my accident, still looking very badly disfigured, I travelled
> to India. There, and in Iran and Afghanistan, my face was rarely given the
> slightest attention. Heavily scarred faces are regular sights, as disfiguring dis-
> eases and accidents are commonplace, while plastic surgery is not widely
> available in these countries. I could quite easily have lived and worked there
> with no further surgery. But on my return, a trip on the London Underground
> was enough to convince me that I need more reconstruction to live and work in
> Britain.[110]

As a result of the social cost—a difficulty in merely living and working—
incurred as a result of a disfiguring facial injury within the framework of our
Western socio-cultural norms, the plastic surgery performed to correct this
individual's disfiguring facial burns is considered medical treatment, rather
than an elective cosmetic enhancement.

Acceptable appearance is, hence, largely a matter of context. As cosmetic
surgery becomes a cultural practice undertaken by more and more people, the
more 'normal' surgically altered bodies will become. Although some critics
argue that "the number of women who do opt for cosmetic surgery is almost
negligible compared to the number of women who do not,"[111] what is at
stake is not merely how many individuals seek out surgery in the present day,
but whether these practices are becoming *normalized*, changing expectations
of what it means 'to have' and 'to be' a body, with real consequences for
future generations of girls and women. The more established a norm of
appearance or a body practice becomes, the more difficult, or socially costly,
it is to resist adhering to it, transforming the thresholds for body shame and
raising the bar even further for what is considered an acceptable or reasonable level of attractiveness. The worry is, of course, that those who refuse
enhancement procedures, aesthetic or otherwise, are, as Gail Weiss warns,
"regarded as not only *aesthetically deficient* but also *morally blame-
worthy*."[112]

With practices like cosmetic surgery becoming normalized what we see is
not just the "medicalization of the body" through aesthetic norms, but also
what we might consider a "'demedicalization' of medicine."[113] The disturbing post-surgical near-future society Jeanette Winterson describes in her novel *The Stone Gods* (2009), reads as the inevitable conclusion to this trend

which sets no limits to the changes we can make to the body through aesthetic medicine:

> Celebrities are under pressure, no doubt about it. We are all young and beautiful now, so how can they stay ahead of the game? Most of them have macrosurgery. Their boobs swell up like beach balls, and their dicks go up and down like beach umbrellas. They are surgically stretched to be taller, and steroids give them muscle-growth that turns them into star-gods. Their body parts are bio-enhanced, and their hair can do clever things like change colour to match their outfits. They are everything that science and money can buy. [114]

Through satirical passages such as this one, Winterson raises important questions about where narrowing standards of enhancement and appearance will take us, imploring us to ask whether being "everything that science and money can buy" is really all we hope for. In fact, the neoliberal emphasis on self-transformation coupled with the novelty of cutting-edge medical practices, and the profits for powerful industries generated by both, should not prevent us from seeing the further social and moral inequalities for marginalized groups engendered by these sorts of practices. If technologies are developed merely as a result of the impersonal demands of the free market spurred on by the pride of human achievements, then the post-surgical, sexist and inequality-rife dystopia Winterson describes in *The Stone Gods* reads as the inevitable conclusion to a trend that sets no limits on the changes we can make to bodies under the guise of 'choice' and self-improvement. [115] What these reflections demonstrate is that the deeper problems of the human condition and of social inequalities, particularly those underpinned by body shame and political struggles for recognition and (in)visibility, require more than the surface fixes offered by consumption, technological innovation, and narcissistic body projects.

CONCLUSION

The theoretical approaches of phenomenology and social constructionism in many ways capture the often contradictory and competing experiential states of contemporary women and their drive for bodily (in)visibility in choices to engage in cosmetic surgery practices. When seen through the lens of phenomenology, where in the classical Husserlian formulation, as discussed in chapter 2, the body is the 'organ of the will' and facilitates one's successful relation to the lifeworld, women are willing to partake in practices such as cosmetic surgery in order to facilitate their daily existence through an augmentation of social capital and power. The three main arguments employed in defense of cosmetic surgery—(1) It eliminates psychological suffering; (2) It can enhance one's social capital; and (3) It is socially and personally empowering—hinge on the idea that, when considered from the point of view of the individual subject, cosmetic surgery can facilitate one's successful intentional action, eliminating bodily dys-appearance and enhancing one's social capital and (in)visibility. As such, it is purportedly for the benefit of the subject and a practice that is reasonably and autonomously pursued.

However, as we have seen, social thinkers criticize phenomenology for not taking into account social forces that have an effect on and, in many cases, delimit and define embodied experiences. Phenomenology gives a largely individualistic view of the body subject, focusing on action, perception and motility, while giving less consideration to intersubjective, sociocultural and political forces. As Linda Martin Alcoff explains, social critics of phenomenology charge it with taking "subjectivity and subjective experience as cause and foundation when in reality they are mere epiphenomenon and effect."[116] As such, looking at broader social structures which frame experiences is key. Social constructionist accounts of women's embodiment, from which the classic feminist critique of cosmetic surgery arises, paint a much bleaker picture in which women might consider themselves to be making 'free' and 'informed' decisions because they retain "effective agency," but in reality their choices are characterized by "false consciousness," confined within the tight parameters of an oppressive cultural regime.[117]

As such, phenomenology and social constructionism can be employed to characterise the contradictory positions of what is termed the "structure-agency debate"[118] in the cosmetic surgery literature and which have been discussed throughout this chapter. On one side of this debate, women are victims of the pernicious disciplinary politics of normalization where recurrent and patterned forces delimit and influence choices and opportunities (structure), while on the other side of the debate, women make autonomous choices to engage in normalizing practices in order to enhance their social capital or power (agency).

However, characterizing women as *either* passive victims *or* empowered agents is too simplistic. The structure-agency debate does not leave much space to consider the complex state of mind of women who are struggling with negative self-conscious emotions, such as chronic body shame. Most ordinary women operate with a paradoxical and contradictory state of mind; rather than being duped and deluded, they are often fully aware of the coercive and sometimes harmful nature of beauty norms, but at the same time, however, are unwilling or unable to give up the social capital that conforming to these norms affords. We do not make choices in a self-contained cognitive bubble, but are embodied, affective, social beings, constantly struggling to confer a sense of belongingness and acceptance while negotiating the broader normative frameworks and power structures that enframe us. As long as our contemporary frameworks of biomedicine and neoliberalism do not challenge their patriarchal origins and continue to position women in an undermined position due to shame-inducing structures, practices, institutions and values, then women, undermined by insecurities about their bodies, will be willing to go to great lengths to secure their sense of acceptance and belonging. As discussed in chapter 2, the desire to avoid body shame, and to feel secure with one's social bonds, can far surpasses the desire to avoid physical pain. Recalling Michelle, undergoing rhinoplasty (a surgical procedure with serious risks and a long, painful recovery time) is preferable to living with the pain of body shame.

Understanding the power of body shame and the concomitant drive for bodily (in)visibility, through the phenomenological and social constructionist accounts, yields a richer understanding of the mechanisms behind the drive for normalization of the body for contemporary women and, furthermore, an understanding of how beauty practices are being increasingly conflated with biomedical discourse. As normative aesthetic standards strive to ever unattainable ideals, more elaborate, expensive and specialized beauty practices, through the guise of medicine, have been, and will continue to be, developed. The desire for anonymity, whose blandness ensures a general social acceptance, coupled with the desire for health, whose physical ease ensures agency and intentionality, are driving women to see cosmetic surgery as a viable means to ensure the avoidance of stigma and the concomitant augmentation of social capital. The drive to embody the normate yet to be oneself, to become ordinary yet remain individual, to be indistinguishable but unique demonstrates this seemingly contradictory state of wanting to be seen and 'in play,' but to remain invisible: to be an (in)visible body.

When considering the political implications of visibility and invisibility, especially for marginalized groups, it becomes apparent that cosmetic surgery practices are not merely about aesthetics, and hence somehow politically trivial. Instead, these practices intersect the cultural politics of shame and issues regarding dominance, race, gender, disability and struggles for social and political inclusion. As Edmonds notes, cosmetic surgery is intimately tied up with the social exclusion of marginalised groups and this is masked by its medicalization, and hence apparent inherent legitimacy, and also by its tendency to isolate individuals and to position aesthetic norms as a personal rather than political concern. Edmonds argues that cosmetic surgery, "enables the aged, the abandoned, the unemployed, the nonwhite, the unloved, to *name* their condition an aesthetic defect and objectify it in their bodies."[119] Instead of seeing their exclusion as a political problem arising from broader social structures which inherently disadvantage or disempower them, marginalized people are felt to be responsible for their own exclusion. It is precisely this tendency within neoliberalism, which emphasises 'personal choice' and 'self-transformation,' that collapses serious political injustices into issues that can be remedied through consumer choices. This "repressive politics of personal responsibility,"[120] means that those who are experiencing social exclusion as a result of the body not conforming to the prevailing sexist, ageist, racist, able-ist normative values see this as a personal failing—their shame is legitimated—and they merely need to invest in a product, service or procedure that can ameliorate their embodied dissatisfaction. As Edmonds notes: "There now seems to be an almost inverse process of reclassifying the socially excluded as 'aesthetically suffering.'"[121] The point is that cosmetic surgery, driven by body shame, is being utilized by marginalized individuals—female, disabled, raced, transgendered and others—as a means to achieve recognition through (in)visibility.

NOTES

1. Debra Gimlin, "Cosmetic Surgery: Paying for Your Beauty," in *Feminist Frontiers, 6th Edition*, eds. L. Richardson, V. Taylor, and N. Whittier (New York: McGraw-Hill, 2004), 95.

2. Foucault intended his reflections in *Discipline and Punish* to be an exploration of the consequences and implications which arose as a result of the shift from a system of justice and punishment that expresses itself through the violent spectacle of public execution to a system that uses incarceration, control and confinement as a source of retribution. He famously opens *Discipline and Punish* with the graphic description of the torture and quartering of a condemned man, Damiens the regicide, as recounted by the *Gazette d'Amsterdam* on April 1, 1757: "the flesh will be torn from his breasts, arms thighs and calves with red-hot pincers, his right hand . . . burnt away with sulphur, and, on those places where the flesh will be torn away, poured molten lead, boiling oil, burning resin, wax and sulphur . . . and then his body drawn and quartered by four horses." Foucault, *Discipline and Punish*, 3–5.

3. A note on terminology: cosmetic (or aesthetic) surgery is used to denote elective and medically unnecessary surgery performed solely to enhance the appearance of otherwise healthy patients. Plastic surgery, in contrast, is a medical specialty which is concerned with the restoration of form and function and includes reconstructive surgery, microsurgery and the treatment of burns. Although cosmetic surgery is a sub-speciality of plastic surgery, it should be noted that much plastic surgery is not cosmetic, as it is considered *treatment* rather than *enhancement*. For the purposes of this work, I will use the term 'cosmetic surgery' to denote elective surgery that is undertaken for solely aesthetic reasons and also to denote surgeries that are undertaken for purportedly psychological reasons.

4. See: Deborah A. Sullivan, *Cosmetic Surgery: The Cutting Edge of Commercial Medicine in America* (New Jersey: Rutgers University Press, 2001).

5. Gilman, *Making the Body Beautiful*, xviii–xix.

6. As market demand has increased dramatically, the cost of the most popular cosmetic procedures has dropped considerably. Almost 70 percent of cosmetic surgery recipients have annual incomes of less than US$40,000. Furthermore, in some countries, such as Brazil, loans are frequently and readily given for cosmetic procedures. For instance, see: Rosemarie Tong and Hilde Lindemann, "Beauty Under the Knife: A Feminist Appraisal of Cosmetic Surgery," in *Cutting to the Core: Exploring the Ethics of Contested Surgeries*, ed. David Benatar (Lanham, MD: Rowman & Littlefield, 2006). Also see: Alexander Edmonds, "'Engineering the Erotic': Aesthetic Medicine and Modernization in Brazil," in *Cosmetic Surgery: A Feminist Primer*, eds. Cressida J. Heyes and Meredith Jones (Farnham, UK: Ashgate Publishing Company, 2009).

7. Botox is the commercial name for Botulinum Toxin Type A, a diluted form of a lethal drug which paralyses muscle tissue preventing the formation of wrinkles while eradicating existing lines. Botox is by far the most popular non-surgical cosmetic procedure.

8. ASAPS, "Cosmetic Surgery National Data Bank Statistics," ed. The American Society for Aesthetic Plastic Surgery (New York, 2013), 5.

9. See: John Connell, "Medical Tourism: Sea, Sun, Sand and . . . Surgery," *Medical Tourism* vol. 27, no. 1093–1100 (2006).

10. ASAPS, "Cosmetic Surgery National Data Bank Statistics," 3.

11. Cressida J. Heyes and Meredith Jones, "Cosmetic Surgery in the Age of Gender," in *Cosmetic Surgery: A Feminist Primer*, eds. Cressida J. Heyes and Meredith Jones (Farnham, UK: Ashgate Publishing Company, 2009), 3.

12. Ibid., 12. See also: Suzanne Fraser, "Agency Made Over?: Cosmetic Surgery and Femininity in Women's Magazines and Makeover Television," in *Cosmetic Surgery: A Feminist Primer*, eds. Cressida J. Heyes and Meredith Jones (Farnham, UK: Ashgate Publishing Company, 2009), 109–110.

13. See: Kathy Davis, "'A Dubious Equality': Men, Women and Cosmetic Surgery," *Body and Society* vol. 8, no. 1 (2002). However, these conceptions about masculinity and cosmetic surgery are shifting. See, for example: Brenda R. Weber, "What Makes the Man?: Television Makeovers, Made-Over Masculinity, and Male Body Image," *International Journal of Men's Health* vol. 5, no. 3 (2006).

14. For a discussion on the Dutch regulations regarding publicly funded cosmetic surgery procedures see: Henri Wijsbek, "How to Regulate a Practice: The Case of Cosmetic Surgery," *Ethical Theory and Moral Practice* vol. 4 (2001).

15. Kathy Davis, *Dubious Equalities and Embodied Differences: Cultural Studies on Cosmetic Surgery* (New York: Rowman & Littlefield Publishers, 2003), 76.

16. Ibid., 85.

17. Northrop, *Reflecting on Cosmetic Surgery*, 6.

18. See: Henri Wijsbek, "The Pursuit of Beauty: The Enforcement of Aesthetics or a Freely Adopted Lifestyle?," *Journal of Medical Ethics* vol. 26 (2000), 63–64. See also: Stephen Coleman, "A Defense of Cosmetic Surgery," in *Cutting to the Core: Exploring the Ethics of Contested Surgeries*, ed. David Benatar (Lanham, MD: Rowman & Littlefield, 2006).

19. See: Heyes, "Normalisation and the Psychic Life of Cosmetic Surgery," 63.

20. Thomas Pruzinsky, "Psychological Factors in Cosmetic Surgery: Recent Developments in Patient Care," *Plastic Surgery Nursing* vol. 13, no. 2 (1993), 64. Cited in: Suzanne Fraser, "The Agent Within: Agency Repertoires in Medical Discourse on Cosmetic Surgery," *Australian Feminist Studies* vol. 18, no. 4 (2003), 33.

21. Fraser, "The Agent Within," 33.

22. Alexander Edmonds, *Pretty Modern: Beauty, Sex and Plastic Surgery in Brazil* (Durham: Duke University Press, 2010), 114.

23. Ibid.

24. See: Luna Dolezal, "The Body, Gender, and Biotechnology in Jeanette Winterson's *The Stone Gods*," *Literature and Medicine* Forthcoming (2014).

25. Rachel Alpha Johnston Hurst, "Negotiating Femininity With and Through Mother-Daughter and Patient-Surgeon Relationships in Cosmetic Surgery Narratives," *Women's Studies International Forum* vol. 35 (2012), 447.

26. Ibid.

27. Edmonds, *Pretty Modern*, 115.

28. Davis, *Dubious Equalities and Embodied Differences*, 62.

29. Kathy Davis, "'My Body is My Art': Cosmetic Surgery as Feminist Utopia," in *Feminist Theory and the Body: A Reader*, eds. Janet Price and Margrit Shildrick (Edinburgh: Edinburgh University Press, 1999), 455.

30. Ibid., 460.

31. Debra Gimlin notes that in other healthcare systems where cosmetic surgery is unavailable on the national health service and comes at a great personal expense to its recipients, such as in the United States, different motivations may be cited by cosmetic surgery recipients, such as individual autonomy and choice. See: Debra Gimlin, "Accounting for Cosmetic Surgery in the USA and Great Britain: A Cross-Cultural Analysis of Women's Narratives," *Body and Society* vol. 13, no. 1 (2007), 45.

32. Rebecca Huss-Ashmore, "'The Real Me': Therapeutic Narrative in Cosmetic Surgery," *Expedition* vol. 42, no. 3 (2000).

33. Debra Gimlin, "The Absent Body Project: Cosmetic Surgery as a Response to Bodily Dys-Appearance," *Sociology* vol. 40, no. 4 (2006), 704.

34. Ibid.: 711, 713.

35. Patricia Gagné and Deanna McGaughey, "Designing Women: Cultural Hegemony and the Exercise of Power among Women Who Have Undergone Elective Mammoplasty," *Gender and Society* vol. 16, no. 6 (2002), 821.

36. Gimlin, "Accounting for Cosmetic Surgery in the USA and Great Britain," 52.

37. Kathy Davis, *Reshaping the Female Body: The Dilemma of Cosmetic Surgery* (London: Routledge, 1995), 102.

38. Davis, *Dubious Equalities and Embodied Differences*, 77. It should of course be acknowledged that some people undertake cosmetic surgery in order to distinguish or differentiate their bodies. Ruth Holliday and Jacqueline Sanchez Taylor cite the examples of several 'non-normative' surgeries. See: Ruth Holliday and Jacqueline Sanchez Taylor, "Aesthetic Surgery As False Beauty," *Feminist Theory* vol. 7, no. 2 (2006). Consider also the surgeries undertaken by the French feminist performance artist ORLAN as part of her art practice. See, for example: Davis, "'My Body is My Art.'"

39. Nikki Sullivan, "'BIID'?: Queer (Dis)Orientations and the Phenomenology of 'Home,'" in *Feminist Phenomenology and Medicine*, eds. Lisa Folkmarson Käll and Kristin Zeiler (Albany: SUNY Press, 2014), 123.

40. See: Cressida J. Heyes, *Self-Transformations: Foucault, Ethics and Normalized Bodies*. (Oxford: Oxford University Press, 2007).

41. Sullivan, "'BIID?,'" 120.

42. Lanei Rodemeyer, "Feminism, Phenomenology and Hormones" in *Feminist Phenomenology and Medicine*, eds. Lisa Folkmarson Käll and Kristin Zeiler (Albany: SUNY Press, 2014), 190–192.

43. Ibid., 191.

44. Ibid.

45. For instance see: Catherine Hakim, *Honey Money: The Power of Erotic Capital*, (London: Allen Lane, 2011).

46. See, for instance: Jonathan Watts, "A Tall Order," *The Guardian*, Monday, 15 December 2003.

47. Coleman, "A Defense of Cosmetic Surgery," 176. Emphasis in original.

48. Ibid.

49. Ibid.

50. For a feminist discussion of medicalization and women's bodies see: Catherine Kohler Riessman, "Women and Medicalization: A New Perspective," in *The Politics of Women's Bodies: Sexuality, Appearance and Behaviour*, ed. Rose Weitz (Oxford: Oxford University Press, 2003). Furthermore, as Virginia Blum illustrates, heterosexual patriarchal dynamics— where women are passive and dominated and men are active and dominating—are played out in the male surgeon/female patient relationship. She writes: "insofar as conventional heterosexual male and female sexualities are experienced psychically and represented culturewide as the relationship between the one who penetrates and the one penetrated, surgical interventions can function as very eroticized versions of the sexual act." Virginia L. Blum, *Flesh Wounds: The Culture of Cosmetic Surgery* (Berkeley: University of California Press, 2003), 45.

51. These quotes come from advertisements featured in *Vogue* magazine (British edition, June 2011) and *In Style* magazine (May 2011).

52. Edmonds, *Pretty Modern*, 114.

53. Kathryn Pauly Morgan, "Women and the Knife: Cosmetic Surgery and the Colonization of Women's Bodies," in *The Politics of Women's Bodies: Sexuality, Appearance and Behaviour*, ed. Rose Weitz (Oxford: Oxford University Press, 1998), 151.

54. Keith Robertson, "Liposuction," *Rejuvenate*, Autumn 2007, 10–11.

55. Foucault, *Discipline and Punish*, 199.

56. Michel Foucault, *The Birth of the Clinic: An Archaeology of Medical Perception*, trans. A. M. Sheridan (London: Routledge, 2003).

57. Nelson Powell and Brian Humphreys, *Proportions of the Aesthetic Face* (*American Academy of Facial Plastic and Reconstructive Surgery Monograph*) (New York: Thieme Publishing Group, 1984).

58. Llewellyn Negrin, "Cosmetic Surgery and the Eclipse of Identity," *Body and Society* vol. 8, no. 4 (2002): 27.

59. Eugenia Kaw, "Medicalization of Racial Features: Asian American Women and Cosmetic Surgery," *Medical Anthropology Quarterly* vol. 7, no. 1 (1993).

60. Cressida J. Heyes, "All Cosmetic Surgery is 'Ethnic': Asian Eyelids, Feminist Indignation, and the Politics of Whiteness," in *Cosmetic Surgery: A Feminist Primer*, eds. Cressida J. Heyes and Meredith Jones (Farnham, UK: Ashgate Publishing Company, 2009), 191.

61. In 2013, 22 percent of all cosmetic procedures were performed on racial and ethnic minorities in the United States. It is unclear how many of these procedures can be considered to be 'ethnic cosmetic surgery' in the sense that they are normalizing to a white aesthetic ideal.

62. Edmonds, *Pretty Modern*, 145.

63. Heyes, *Self-Transformations*, 99.

64. Heyes, "All Cosmetic Surgery is 'Ethnic,'" 203.

65. Heyes, *Self-Transformations*, 98.

66. See: Sara Goering, "Conformity Through Cosmetic Surgery: The Medical Erasure of Race and Disability," in *Science and Other Cultures*, eds. Robert Figueroa and Sandra Harding (New York: Routledge, 2003).

67. E. Lewandowicz and J. Kruk-Jeromin, "The Indications and Plan of Plastic Operations in Children with Down's Syndrome.," *Acta Chirurgiae Plasticae* vol. 37, no. 2 (1995).

68. Alastair V. Campbell, *The Body in Bioethics* (London: Routledge, 2009), 82–83.

69. Morgan, "Women and the Knife," 157.

70. Bordo, *Twilight Zones*, 44

71. Edmonds, *Pretty Modern*, 115.

72. Bordo, *Twilight Zones*, 44.

73. Morgan, "Women and the Knife," 148. Emphasis in original.

74. Heyes, *Self-Transformations*, 106.

75. Although there are very low mortality rates in cosmetic surgery (the ASAPS estimates about one death in fifty thousand procedures) there are many potential complications that come with general anaesthetic and surgery of any kind. Furthermore, cosmetic surgery runs the further risks of infection, bleeding, blood clots, skin death or necrosis, asymmetry, numbness or tingling, skin irregularities and scarring. Furthermore, recovery can be painful and prolonged.

76. Anthony Elliott, *Making the Cut: How Cosmetic Surgery Is Transforming Our Lives*, (London: Reaktion Books, 2008), 9.

77. Northrop, *Reflecting on Cosmetic Surgery*, 110.

78. Ibid., 173.

79. Katherine J. Morris, "The Graceful, the Ungraceful and the Disgraceful," in *Reading Sartre: On Phenomenology and Existentialism*, ed. J. Webber (London: Routledge, 2011), 134.

80. Davis, *Reshaping the Female Body*, 85.

81. Ibid., 83.

82. Northrop, *Reflecting on Cosmetic Surgery*: 171.

83. Blum, *Flesh Wounds*, 274–275.

84. See, for example Heyes's discussion of transgender in chapter 2, 'Feminist Solidarity after Queer Theory,' in: Heyes, *Self-Transformations*, 38–62.

85. Bordo, "Twenty Years in the Twilight Zone," 24.

86. See, for example: Cressida J. Heyes, "Diagnosing Culture: Body Dysmorphic Disorder and Cosmetic Surgery," *Body and Society* vol. 15, no. 4 (2009): 79–80. Also see: Gilman, *Making the Body Beautiful*, 36–42.

87. See: Virginia Braun, "Selling the 'Perfect' Vulva," in *Cosmetic Surgery: A Feminist Primer*, eds. Cressida J. Heyes and Meredith Jones (Farnham, UK: Ashgate Publishing Company, 2009).

88. Bordo, "Twenty Years in the Twilight Zone," 28.

89. Leder, *The Absent Body*, 98.

90. Northrop, *Reflecting on Cosmetic Surgery*, 172.

91. Ibid., 178.
92. Heyes, "Normalisation and the Psychic Life of Cosmetic Surgery," 60, 67.
93. See: Ibid., 63.
94. David B. Sarwer, "Cosmetic Surgery and Changes in Body Image," in *Body Image: A Handbook of Theory, Research and Clinical Practice*, ed. T. H. Cash and T. Pruzinsky (New York: The Guilford Press, 2002), 425. Emphasis added.
95. Blum, *Flesh Wounds*, 274.
96. See: Heyes, "Diagnosing Culture," 86.
97. Individuals suffering from BDD regularly seek out cosmetic surgery. For instance, in a sample of 188 individuals with BDD, Phillips and Diaz found that 131 sought out cosmetic surgery and 109 ended up receiving cosmetic surgical, dental, dermatological or other medical treatments. However, the majority of people with BDD don't benefit from cosmetic treatments and feel their appearance hasn't improved at all or has maybe even worsened. See: Phillips and Diaz, "Gender Differences in Body Dysmorphic Disorder."
98. Heyes cites the example of a risk management chapter in a cosmetic surgery textbook entitled 'Guidelines for Preoperative Screening of Patients,' where patients are explicitly classified into types, such as 'the VIP,' 'demanding' and 'secretive,' in order to determine those unlikely to benefit from surgery. See: Heyes, "Diagnosing Culture," 87.
99. See: Ibid.
100. Quoted in: Bordo, "Twenty Years in the Twilight Zone," 26–27.
101. Eva Wiseman, "Would Madam Like a Nose Job with Her Sandwich," *The Observer Magazine* 2010, 56. Emphasis added.
102. Davis, *Dubious Equalities and Embodied Differences*, 76–77.
103. Northrop, *Reflecting on Cosmetic Surgery*, 5.
104. Heyes, "Diagnosing Culture," 77.
105. Ibid., 78.
106. Alex Kuczynski, *Beauty Junkies: Under the Skin of the Cosmetic Surgery Industry* (London: Vermilion, 2007), 101. The British Government Department of Health information brochure for those seeking out cosmetic surgery implicitly questions this conception of cosmetic surgery as offering a psychological 'cure,' without explicitly condemning these practices. It urges cosmetic surgery patients to reconsider their "reasons" and "expectations" for seeking out surgery, and to perhaps instead seek out a counselor or psychologist, the brochure asks: "Is it reasonable or likely that a change in your appearance will radically change your life?" "Information for Patients: Considering Cosmetic Surgery," ed. Department of Health (UK) (2005).
107. Davis, *Dubious Equalities and Embodied Differences*, 74.
108. Davis, "'My Body is My Art,'" 460.
109. Edmonds, *Pretty Modern*, 114.
110. Quoted in: Inez de Beaufort et al., "Beauty and the Doctor: Moral Issues in Health Care with Regard to Appearance," ed. European Commission Research on Bioethics (Erasmus University, Rotterdam, 2000).
111. Wijsbek, "The Pursuit of Beauty," 456.
112. Gail Weiss, "Uncosmetic Surgeries in an Age of Normativity," in *Feminist Phenomenology and Medicine*, eds. Kristin Zeiler and Lisa Folkmarson Käll (Albany: SUNY Press, 2014), 105. Emphasis in original.
113. Edmonds, *Pretty Modern*, 117.
114. Jeanette Winterson, *The Stone Gods* (London: Penguin, 2009), 19.
115. See: Dolezal, "The Body, Gender, and Biotechnology in Jeanette Winterson's *The Stone Gods*."
116. Linda Martin Alcoff, "Merleau-Ponty and Feminist Theory on Experience," in *Chiasms: Merleau-Ponty's Notion of Flesh*, eds. Fred Evans and Leonard Lawlor (Albany: SUNY Press, 2000), 252.
117. See: Diana Tietjens Meyers, "Feminism and Women's Autonomy: The Challenge of Female Genital Cutting," *Metaphilosophy* vol. 31, no. 5 (2000).
118. Victoria Pitts-Taylor, "Becoming/Being a Cosmetic Surgery Patient: Semantic Instability and the Intersubjective Self," *Studies in Gender and Sexuality* vol. 10 (2009), 120.
119. Edmonds, *Pretty Modern*, 114.

120. Phipps, *The Politics of the Body*, 18.
121. Edmonds, *Pretty Modern*, 114.

Conclusion

This book has sought to investigate the concept of body shame and explore its significance when considering philosophical accounts of embodied subjectivity, especially aiming to provide phenomenological reflections on how the body is shaped by social forces. As we have seen, body shame as a topic of theoretical inquiry is compelling because it reaches to the heart of what it means to be human. It is fundamental not only to how we experience our own bodies, playing a key role in the construction of the body schema, the habit body and the 'seen body,' but, furthermore, it is also a fundamental feature of intersubjective relations, shaping our experience of Others and the broader milieu. In this sense, shame is integral for identity formation and plays a key role in development and socialization; it shapes us and keeps us in check. As we have seen, shame does not occur in an isolated subject, sealed off from others and the world, instead it is, as Seigworth and Gregg aptly describe, a "specific explosion of mind, body, place and history."[1] In short, to come to an understanding of how individual bodies are shaped by the broader social world and its normative forces, I have argued that we must investigate shame.

To this end, chapters 1 to 3 explored several leading philosophical accounts of embodiment in order to demonstrate that body shame is a necessary and inevitable component of embodied subjectivity. In chapter 4, a phenomenology of self-presentation was outlined, discussing body shame's fundamental role in social interaction and cultural politics. Chapters 5 and 6, through a feminist analysis of appearance management and cosmetic surgery, explored the oppressive potential of body shame within intersubjective, social and political relations.

In chapter 1, shame was introduced as a philosophical and existential concept. In particular, body shame was defined and the cases of acute body shame and chronic body shame were delimited. It is worth reiterating the terminological issues. In its acute form, where body shame arises as a result of minor and unexpected infractions as a result of the body or comportment, body shame is more commonly termed 'embarrassment.' For the purposes of simplicity, I employed the term 'shame' throughout this work to indicate a whole range of self-conscious emotions including embarrassment, humiliation, mortification, and so forth. Employing the term 'shame,' I did not wish to offer an exaggerated account of social reality and at times 'shame' in fact indicated 'milder' or less intense affects such as embarrassment or social anxiety.

It was seen that body shame is an experience that has three layers or aspects: the personal, the intersubjective and the socio-cultural and political. As such, in order to elucidate the significance of body shame, chapters 2 and 3 explored these three layers in turn, focusing on the experiences of bodily visibility and invisibility in particular, while also offering a critical analysis of several leading philosophical accounts of embodied subjectivity through phenomenology and social theory.

In chapter 2, a phenomenological account of embodiment was examined primarily through the work of Edmund Husserl and Maurice Merleau-Ponty. This account revealed the conditions of meaningful embodied experience, exploring features of embodiment such as motor intentionality, the habit body, the body schema, skill acquisition, dys-appearance and bodily invisibility and visibility. These key phenomenological features of embodiment were seen to be integral to understanding and elucidating the shame experience. In this chapter, I also considered Jean-Paul Sartre's account of the intersubjective constitution of reflective self-consciousness, exploring the experience of body shame as it arises within intercorporeal relations. As we saw, Sartre's phenomenological ontology is concerned with the role of the Other in the constitution of individual embodied subjectivity. Sartre argues that reflective self-awareness only arises as a result of intersubjective relations; the subject must be 'seen' by others in order to be able to 'see' the self. Shame is not insignificant to Sartre. Indeed, he discusses it at some length and posits shame as a structural, and necessary, part of intersubjective embodied relations. In this chapter, the experiences of the 'seen body,' objectification and alienation which occur in body shame were examined. Hence, in chapter 2, I provided some reflections on a possible phenomenology of body shame, examining social dys-appearance and the experience of 'binding.' Although the phenomenological account of body shame provides an important description of its structural and experiential features, its focus is largely limited to the individual subject.

While Sartre's account does elucidate the experience of shame within intersubjective and self-evaluative experiences, he largely omits any analysis of broader social structures, such as institutions and social, cultural and political norms, which shape and determine shame experiences. Hence, in chapter 3, I turned to consider the work of two social thinkers, Michel Foucault and Norbert Elias, both of whom give sustained attention to describing the social shaping of the body. Both Foucault and Elias use analyses of historical change and socio-cultural structures in order to better understand contemporary modes of body management. Criticizing phenomenological approaches to embodied subjectivity, Foucault offers a critical historical analysis of the manner in which bodies are embedded into social systems and institutions and how those structures can colour and shape aspects of embodied life. Although Foucault does not explicitly discuss shame in his analysis of discipline and embodiment, key to his discussion are several features of the shame experience, such as surveillance, objectification, alienation, internalization and normalization.

Norbert Elias, on the other hand, explicitly draws out how shame is an important mechanism at play when understanding how the body subject takes on particular modes of body comportment within certain social contexts. In his theory of the civilizing process, Elias draws connections between the seen body, social control, body shame, normalization and internalization, demonstrating the interdependence of bodies and the importance of maintaining social bonds. As we have seen, the civilizing process is driven by a desire to avoid social exclusion, or stigma, and to secure and maintain social standing, hence ensuring acceptance and recognition within the social group.

As noted, there is an interesting tension between phenomenological and social constructionist accounts of embodiment; they seem to give two opposing, yet undeniably existent, views. On the one hand, phenomenology describes the body subject as a constituting agent, where the body acts as 'the organ of the will' opening a field of meaningful engagement with the world. On the other hand, social constructionism describes a body shaped and constrained by external social contingencies; the body that Foucault describes (in his early work at least) is, for the most part, docile and disciplined and scant attention is paid to how the subject experiences the power structures which shape and tame the body. Forging a connection between the two opposing views of phenomenology and social constructionism through an understanding of the role of body shame and the phenomenology of self-presentation was, in part, the aim of chapter 4. Looking at these two philosophical approaches together, as we have seen, gives a richer and more complete account of the comprehensive conditions of situated embodied existence. Furthermore, it has been seen that body shame is a structural and necessary part of embodied experience; it plays a fundamental role in the formation of the body schema and the habit body, in motor intentionality and in skill acquisition. Hence, as an experience that can be described phenomenologically, but is at the same time determined by prevailing norms and mores, body shame gives insight into precisely how the body is shaped by social forces.

Moreover, the ideas explored in the work of Sartre, Foucault and Elias demonstrate that impression management and self-presentation are central to embodied life. It is not as though self-presentation follows as some sort of second order concern after phenomenological experiences of motor action and perception are established. Instead, as we have seen, these features of experience are entangled such that one cannot be said to precede the other. The seen body, like the body schema, isn't optional or secondary to consciousness, but instead is an inherent part of the structure of reflective self-awareness. As such, self-presentation and body management play constitutive roles in subjectivity. Furthermore, body shame is a structural feature in the constant production of subjectivity and reflective self-consciousness.

As a result, the phenomenological characteristics of body shame coupled with its inherent social nature, play an important role in understanding how the subject acquires a particular body idiom, and is 'shaped' by the cultural, institutional and social milieu of which it is a part. Body shame can tell us something about how the individual body is connected to, and ultimately shaped by, socio-cultural norms and mores without reducing the description of the body subject to one of social determinism where the subject is inscribed by external forces, lacking autonomy and agency. Understanding body shame, and its ubiquity in social relations, demonstrates that self-presentation, bodily visibility and (in)visiblity are neither trivial nor insignificant, but instead these concerns play constitutive and foundational roles in subjectivity. Essential features of embodiment such as skill acquisition and the body schema are shaped by the incessant desire to avoid, circumvent and minimize intrusions of body shame. When considered in this light, shame (or the possibility of shame) is not only ubiquitous, but in some cases it is necessary.

However, as noted in chapter 4 in the discussion of the cultural politics of shame, there are also times when body shame can become chronic and, as a result, oppressive. Instead of being instrumental for realizing the full expression of embodied social life, chronic body shame can become compromising. Body shame is intimately linked to the powerful fear of stigma and social exclusion. It acts as a mechanism that ensures one's recognition and belongingness within a social group. When it is mobilized in order to disadvantage a marginalized group, body shame can have political consequences. Overcoming shame is central to the struggle for recognition, both in terms of interpersonal relations, and also in terms of the struggle for rights and social standing within one's social group. As a result, concerns around self-presentation and avoiding body shame, especially with regard to normalized standards, are far from trivial. In fact, when it comes to the body within social relations, looks and appearances are crucial. Flawed or failed self-presentation can have devastating consequences. In chapters 5 and 6, these themes were explored with respect to the experience of Western women, regarding appearance management and beauty norms within the neoliberal, patriarchal structures of late modernity.

In chapter 5, I discussed the relationship between shame, gender and the female body. In this chapter, the themes of surveillance, objectification, alienation and internalization, as they relate to the experience of female embodiment, were revisited. Furthermore, the pernicious normalizing and homogenizing tendencies of contemporary neoliberalism were examined, especially when considering the internalization of norms regarding appearance. It was demonstrated that body shame plays a central role in female embodiment and that this can have negative consequences for women in terms of their agency, transcendence and subjectivity.

Chapter 6 was concerned with a feminist analysis of cosmetic surgery and body shame. It was shown that cosmetic surgery is often regarded as a practice that can ameliorate psychological dissatisfaction with body image and alleviate chronic body shame. However, I argued that body shame is often exacerbated, rather than eradicated, by the cosmetic surgery industry. Examining the conflation of beauty and biomedicine as occurs in cosmetic surgery practices, particularly as it affects women, the themes of surveillance, normalization, internalization and objectification were again explored. It was demonstrated that if women are making decisions about cosmetic surgery from a place of body shame and emotional vulnerability, within an oppressive social system, then the rhetoric of empowerment and personal responsibility frequently employed by the cosmetic surgery industry must be critically examined.

When considering the political implications of visibility and invisibility, especially for marginalized groups, it is apparent that cosmetic surgery practices are not merely about aesthetics, and hence somehow politically trivial. Instead, these practices intersect the cultural politics of shame and issues regarding dominance, race, gender, disability and struggles for social and political inclusion. Cosmetic surgery is intimately tied up with the social exclusion of marginalised groups and this is masked by its medicalization, and hence inherent legitimacy, and also by its tendency to isolate individuals and to position aesthetic concerns as personal, rather than political. Instead of seeing their exclusion as a political problem arising from broader social structures which inherently disadvantage or disempower them, marginalized individuals are made to feel responsible for their own exclusion. It is precisely this tendency within neoliberalism, which emphasises 'personal choice' and 'self-transformation,' that collapses serious political injustices into issues that can be remedied through consumer choices. The point is that cosmetic surgery, driven by body shame, is being utilized by marginalized bodies—female, disabled, raced, transgendered and others—to attempt to achieve recognition or (in)visibility.

As I noted in the introduction, I covered a lot of conceptual ground in this work, and naturally, due to space restraints, many of the topics I broached were not able to be explored fully. In particular, I did not discuss child development or the formation of reflective self-consciousness in infants. Although I examined various manifestations of body shame, I did not attempt to unify body shame with other varieties of shame, nor did I differentiate shame from other self-conscious emotions. Furthermore, I did not discuss psychoanalytic theories of shame, nor any theories of emotions or of emotion types. I did not discuss the origins or exhaustively define the features of the concepts of stigma, recognition, acceptance and belonging. Furthermore, in my analysis of chronic body shame, the cultural politics of shame, beauty ideals and cosmetic surgery, I mentioned but did not explore at length several issues in bioethics, such as autonomy, medical consent, medical necessity and the treatment/enhancement distinction.

Hence, there are many research directions that are opened up when considering body shame, as it is a concept that straddles a multitude of disciplines and thematic areas. When considering the oppressive potential of chronic body shame, exploring the consequences of emotional vulnerability is of great interest when considering issues such as autonomy and justice within bioethics, especially when critically examining medical consumerism and enhancement practices such as cosmetic surgery. Investigating the manner through which body shame is cultivated by the beauty-biomedicine industry through marketing strategies and beauty-health discourse is perhaps one way a site of criticism and resistance can be established.

In my own experience, cultivating a sense of meaningful autonomy and resisting norms and discipline does not involve dissolving power relations, but rather involves coming to an awareness of the power relations at play in one's own life. This awareness for me has arisen in part through research and scholarship, but also in a very significant way, through engaging in introspective body practices. The transformative potential of body practices is an insight that Foucault develops in his later work when considering the care of the self. He argues that through engaging in certain reflexive body practices one can establish a critical and reflexive relation to oneself and fashion one's own subjectivity. Through caring for oneself, Foucault argues, the body becomes a vital site for self-knowledge and self-transformation.[2]

For me, certain introspective body practices have provided me with an alternative way to regard my own body and self, cultivating an inner sensitivity, so non-observable attributes of my body, such as how I feel or my embodied capacities, are given more regard than external comparisons to normalized ideals regarding appearance. As such, I agree with Cressida Heyes's insightful reflections on the possible role that introspective body practices can play in one's own journey of self-transformation. In her book *Self-Transformations*, Heyes discusses how practices like yoga can help

phenomenology is constantly in motion – doesn't seek for solutions or resolution so much as continued contextual analysis.

women find an alternative to the normalizing body pressures that infuse modern life.[3] Instead of encouraging women to strive for impossible body ideals and perhaps turn to other body-shaping activities, such as dieting or cosmetic surgery, an introspective body practice can cultivate an alternative awareness and understanding of one's own body. Yoga and other practices like it, which have the potential to operate outside the limiting logics of consumerism, neoliberalism and scientific discourse, provide an alternative and compassionate vocabulary with which one can regard the body and the self; this is a vocabulary beyond comparisons and criticisms and outside of the limiting shame-inducing logic under which women's bodies are usually positioned.[4] The body's uniqueness is not compared to some ideal and through these practices new ways to understand and relate to one's self and one's body can be established, and transformation and healing can take place. Through this sort of inquiry, discovering individual and collective strategies to forge embodied resistance to the normalizing tendencies of neoliberal patriarchy is a fruitful and important area for further research and feminist reflection.

This book has sought to demonstrate that body shame is far from an experience of marginal importance, but instead is an integral part of embodied subjectivity. As an experience which bridges our personal, individual and embodied experience with the social world which contains us, body shame can shed light on how the social is embodied; that is, how the body—experienced in its phenomenological primacy by the subject—becomes a social and cultural artifact, shaped by external forces and demands. In short, when investigating the nature of embodied subjectivity and the inseparability of the subject, body and world, it has been seen that body shame is not only important, but is paramount.

NOTES

1. Gregory J. Seigworth and Melissa Gregg, "An Inventory of Shimmers," in *The Affect Theory Reader*, eds. Gregory J. Seigworth and Melissa Gregg (Durham: Duke University Press, 2010), 81.

2. See, for example: Foucault, "Technologies of the Self."

3. See: Heyes, *Self-Transformations*, 128–132.

4. However, it should be noted that practices like yoga have been colonized by the limiting logic of neoliberal consumerism, especially with respect to women's bodies. The contemporary 'yoga industry' propagates limiting ideas about ideal and acceptable bodies which for the most part follow the narrow normative standards of the mainstream beauty, diet, grooming and fashion industries. See: Luna Dolezal,"Yoga for Women: The Problem of Beautiful Bodies," in *Yoga—Philosophy For Everyone: Bending Mind and Body*, ed. Liz Stillwaggon Swan (Wiley Blackwell, 2011).

Bibliography

Ahmed, Sara. *The Cultural Politics of Emotion*. Edinburgh: Edinburgh University Press, 2004.

Alcoff, Linda Martin. "Merleau-Ponty and Feminist Theory on Experience." In *Chiasms: Merleau-Ponty's Notion of Flesh*, edited by Fred Evans and Leonard Lawlor. Albany: SUNY Press, 2000.

Andrews, Bernice. "Bodily Shame as a Mediator between Abusive Experiences and Depression." *Journal of Abnormal Psychology* vol. 104 (1995): 277–285.

Aquinas, St. Thomas. *Summa Theologae, Volume 21*. Translated by John Patrick Reid. London: Blackfriars, 1965.

Aristotle. *The 'Art' of Rhetoric*. Translated by John Henry Freese. Cambridge: Harvard University Press, 1994.

———. *The Nicomachean Ethics*. Translated by J. A. K. Thomson. London: Penguin Books, 2004.

———. *The Nicomachean Ethics*. Translated by David Ross. Edited by Lesley Brown. Oxford: Oxford University Press, 2009.

ASAPS. "Cosmetic Surgery National Data Bank Statistics." edited by The American Society for Aesthetic Plastic Surgery. New York, 2013.

Babock, Mary K., and John Sabini. "On Differentiating Embarrassment from Shame." *European Journal of Social Psychology* vol. 20, no. 2 (1990): 151–169.

Bartky, Sandra Lee. *Femininity and Domination: Studies in the Phenomenology of Oppression*. London: Routledge, 1990.

Baumeister, Roy F., and Mark R. Leary. "The Need to Belong: Desire for Interpersonal Attachments as a Fundamental Human Motivation." *Psychological Bulletin* vol. 117, no. 3 (1995): 497–529.

Beaufort, Inez de, Ineke Bolt, Medard Hilhorst, and Henri Wijsbek. "Beauty and the Doctor: Moral Issues in Health Care with Regard to Appearance." edited by European Commission Research on Bioethics. Rotterdam: Erasmus University, 2000.

Behnke, Elizabeth A. "Edmund Husserl's Contribution to Phenomenology of the Body in Ideas II." In *Phenomenology: Critical Concepts in Philosophy—Volume 2*, edited by Dermot Moran and Lester E. Embree, 235–264. Oxon: Routledge, 2004.

———. "The Socially Shaped Body and the Critique of Corporeal Experience." In *Sartre on the Body*, edited by Katherine J. Morris, 231–255. Baginstoke, Hampshire: Palgrave Macmillan, 2010.

———. "World without Opposite/Flesh of the World (a Carnal Introduction)." Paper presented at the Merleau-Ponty Circle, Ninth Annual Meeting, Concordia University, Montreal, September 1984.

Bentham, Jeremy. *The Panopticon Writings*. Edited by Miran Bozovic. London: Verso, 1995.

Berger, John. *Ways of Seeing*. London: Penguin, 1972.

Berlant, Lauren, Sina Najafi, and David Serlin. "The Broken Circuit: An Interview with Lauren Berlant." *Cabinet*, no. 31 (2008).

Blum, Virginia L. *Flesh Wounds: The Culture of Cosmetic Surgery*. Berkeley: University of California Press, 2003.

Bordo, Susan. "Twenty Years in the Twilight Zone." In *Cosmetic Surgery: A Feminist Primer*, edited by Cressida J. Heyes and Meredith Jones, 21–33. Farnham, UK: Ashgate Publishing Company, 2009.

———. *Twilight Zones: The Hidden Life of Cultural Images from Plato to O.J.* Berkeley: University of California Press, 1997.

———. *Unbearable Weight: Feminism, Western Culture and the Body, 10th Anniversary Edition*. Berkeley: University of California Press, 2003.

Bourdieu, Pierre. *Distinction: A Social Critique of the Judgement of Taste*. Translated by Richard Nice. London: Routledge, 1984.

———. "The Forms of Capital." In *Handbook of Theory of Research for the Sociology of Education*, edited by J. E. Richardson, 241–258. Santa Barbara: Greenwood Press, 1986.

———. *Outline of a Theory of Practice*. Translated by Richard Nice. Cambridge: Cambridge University Press, 1977.

Bourdieu, Pierre, and Loic Wacquant. *An Invitation to Reflexive Sociology*. Translated by Loic Wacquant. Cambridge: Polity, 1992.

Bouson, J. Brooks. *Embodied Shame: Uncovering Female Shame in Contemporary Women's Writings*. Albany: SUNY Press, 2009.

Braun, Virginia. "Selling the 'Perfect' Vulva." In *Cosmetic Surgery: A Feminist Primer*, edited by Cressida J. Heyes and Meredith Jones. Farnham, UK: Ashgate Publishing Company, 2009.

Brumberg, Joan Jacobs. *The Body Project: An Intimate History of American Girls*. New York: Random House, 1997.

Burkitt, Ian. "Overcoming Metaphysics: Elias and Foucault on Power and Freedom." *Philosophy of the Social Sciences* vol. 23, no. 1 (1993): 50–72.

Butler, Judith. *Gender Trouble: Feminism and the Subversion of Identity*. London: Routledge, 1990.

———. "Sexual Ideology and Phenomenological Description: A Feminist Critique of Merleau-Ponty's Phenomenology of Perception." In *The Thinking Muse*, edited by Jeffner Allen and Iris Marion Young. Bloomington: Indiana University Press, 1989.

Buytendijk, F. J. J. *Prolegomena to an Anthropological Physiology*. Translated by A. I. Orr. Pittsburgh: Duquesne University Press, 1964.

Calhoun, Cheshire. "An Apology for Moral Shame." *The Journal of Political Philosophy* vol. 12, no. 2 (2004): 127–146.

Campbell, Alastair V. *The Body in Bioethics*. London: Routledge, 2009.

Cole, Jonathan. *Pride and a Daily Marathon*. Cambridge: MIT Press, 1995.

Coleman, Stephen. "A Defense of Cosmetic Surgery." In *Cutting to the Core: Exploring the Ethics of Contested Surgeries*, edited by David Benatar, 171–182. Lanham, MD: Rowman & Littlefield, 2006.

Connell, John. "Medical Tourism: Sea, Sun, Sand and . . . Surgery." *Medical Tourism* vol. 27, (2006): 1093–1100

Cooley, Charles H. *Human Nature and the Social Order*. Glencoe, Illinois: The Free Press, 1956.

Cox, Gary. *The Sartre Dictionary*. London: Continuum, 2008.

Crossley, Nick. *Reflexive Embodiment in Contemporary Society*. New York: Open University Press, 2006.

Crozier, W. Ray. "Blushing, Shame and Social Anxiety." In *Body Shame: Conceptualisation, Research and Treatment*, edited by Paul Gilbert and Jeremy Miles, 205–218. New York: Brunner-Routledge, 2002.

———. "Social Psychological Perspectives on Shyness, Embarrassment, and Shame." In *Shyness and Embarrassment: Perspectives from Social Psychology*, edited by W. Ray Crozier. Cambridge: Cambridge University Press, 1990.

Damasio, Antonio R. *Descartes' Error: Emotion, Reason and the Human Brain.* New York: Avon Books, 1994.

Darwin, Charles. *The Expression of the Emotions in Man and Animals.* Chicago: Chicago University Press, 1965.

Davis, Kathy. *Dubious Equalities and Embodied Differences: Cultural Studies on Cosmetic Surgery.* New York: Rowman & Littlefield Publishers, 2003.

———. "'a Dubious Equality': Men, Women and Cosmetic Surgery." *Body and Society* vol. 8, no. 1 (2002): 49–65.

———. "'My Body Is My Art': Cosmetic Surgery as Feminist Utopia." In *Feminist Theory and the Body: A Reader,* edited by Janet Price Margrit Shildrick. Edinburgh: Edinburgh University Press, 1999.

———. *Reshaping the Female Body: The Dilemma of Cosmetic Surgery.* London: Routledge, 1995.

de Beauvoir, Simone. *The Second Sex.* Translated by H. M. Parshley. London: Vintage, 1997.

Deonna, Julien A., and Fabrice Teroni. "The Self of Shame." In *Emotions, Ethics and Authenticity,* edited by Mikko Salmela and Verena Mayer, 33–50. Amsterdam: John Benjamins Publishing Company, 2009.

Deonna, Julien A., Raffaele Rodogno, and Fabrice Teroni. *In Defense of Shame: The Faces of an Emotion.* Oxford: Oxford University Press, 2012.

Descartes, Rene. *The Passions of the Soul.* Translated by Stephen H. Voss. Indianapolis: Hackett Publishing Company, 1989.

Dillon, Martin C. *Merleau-Ponty's Ontology.* Evanston: Northwestern University Press, 1962.

Diprose, Rosalyn. *Corporeal Generosity: On Giving with Nietzsche, Merleau-Ponty, and Levinas.* Albany: SUNY Press, 2002.

———. "'Where' Your People from, Girl?': Belonging to Race, Gender, and Place *beneath Clouds.*" *differences: A Journal of Feminist Cultural Studies* vol. 19, no. 3 (2008): 28–58.

Dobscha, Susan. "The Changing Image of Women in American Society: What Do Pregnant Women Represent in Advertising?" *Advertising and Society Review* vol. 7, no. 3 (2006).

Dolezal, Luna. "The (In)visible Body: Feminism, Phenomenology and the Case of Cosmetic Surgery." *Hypatia* vol. 25, no. 2 (2010): 357–375.

———. "The Body, Gender, and Biotechnology in Jeanette Winterson's *The Stone Gods.*" *Literature and Medicine,* Forthcoming (2014).

———. "Reconsidering the Look in Sartre's *Being and Nothingness.*" *Sartre Studies International* vol. 18, no. 1 (2012): 9–28.

———. "The Remote Body: The Phenomenology of Telepresence and Reembodiment." *Human Technology* vol. 5, no. 2 (2009): 208–226.

———. "Yoga for Women: The Problem of Beautiful Bodies," in *Yoga—Philosophy For Everyone: Bending Mind and Body,* edited by Liz Stillwaggon Swan (Wiley Blackwell, 2011).

Dreyfus, Hubert L. "The Challenge of Merleau-Ponty's Phenomenology of Embodiment for Cognitive Science." In *Perspectives on Embodiment: The Intersections of Nature and Culture,* edited by Honi Fern Haber and Gail Weiss, 103–120. New York: Routledge, 1999.

———. "A Phenomenology of Skill Acquisition as the Basis for a Merleau-Pontian Non-Representationalist Cognitive Science." University of California, Berkeley http://ist-socrates.berkeley.edu/~hdreyfus/pdf/MerleauPontySkillCogSci.pdf (Accessed 9 September 2014).

Dworkin, Andrea. *Women-Hating.* New York: Dutton, 1974.

Earle, Sarah. "'Boobs and Bumps': Fatness and Women's Experience of Pregnancy." *Women's Studies International Forum* vol. 26, no. 3 (2003): 245–252.

Edelstein, R. S., and P. R. Shaver. "A Cross-Cultural Examination of Lexican Studies of Self-Conscious Emotions." In *The Self-Conscious Emotions: Theory and Research,* edited by J. L. Tracy, R. W. Robins and J. P. Tangney. New York: Guildford Press, 2007.

Edmonds, Alexander. "'Engineering the Erotic': Aesthetic Medicine and Modernization in Brazil." In *Cosmetic Surgery: A Feminist Primer,* edited by Cressida J. Heyes and Meredith Jones, 153–169. Farnham, UK: Ashgate Publishing Company, 2009.

————. *Pretty Modern: Beauty, Sex and Plastic Surgery in Brazil.* Durham: Duke University Press, 2010.

Elias, Norbert. *The Civilizing Process: Sociogenetic and Psychogenic Investigations, Revised Edition.* Translated by Edmund Jephcott. Edited by Eric Dunning, Johan Goudsblom and Stephen Mennell. Oxford: Blackwell, 1994.

————. *The Court Society.* Translated by Edmund Jeffcott. Oxford: Basil Blackwell Publisher, 1983.

————. "Homo Clausus: The Thinking Statues." In *On Civilization, Power, and Knowledge*, edited by Stephen Mennell and Johan Goudsblom, 269–289. Chicago: The University of Chicago Press, 1998.

————. *What Is Sociology?* Translated by Grace Morrissey and Stephen Mennell. London: Hutchinson, 1978.

Elliott, Anthony. *Making the Cut: How Cosmetic Surgery Is Transforming Our Lives.* London: Reaktion Books, 2008.

Fanon, Frantz. *Black Skin, White Masks.* Translated by Charles Lam Markman. London: Paladin, 1970.

Fisher, Linda, and Lester Embree, eds. *Feminist Phenomenology.* Kluwer Academic Publishers, 2000.

Foucault, Michel. *The Birth of the Clinic: An Archaeology of Medical Perception.* Translated by A. M. Sheridan. London: Routledge, 2003.

————. *Discipline and Punish: The Birth of the Prison.* Translated by Alan Sheridan. New York: Vintage Books, 1995.

————. "Dream, Imagination and Existence: An Introduction to Ludwig Binswanger's 'Dream and Existence.'" *Review of Existential Psychology and Psychiatry* vol. 19, no. 1 (1984–85).

————. "Forward to the English Edition." In *The Order of Things*, ix–xv. London: Routledge, 2002.

————. "Nietzsche, Genealogy, History." In *The Foucault Reader* edited by Paul Rabinow, 76–100. London: Penguin, 1984.

————. *Power/Knowledge: Selected Interviews and Other Writings, 1972–77.* Translated by Colin Gordon, Leo Marshall, John Mepham and Kate Soper. Edited by Colin Gordon. Brighton: Harvester, 1980.

————. *'Society Must Be Defended': Lectures at the College De France, 1975–1976.* Translated by David Macey. Edited by Mauro Bertani and Alessandro Fortuna. New York: Picador, 2003.

————. "The Subject and Power." In *Michel Foucault: Beyond Structuralism and Hermeneutics*, edited by Hubert Dreyfus and Paul Rabinow, 208–226. Hertfordshire: Harvester Wheatsheaf, 1982.

————. "Technologies of the Self." In *Technologies of the Self: A Seminar with Michel Foucault*, edited by Luther H. Martin, Huck Gutman and Patrick H. Hutton, 16–49. London: Tavistock, 1988.

————. *The Will to Knowledge: The History of Sexuality, Volume 1.* Translated by Robert Hurley. London: Penguin, 1998.

Fraser, Suzanne. "Agency Made Over?: Cosmetic Surgery and Femininity in Women's Magazines and Makeover Television." In *Cosmetic Surgery: A Feminist Primer*, edited by Cressida J. Heyes and Meredith Jones, 99–115. Farnham, UK: Ashgate Publishing Company, 2009.

————. "The Agent Within: Agency Repertoires in Medical Discourse on Cosmetic Surgery." *Australian Feminist Studies* vol. 18, no. 4 (2003): 27–44.

Fredrickson, Barbara L., and Tomi-Ann Roberts. "Objectification Theory: Toward Understanding Women's Lived Experiences and Mental Health Risks." *Psychology of Women Quarterly* vol. 21, (1997): 173–206.

Fredrickson, Barbara L., Tomi-Ann Roberts, Stephanie M. Noll, Diane M. Quinn, and Jean M. Twenge. "That Swimsuit Becomes You: Sex Differences in Self-Objectification, Restrained Eating, and Math Performance." *Journal of Personality and Social Psychology* vol. 75, no. 1 (1998): 269–284.

Frost, Liz. "'Doing Looks': Women, Appearance and Mental Health." In *Women's Bodies: Discipline and Transgression*, edited by Jane Arthur and Jean Grimshaw, 117–136. London: Cassell, 1999.

———. "Theorizing the Young Woman in the Body." *Body and Society* vol. 11, no. 1 (2005): 63–85.

Fuchs, Thomas. "The Phenomenology of Shame, Guilt and Body in Body Dysmorphic Disorder and Depression." *Journal of Phenomenological Psychology* vol. 33, no. 2 (2003): 223–243.

Gagné, Patricia, and Deanna McGaughey. "Designing Women: Cultural Hegemony and the Exercise of Power among Women Who Have Undergone Elective Mammoplasty." *Gender and Society* vol. 16, no. 6 (2002): 814–838.

Gallagher, Shaun. "Lived Body and Environment." In *Phenomenology: Critical Concepts in Philosophy—Volume 2*, edited by Dermot Moran and Lester E. Embree, 265–293. Oxon: Routledge, 2004.

Gallagher, Shaun, and Jonathan Cole. "Body Image and Body Schema in a Deafferented Subject." In *Body and Flesh: A Philosophical Reader*, edited by Donn Welton, 131–147. Oxford: Blackwell, 1998.

Gilbert, Paul. "Body Shame: A Biopsychological Conceptualisation and Overview, with Treatment Implications." In *Body Shame: Conceptualisation, Research and Treatment*, edited by Paul Gilbert and Jeremy Miles, 3–54. New York: Brunner-Routledge, 2002.

Gilbert, Paul, and Jeremy Miles, eds. *Body Shame: Conceptualisation, Research and Treatment*. London: Routledge, 2002.

Gilman, Sander L. *Making the Body Beautiful: A Cultural History of Aesthetic Surgery*. Princeton: Princeton University Press, 1999.

Gimlin, Debra. "The Absent Body Project: Cosmetic Surgery as a Response to Bodily Dys-Appearance." *Sociology* vol. 40, no. 4 (2006): 699–716.

———. "Accounting for Cosmetic Surgery in the USA and Great Britain: A Cross-Cultural Analysis of Women's Narratives." *Body and Society* vol. 13, no. 1 (2007): 41–60.

———. "Cosmetic Surgery: Paying for Your Beauty." In *Feminist Frontiers, 6th Edition*, edited by L. Richardson, V. Taylor and N. Whittier, 94–109. New York: McGraw-Hill, 2004.

Goering, Sara. "Conformity through Cosmetic Surgery: The Medical Erasure of Race and Disability." In *Science and Other Cultures*, edited by Robert Figueroa and Sandra Harding, 172–188. New York: Routledge, 2003.

Goffman, Erving. *Behaviour in Public Places: Notes on the Social Organization of Gatherings*. New York: The Free Press, 1963.

———. *Interaction Ritual: Essays on Face-to-Face Behaviour*. New York: Pantheon Books, 1967.

———. *The Presentation of Self in Everyday Life*. Middlesex: Penguin Books, 1959.

———. *Stigma: Notes on the Management of Spoiled Identity*. London: Penguin Books, 1990.

———. *Strategic Interaction*. Philadelphia: University of Pennsylvania Press, 1969.

Grene, Marjorie. *Sartre*. Lanham, MD: University Press of America, 1983.

———. "Sartre and the Other." *Proceedings and Addresses of the American Philosophical Association* vol. 45, (1971–1972): 22–41.

Grimshaw, Jean. "Working out with Merleau-Ponty." In *Women's Bodies: Discipline and Transgression*, edited by Jane Arthurs and Jean Grimshaw, 91–116. London: Cassell, 1999.

Guenther, Lisa. "Shame and the Temporality of Social Life." *Continental Philosophy Review* vol. 44, no. 1 (2011): 23–39.

Hakim, Catherine. *Honey Money: The Power of Erotic Capital*. London: Allen Lane, 2011.

Harrington, Austin. "Introduction: What Is Social Theory?" *Modern Social Theory: An Introduction* edited by Austin Harrington. Oxford: Oxford University Press, 2005.

Harris-Moore, Deborah. *Media and the Rhetoric of Body Perfection: Cosmetic Surgery, Weight Loss and Beauty in Popular Culture*. Farnham, UK: Ashgate, 2014.

Heyes, Cressida J. "All Cosmetic Surgery Is 'Ethnic': Asian Eyelids, Feminist Indignation, and the Politics of Whiteness." In *Cosmetic Surgery: A Feminist Primer*, edited by Cressida J. Heyes and Meredith Jones, 191–205. Farnham, UK: Ashgate Publishing Company, 2009.

———. "Diagnosing Culture: Body Dysmorphic Disorder and Cosmetic Surgery." *Body and Society* vol. 15, no. 4 (2009): 73–93.

———. "Normalisation and the Psychic Life of Cosmetic Surgery." *Australian Feminist Studies* vol. 22, no. 52 (2007): 55–71.

———. *Self-Transformations: Foucault, Ethics and Normalized Bodies.* Oxford: Oxford University Press, 2007.

Heyes, Cressida J., and Meredith Jones. "Cosmetic Surgery in the Age of Gender." In *Cosmetic Surgery: A Feminist Primer*, edited by Cressida J. Heyes and Meredith Jones, 1–17. Farnham, UK: Ashgate Publishing Company, 2009.

———, eds. *Cosmetic Surgery: A Feminist Primer.* Farnham, UK: Ashgate Publishing Company, 2009.

Holliday, Ruth, and Jacqueline Sanchez Taylor. "Aesthetic Surgery as False Beauty." *Feminist Theory* vol. 7, no. 2 (2006): 179–195.

Honneth, Axel. "Invisibility: On the Epistemology of 'Recognition.'" *Aristotelian Society Supplementary Volume* 75, no. 1 (2001): 111–126.

———. *The Struggle for Recognition: The Moral Grammar of Social Conflicts.* Translated by Joel Anderson. Cambridge, UK: Polity, 1995.

Hurst, Rachel Alpha Johnston. "Negotiating Femininity with and through Mother-Daughter and Patient-Surgeon Relationships in Cosmetic Surgery Narratives." *Women's Studies International Forum* vol. 35 (2012): 447–457.

Huss-Ashmore, Rebecca. "'the Real Me': Therapeutic Narrative in Cosmetic Surgery." *Expedition* vol. 42, no. 3 (2000): 26–38.

Husserl, Edmund. *Cartesian Meditations: An Introduction to Phenomenology.* Translated by Dorion Cairns. Dordrecht, The Netherlands: Kluwer Academic Publishers, 1977.

———. *Ideas Pertaining to a Pure Phenomenology and to a Phenomenological Philosophy—First Book.* Translated by F. Kersten. Dordrecht, The Netherlands: Kluwer Academic Publishers, 1982.

———. *Ideas Pertaining to a Pure Phenomenology and to a Phenomenological Philosophy - Second Book.* Translated by R. Rojcewicz and A. Schuwer. Dordrecht, The Netherlands: Kluwer Academic Publishers, 1989.

———. *Thing and Space: Lectures of 1907.* Translated by R. Rojcewicz. New York: Springer, 1997.

Hutchinson, Phil. *Shame and Philosophy: An Investigation in the Philosophy of Emotions and Ethics.* New York: Palgrave Macmillan, 2008.

"Information for Patients: Considering Cosmetic Surgery." edited by Department of Health (UK), 2005.

Jay, Martin. *Downcast Eyes: The Denigration of Vision in Twentieth-Century French Thought.* Berkeley: University of California Press, 1994.

Käll, Lisa Folkmarson, and Kristin Zeiler. "Why Feminist Phenomenology and Medicine?" *Feminist Phenomenology and Medicine*, edited by Lisa Folkmarson Käll and Kristin Zeiler, 1–25. Albany: SUNY Press, 2014.

Kaufman, Gershen. *Shame: The Power of Caring.* Rochester: Schenkman Boooks, 1992.

———. *The Psychology of Shame: Theory and Treatment of Shame Based Syndromes.* London: Routledge, 1993.

Kaw, Eugenia. "Medicalization of Racial Features: Asian American Women and Cosmetic Surgery." *Medical Anthropology Quarterly* vol. 7, no. 1 (1993): 74–89.

Keltner, Dacher, and Brenda N. Buswell. "Evidence for the Distinctness of Embarrassment, Shame and Guilt: A Study of Recalled Antecedents and Facial Expressions of Emotion." *Cognition and Emotion* vol. 10, no. 2 (1996): 155–171.

Klein, Ernest. *A Comprehensive Etymological Dictionary of the English Language.* Amsterdam: Elsevier Publishing Co., 1967.

Konings, Martijn. "Rethinking Neoliberalism and the Crisis: Beyond the Re-Regulation Agenda." In *The Great Credit Crash*, edited by Martijn Konings. London: Verso, 2010.

Kuczynski, Alex. *Beauty Junkies: Under the Skin of the Cosmetic Surgery Industry.* London: Vermilion, 2007.

Kurzban, Robert. "Evolutionary Origins of Stigmatization: The Functions of Social Exclusion." *Psychological Bulletin* vol. 127, no. 2 (2001): 187–208.

Lashbrook, Jeffrey T. "Fitting In: Exploring the Emotional Dimension of Adolescent Pressure." *Adolescence* vol. 35, no. 140 (2000): 747–757.

Leary, Mark R. *Self-Presentation: Impression Management and Interpersonal Behaviour.* Madison: Brown & Benchmark, 1995.

Leder, Drew. *The Absent Body.* Chicago: University of Chicago Press, 1990.

Lee, Emily S. "Madness and Judiciousness: A Phenomenological Reading of a Black Woman's Encounter with a Saleschild." In *Covergences: Black Feminism and Continental Philosophy,* edited by Maria del Guadalupe Davidson, Kathryn T. Gines and Donna-Dale L. Marcano, 185–199. Albany: SUNY Press, 2010.

Lee, J. "Menarche and the (Hetero)Sexualization of the Female Body." In *The Politics of Women's Bodies: Sexuality, Appearance and Behaviour,* edited by Rose Weitz. Oxford: Oxford University Press, 1998.

Lee, Robert G., and Gordon Wheeler, eds. *The Voice of Shame: Silence and Connection in Psychotherapy.* San Francisco: Jossey-Bass, 1996.

Lehtinen, Ullaliina. "How Does One Know What Shame Is? Epistemology, Emotions and Forms of Life in Juxtaposition." *Hypatia* vol. 13, no. 1 (1998): 56–77.

Levinas, Emmanuel. *Totality and Infinity: An Essay on Exteriority,* translated by Alfonso Lingus. The Hague: Nijhoff, 1979.

Lewandowicz, E., and J. Kruk-Jeromin. "The Indications and Plan of Plastic Operations in Children with Down's Syndrome." *Acta Chirurgiae Plasticae* vol. 37, no. 2 (1995): 40–44.

Lewis, Helen B. *Shame and Guilt in Neurosis.* New York: International Universities Press, 1971.

———, ed. *The Role of Shame in Symptom Formation.* East Sussex: Psychology Press, 1987.

Lewis, Michael. "Embarrassment: The Emotion of Self-Exposure and Evaluation." In *Self-Conscious Emotions: The Psychology of Shame, Guilt, Embarrassment and Pride,* edited by June Price Tangney and Kurt W. Fischer. New York: The Guilford Press, 1995.

Liddell, Henry George, and Robert Scott, eds. *An Intermediate Greek-English Lexicon.* Oxford: Oxford University Press, 1889.

Martin, Courtney E. *Perfect Girls, Starving Daughters: The Frightening New Normality of Hating Your Body.* London: Piatkus Books, 2007.

Matlin, M. W. *The Psychology of Women.* New York: Holt, Rinehart and Winston, 1987.

Matos, Marcela, and Jose Pinto-Gouveia. "Shame as Traumatic Memory." *Clinical Psychology and Psychotherapy* 17 (2010): 299–312.

Mauss, Marcel. "Techniques of the Body." In *The Body: A Reader,* edited by Mariam Fraser and Monica Greco, 73–77. London: Routledge, 2005.

McKinley, Nita Mary. "Feminist Perspectives and Objectified Body Consciousness." In *Body Image: A Handbook of Theory, Research and Clinical Practice,* edited by T. H. Cash and T. Pruzinsky. New York: The Guilford Press, 2002.

———. "Women and Objectified Body Consciousness: Mothers' and Daughters' Body Experience in Cultural, Developmental, and Familial Context." *Developmental Psychology* vol. 35, no. 3 (1999): 760–769.

Merleau-Ponty, Maurice. "The Child's Relations with Others." In *The Primacy of Perception,* edited by James M. Edie, 96–155. Evanston: Northwestern University Press, 1964.

———. "Eye and Mind." Translated by Carleton Dallery. In *The Primacy of Perception.* Evanston: Northwestern University Press, 1964. 159–90.

———. *Nature: Course Notes from the Collège De France.* Translated by Robert Vallier. Evanston: Northwestern University Press, 2003.

———. *Phenomenology of Perception.* Translated by Colin Smith. London: Routledge, 2006.

———. *Sense and Non-Sense.* Translated by Hubert L. Dreyfus and Patricia Allen Dreyfus. Evanston: Northwestern University Press, 1964.

———. *Signs.* Translated by Richard C. McCleary. Evanston: Northwestern University Press, 1964.

———. "An Unpublished Text by Maurice Merleau-Ponty: A Prospectus of His Work." In *The Primacy of Perception,* 3–11, 1964.

————. *The Visible and the Invisible*. Translated by Alphonso Lingus. Edited by Claude Lefort. Evanston: Northwestern University Press, 1968.

Metge, Joan. *In and out of Touch: Whakamaa in Cross Cultural Perspective*. Wellington: Victoria University Press, 1986.

Meyers, Diana Tietjens. "Feminism and Women's Autonomy: The Challenge of Female Genital Cutting." *Metaphilosophy* vol. 31, no. 5 (2000): 469–489.

Miller, Rowland S. *Embarrassment: Poise and Peril in Everyday Life*. New York: The Guilford Press, 1996.

Miller, Rowland S., and June Price Tangney. "Differentiating Embarrassment and Shame." *Journal of Social and Clinical Psychology* vol. 13, (1994): 273–287.

Mirowski, Philip. *Never Let a Good Crisis Go to Waste: How Neoliberalism Survived the Financial Meltdown*. London: Verso, 2013.

Mohanty, J. N. "Intentionality and the Mind/Body Problem." In *Phenomenology: Critical Concepts in Philosophy—Volume 2*, edited by Dermot Moran and Lester E. Embree, 316–332. Oxon: Routledge, 2004.

Moran, Dermot. *Edmund Husserl: Founder of Phenomenology*. Cambridge: Polity Press, 2005.

Morgan, Kathryn Pauly. "Women and the Knife: Cosmetic Surgery and the Colonization of Women's Bodies." In *The Politics of Women's Bodies: Sexuality, Appearance and Behaviour*, edited by Rose Weitz, 147–166. Oxford: Oxford University Press, 1998.

Morris, Katherine J. "Merleau-Ponty on Understanding *Other* Others." In *Body/Self/Other: The Phenomenology of Social Encounters*, edited by Luna Dolezal and Danielle Petherbridge. Albany: SUNY Press, Forthcoming.

————. *Starting with Merleau-Ponty*. London: Continuum, 2012.

————. "The Graceful, the Ungraceful and the Disgraceful." In *Reading Sartre: On Phenomenology and Existentialism*, edited by J. Webber, 130–144. London: Routledge, 2011.

————. "The Phenomenology of Body Dysmorphic Disorder: A Sartrean Analysis." In *Nature and Narrative: An Introduction to the New Philosophy of Psychiatry*, edited by Bill Fulford, et al. Oxford: Oxford University Press, 2003.

Morris, Phyllis Sutton. "Sartre on Objectification: A Feminist Perspective." In *Feminist Interpretations of Jean-Paul Sartre*, edited by Julien S. Murphy, 64–89. University Park, PA: The Pennsylvania State University Press, 1999.

Morrison, Toni. *The Bluest Eye*. London: Vintage, 1999.

Morwood, James, and John Taylor, eds. *Pocket Oxford Classical Greek Dictionary*. Oxford: Oxford University Press, 2002.

Nathanson, Donald L. *Shame and Pride: Affect, Sex and the Birth of the Self*. New York: W. W. Norton and Company, 1992.

Negrin, Llewellyn. "Cosmetic Surgery and the Eclipse of Identity." *Body and Society* vol. 8, no. 4 (2002): 21–42.

Nietzsche, Friedrich. *Daybreak: Thoughts on the Prejudices of Morality*. Translated by R. J. Hollingdale. Edited by Maudemarue Clark and Brian Leiter. Cambridge: Cambridge University Press, 1997.

Northrop, Jane Megan. *Reflecting on Cosmetic Surgery: Body Image, Shame and Narcissism*. London: Routledge, 2012.

Nussbaum, Martha C. *Hiding from Humanity: Disgust, Shame and the Law*. Princeton: Princeton University Press, 2004.

————. "Objectification." *Philosophy and Public Affairs* 24, no. 4 (1995): 249–291.

O'Donohoe, Stephanie. "Yummy Mummies: The Clamor of Glamour in Advertising to Mothers." *Advertising and Society Review* vol. 7, no. 3 (2006).

Orbach, Susie. *Fat Is a Feminist Issue*. London: Arrow Books, 2006.

Paster, Gail Kern. *The Body Embarrassed: Drama and the Disciplines of Shame in Early Modern England*. Cornell: Cornell University Press, 1993.

Pattison, Stephen. *Saving Face: Enfacement, Shame, Theology*. Farnham, Surrey: Ashgate, 2013.

Phillips, Katharine A. *The Broken Mirror: Understanding and Treating Body Dysmorphic Disorder*. Oxford: Oxford University Press, 2005.

Phillips, Katherine A., and S. F. Diaz. "Gender Differences in Body Dysmorphic Disorder." *Journal of Nervous and Mental Diseases* vol. 185, (1997): 570–577.

Phipps, Alison. *The Politics of the Body*. Cambridge, UK: Polity Press, 2014.

Piers, Gerhart. "Shame and Guilt: Part I." In *Shame and Guilt: A Psychoanalytic Study*, edited by Gerhart Piers and M. B. Singer. Springfield, IL: Charles C. Thomas, 1953.

Pinel, Elizabeth C. "Stigma Consciousness: The Psychological Legacy of Social Stereotypes." *Journal of Personality and Social Psychology* vol. 76, no. 1 (1999): 114–128.

Pitts-Taylor, Victoria. "Becoming/Being a Cosmetic Surgery Patient: Semantic Instability and the Intersubjective Self." *Studies in Gender and Sexuality* vol. 10, (2009): 119–128.

Powell, Nelson, and Brian Humphreys. *Proportions of the Aesthetic Face* (*American Academy of Facial Plastic and Reconstructive Surgery Monograph*). New York: Thieme Publishing Group, 1984.

Probyn, Elspeth. *Blush: The Faces of Shame*. Minneapolis: University of Minnesota Press, 2005.

Pruzinsky, Thomas. "Psychological Factors in Cosmetic Surgery: Recent Developments in Patient Care." *Plastic Surgery Nursing* vol. 13, no. 2 (1993): 64–71.

Ratcliffe, Matthew. *Feelings of Being: Phenomenology, Psychiatry and the Sense of Reality*. Oxford: Oxford University Press, 2008.

———. "Touch and Situatedness." *International Journal of Philosophical Studies* 16.3 (2008): 299–322.

Reddy, Vasudevi. *How Infants Know Minds*. Cambridge: Harvard University Press, 2008.

Riessman, Catherine Kohler. "Women and Medicalization: A New Perspective." In *The Politics of Women's Bodies: Sexuality, Appearance and Behaviour*, edited by Rose Weitz, 46–63. Oxford: Oxford University Press, 2003.

Robertson, Keith. "Liposuction." *Rejuvenate*, Autumn 2007, 8–12.

Rodemeyer, Lanei. "Feminism, Phenomenology and Hormones," in *Feminist Phenomenology and Medicine*, edited by Kristin Zeiler and Lisa Folkmarson Käll, 183–200. Albany: SUNY Press, 2014.

Rousseau, Jean-Jacques. *The Confessions*. London: Wordsworth Editions, 1996.

Sabini, John, Brian Garvey, and Amanda L. Hall. "Shame and Embarrassment Revisited." *Personality and Social Psychology Bulletin* vol. 27, (2001): 104–117.

Sacks, Oliver. *The Man Who Mistook His Wife for a Hat*. London: Duckworth, 1985.

Sartre, Jean-Paul. *Anti-Semite and Jew: An Exploration of the Etiology of Hate*. New York: Schocken Press, 1995.

———. *Being and Nothingness: An Essay on Phenomenological Ontology*. Translated by Hazel E. Barnes. London: Routledge, 2003.

———. *Sketch for a Theory of the Emotions*. Translated by Philip Mairet. London: Routledge, 2002.

Sarwer, David B. "Cosmetic Surgery and Changes in Body Image." In *Body Image: A Handbook of Theory, Research and Clinical Practice*, edited by T. H. Cash and T. Pruzinsky, 422–430. New York: The Guilford Press, 2002.

Scheff, Thomas J. *Bloody Revenge: Emotions, Nationalism and War*. Boulder: Westview, 1994.

———. "Elias, Freud and Goffman: Shame as the Master Emotion." In *The Sociology of Norbert Elias*, edited by Steven Loyal and Stephen Quilley, 229–242. Cambridge: Cambridge University Press, 2004.

———. "Shame and the Social Bond: A Sociological Theory." *Sociological Theory* vol. 18, no. 1 (2000): 84–99.

———. "Unpacking the Civilizing Process: Interdependence and Shame." In *Norbert Elias and Human Interdependencies*, edited by Thomas Salumets. Montreal and Kingston: McGill-Queen's University Press, 2001.

Schlink, Bernhard. *The Reader*. Translated by Carol Brown Janeway. London: Phoenix, 1997.

Schroeder, William R. *Continental Philosophy: A Critical Approach*. Oxford: Blackwell Publishing, 2004.

Schudson, Michael. "Embarrassment and Erving Goffman's Idea of Human Nature." *Theory and Society* vol. 13, (1984): 633–648.

Sedgwick, Eve Kosofsky. *Touching Feeling: Affect, Pedagogy, Performativity*. Durham and London: Duke University Press, 2003.

Seigworth, Gregory J., and Melissa Gregg. "An Inventory of Shimmers." In *The Affect Theory Reader*, edited by Gregory J. Seigworth and Melissa Gregg, 1–25. Durham: Duke University Press, 2010.

——, eds. *The Affect Theory Reader*. Durham: Duke University Press, 2010.

Shaver, P., S. Wu, and J. Schwartz. "Cross Cultural Similarities and Differences in Emotion and Its Representation." *Review of Personality and Social Psychology* vol. 13, (1992): 175–212.

Skeggs, Beverly. "Ambivalent Femininities." In *Gender: A Sociological Reader*, edited by Stevi Jackson, 311–325. London: Routledge, 2002.

Slatman, Jenny. *Our Strange Body: Philosophical Reflections on Identity and Medical Interventions*. Amsterdam: Amsterdam University Press, 2014.

Southward, David. "Jane Austen and the Riches of Embarrassment." *Studies in English Literature, 1500–1900* vol. 36, no. 4 (1996): 763–784.

Spinoza. *Ethics*. Translated by G. H. R. Parkinson. Oxford: Oxford University Press, 2000.

Stepian, Aneta. "Understanding Male Shame." *Masculinities: A Journal of Identity and Culture* vol. 1 (2014): 7–27.

Strassberg, Daniel. "'Perhaps Truth Is a Woman': On Shame and Philosophy." In *Philosophy's Moods: The Affective Grounds of Thinking*, edited by Hagi Kenaan and Ilit Ferber, 69–85. London: Springer, 2011.

Straus, Erwin W. "Shame as a Historiological Problem." In *Phenomenological Psychology*. London: Tavistock, 1966.

——. "The Upright Posture." In *Phenomenological Psychology*, 137–165. London: Tavistock Publications, 1966.

Sullivan, Deborah A. *Cosmetic Surgery: The Cutting Edge of Commercial Medicine in America*. New Jersey: Rutgers University Press, 2001.

Sullivan, Nikki. "'BIID'?: Queer (Dis)Orientations and The Phenomenology of 'Home.'" In *Feminist Phenomenology and Medicine*, edited by Kristin Zeiler and Lisa Folkmarson Käll, 119–39. Albany: SUNY Press, 2014.

Tangney, June Price, Rowland S. Miller, Laura Flicker, and Deborah Hill Barlow. "Are Shame, Guilt and Embarrassment Distinct Emotions?" *Journal of Personality and Social Psychology* vol. 70, no. 6 (1996): 1256–1269.

Taylor, Charles. "The Person." In *The Category of the Person*, edited by Michael Carrithers, Steven Collins and Steven Lukes. Cambridge: Cambridge University Press, 1985.

Taylor, Gabriele. *Pride, Shame and Guilt: Emotions of Self Assessment*. Oxford: Clarendon Press, 1985.

Thomson, Rosemarie Garland. *Extraordinary Bodies: Figuring Physical Disability in American Culture and Literature*. New York: Columbia University Press, 1997.

——. "Integrating Disability, Transforming Feminist Theory." *NWSA Journal* vol. 14, no. 3 (2004).

Toadvine, Ted. "Merleau-Ponty's Reading of Husserl: A Chronological Overview." In *Merleau-Ponty's Reading of Husserl*, edited by Ted Toadvine and Lester Embree, 227–286. Dordrecht, The Netherlands: Kluwer Academic Publishers, 2002.

Tomkins, Silvan S. *Affect, Imagery, Consciousness: The Negative Affects, Vol 2*. New York: Springer, 1963.

Tong, Rosemarie, and Hilde Lindemann. "Beauty under the Knife: A Feminist Appraisal of Cosmetic Surgery." In *Cutting to the Core: Exploring the Ethics of Contested Surgeries*, edited by David Benatar, 183–196. Lanham, MD: Rowman & Littlefield, 2006.

Turner, Bryan S. *The Body and Society*. Oxford: Blackwell, 1984.

Tyler, Imogen. "Skin-Tight: Celebrity, Pregnancy and Subjectivity." In *Thinking through the Skin*, edited by Sara Ahmed and Jackie Stacey. London: Routledge, 2001.

Valery, Paul. "Some Simple Reflections on the Body." In *Fragments for a History of the Human Body—Part 2*, edited by Michel Feher, Ramona Naddaff and Nadia Tazi, 395–405. Cambridge, MA: MIT Press, 1989.

van den Berg, J. H. "The Human Body and the Significance of Human Movement: A Phenomenological Study." *Philosophy and Phenomenological Research* vol. 13, no. 2 (1952): 159–183.

Veale, David. "Shame in Body Dysmorphic Disorder." In *Body Shame: Conceptualization, Research and Treatment*, edited by Paul Gilbert and Jeremy Miles, 267–282. New York: Brunner-Routledge, 2002.

Velleman, J. David. "The Genesis of Shame." *Philosophy and Public Affairs* vol. 30, no. 1 (2001): 27–52.

Wallbott, Harald G., and Klaus R. Scherer. "Cultural Determinants in Experiencing Shame and Guilt." In *Self-Conscious Emotions: The Psychology of Shame, Guilt, Embarrassment and Pride*, edited by June Price Tangney and Kurt W. Fischer. New York: The Guilford Press, 1995.

Walter, Natasha. *Living Dolls: The Return of Sexism*. London: Virago, 2010.

Watts, Jonathan. "A Tall Order." *The Guardian*, Monday, 15 December 2003.

Weber, Brenda R. "What Makes the Man?: Television Makeovers, Made-over Masculinity, and Male Body Image." *International Journal of Men's Health* vol. 5, no. 3 (2006): 287–306.

Weiss, Gail. *Body Images: Embodiment as Intercorporeality*. New York: Routledge, 1999.

———. "Uncosmetic Surgeries in an Age of Normativity." In *Feminist Phenomenology and Medicine*, edited by Kristin Zeiler and Lisa Folkmarson Käll, 101–118. Albany: SUNY Press, 2014.

Wijsbek, Henri. "How to Regulate a Practice: The Case of Cosmetic Surgery." *Ethical Theory and Moral Practice* vol. 4, (2001): 59–74.

———. "The Pursuit of Beauty: The Enforcement of Aesthetics or a Freely Adopted Lifestyle?" *Journal of Medical Ethics* vol. 26, (2000): 454–458.

Williams, Bernard. *Shame and Necessity*. Berkeley: University of California Press, 1993.

Winterson, Jeanette. *The Stone Gods*. London: Penguin, 2009.

Wiseman, Eva. "Would Madam Like a Nose Job with Her Sandwich." *The Observer Magazine*, 2010, 56–59.

Wolf, Naomi. *The Beauty Myth*. London: Vintage, 1990.

Woodward, Kathleen. "Traumatic Shame: Toni Morrison, Televisual Culture, and the Cultural Politics of Emotions." *Cultural Critique* vol. 46 (2000): 210–240.

Wong, Ying, and Jeanne Tsai. "Cultural Models of Shame and Guilt." In *The Self-Conscious Emotions: Theory and Research*, edited by Jessica L. Tracy, Richard W. Robins and June Price Tangney, 209–223. New York: Guilford Press, 2007.

Young, Iris Marion. "Throwing Like a Girl." In *Throwing Like a Girl and Other Essays in Feminist Philosophy and Social Theory*. Indianapolis: Indiana University Press, 1990.

Zahavi, Dan. "Shame and the Exposed Self." In *Reading Sartre: On Phenomenology and Existentialism*, edited by Jonathan Webber, 211–226. London: Routledge, 2011.

Zaner, Richard M. *The Context of Self: A Phenomenological Inquiry Using Medicine as a Clue*. Athens, Ohio: Ohio University Press, 1981.

Zeiler, Kristin. A. "Phenomenological Analysis of Bodily Self-Awareness in Pain and Pleasure: On Bodily Dys-Appearance and Eu-Appearance." *Medicine, Health Care and Philosophy* vol. 13, no. 4 (2010): 333–342.

Index

About the Author

Luna Dolezal is an Irish Research Council Postdoctoral ELEVATE Fellow—co-funded by Marie Curie Actions. She is based in the Department of Philosophy, Durham University and the Trinity Long Room Hub, Trinity College Dublin.